For Shutta

Enjoy!

Have Scalpel — Will Travel
Tales of an Itinerant Surgeon

Peter G. Roode, M.D.

Peter G. Roode

10/30/22
@ The FWA Conference

Fulton Books
Meadville, PA

Published by Fulton Books 2022

ISBN 978-1-63860-652-9 (paperback)
ISBN 978-1-63860-721-2 (hardcover)
ISBN 978-1-63860-653-6 (digital)

Printed in the United States of America

Endorsements

Have Scalpel — Will Travel. For a surgeon, it's an alternate lifestyle that is little known in our country. As in the military, the locum tenens life is more than a job, it's an adventure: doing as much as one can with what is readily available to you. One is always deployed, though within the United States, always serving a true need. This book is a must-read for physicians and surgeons—both current and future—as well as members of the general public.

Peter M. Rhee, M.D., FACS
Chief of Trauma, Acute Care Surgery, and Critical Care
Westchester Medical Center,
Valhalla, NY.
Author of *Trauma Red*, the story of how he helped
save Congresswoman Gabby Giffords.

This is a tale of Surgery in austere environments where life hinged on the skill and experience of Dr. Roode. It is an exciting and educational read for surgical and medical professionals and the general public alike. This book provides a rare window into the real world of medical care in smaller hospitals. His account of frontline surgical care clearly demonstrates that patients are saved by clear thinking and judicious action rather than an infinite constellation of high tech "bells and whistles". I highly recommend it!

R. Stephen Smith, MD, FACS
Professor of Surgery
Trauma Medical Director
University of Florida

As a product of a small Minnesota town, a graduate of the Mayo Health System, and a fellow surgeon, I know this collection of stories represents absolute truth. Dr. Roode's surgical skill and care for his patients shine through this collection of patient stories. He is both a gifted story teller and a skilled surgeon. I recommend his memoir to any surgeon considering a career in locum tenens as well as the general public.

Steven J. Hughes, M.D., FACS
Professor of Surgery
Chief Division of Surgical Oncology
Vice-Chairman, General Surgery
University of Florida

A successful physician needs to be a people person.
A successful surgeon needs to be a highly skilled technician.
A successful traveling surgeon needs to be an adventurer.
Peter G. Roode, M.D. is all three and on top of that is a great story teller.

Ron Krablin, M.D.
Retired cardiologist, and a classmate in the pioneer class of 1971
Penn State College of Medicine

My first encounter with the scalpel wielding, peripatetic Dr. Roode was in 1991 when he came to Mobridge, South Dakota to provide surgical services for this community. Not only was he an accomplished surgeon, bringing with him some of his own specialized equipment, but a good pediatric diagnostician as well. I hope you will be enticed to read his surgical escapades in this book.

Leonard Linde, M.D.
Family Practitioner for 40 years in Mobridge, SD

Riveted by the stories, I found the book hard to put down. Dr. Roode's memoir details the adventures and challenges of an itinerant surgeon containing tales of surgical flexibility, improvisation, human tragedy, and success.

Patricia L. Abbitt, M.D.
Professor, Abdominal Imaging
Radiology Department
University of Florida

To a physician who devoted his life to others.
He was named Lukurnyang by his adoptive
tribe—the Murle people of South Sudan

Contents

Foreword

The details of a career as a *locum tenens* in general surgery are found in the pages of *Have Scalpel — Will Travel* by Peter G. Roode, MD. Literature describing the requirements for and outcomes of a *locum tenens* practice is not readily available. A *locum* fills temporary vacancies related to vacation, illness, or a sudden relocation. Assignments are often brief but, on occasion, are extended to meet the needs of an institution. Career opportunities vary—from large clinics with trauma centers to small rural hospitals.

Dr. Roode, a well-trained, competent general surgeon, began practicing surgery in the traditional way. The details that follow delve into the life of a *locum tenens* as he lived it.

Dr. Roode spent much of his childhood in Africa. His father, a physician, served with a church group in South Sudan. Following high school, he attended Rensselaer Polytechnic Institute, graduating with a degree in physics. This led to his employment in the Naval Nuclear Power program led by Admiral Hyman Rickover, who had developed the nuclear-powered ballistic missile submarine, one of the most lethal weapons of war on the planet. It was during this period that the author developed an interest in medicine as a way to help people rather than destroying them with nuclear weapons.

Dr. Roode subsequently matriculated at Penn State College of Medicine in Hershey, Pennsylvania, where he was a member of its first class. The medical school, located in a relatively rural area of central Pennsylvania, did not initially have a large collection of patients to serve as teaching material. Therefore, it was necessary to reach out to medical facilities in the region to fulfill this need. One of those facilities was Geisinger Medical Center, located in Danville, Pennsylvania. It was a growing multispecialty facility that had an accredited general surgery training program. Geisinger's extensive clinical material was also ideal for medical student education. And so Penn State College of Medicine made arrangements to utilize Geisinger as a surgical rotation for medical students.

I was asked to direct that program primarily because of my training at Harvard University, which had included working with undergraduate students. I received an appointment as a Clinical Associate Professor and later as a Clinical Professor of Surgery at the Penn State College of Medicine. Peter Roode was a medical student in one of the early groups. Clearly very interested in surgery, he was highly motivated, often challenging the resident staff regarding diagnosis and treatment plans. He was always on time for surgical rounds, knew their clinical course, and attended surgical procedures even though he knew he would be second or third assistant. It was a pleasure to have him on my service.

Upon graduation from medical school, he chose Geisinger for his surgical education. His medical school advisors were apparently distressed that he would even consider a nonuniversity training program. However, his selection of Geisinger Medical Center was most appropriate based on his ultimate goal.

In this book, Dr. Roode presents a series of clinical experiences at various locations, ranging from large metropolitan medical centers to small rural hospitals. He dramatically demonstrates that severe, complex surgical problems do present at small rural facilities. A *locum* surgeon must be capable of dealing with these problems when they occur, often without the equipment or support available at urban centers. I was especially impressed with his use of peritoneal lavage, a technique popular in the 1960s to detect the presence or absence of intra-abdominal hemorrhage in trauma patients before modern technology, such as computerized tomography or ultrasound was available.

This book by Dr. Roode, *Have Scalpel — Will Travel,* vividly demonstrates two things: first, that the clinical experience is vast and satisfying and, second, that a career as a full-time *locum tenens* surgeon is possible. I highly recommend this book to every surgeon and med student considering such a career, as well as to interested members of the general public.

Carl W. Konvolinka, MD, FACS
Former Chairman, Department of Surgery
Guthrie Clinic, Sayre, Pennsylvania

Retired Clinical Professor of Surgery
Pennsylvania State University
College of Medicine, Hershey, Pennsylvania

Introduction

This book is a collection of human-interest stories of patients that I cared for during my career in *locum tenens* (temporary, fill-in) surgery, which spanned seventeen years in eighteen states. Most of my adventures were in the Midwest, but many took place during numerous tours of duty in Alaska and Hawaii. In all, I undertook 244 assignments at seventy-four different hospitals. During this time, I kept a journal of those patients who were especially challenging or interesting. Many of these stories are illustrative of the complexities inherent in the practice of surgery.

Locum tenens medicine is the practice of filling in for a regular medical practitioner who, for whatever reasons, is away from his or her practice. These temporary absences may be due to vacation, illness, or a call to active military duty. When this occurs, the choice is often between shutting that practice down or hiring temporary help. In addition, hospitals can be placed in an untenable position if the departing physician is the only one in town capable of performing a C-section. Without the ability to provide an emergency operation to deliver a fetus in distress, the entire OB department must also be closed.

Stemming from Latin, *locum tenens* is best translated as "to hold the place of." A number of agencies provide temporary coverage in all medical specialties. When a suitable candidate has been agreed upon, the agency then takes care of the details: travel arrangements, housing, malpractice insurance, and salary for the temporary physician. The hospital or clinic that contracts with the agency can recoup the cost of this service by billing for the services the *locum* physician performs. All in all, it's a win-win situation.

What were the circumstances that led to my involvement in *locum tenens* surgery? I was a member of a multispecialty group in Iowa. Through attrition, the surgery department shrank until I was the sole remaining surgeon, so that I was on call every night. The group then entered a period of turmoil and eventually disbanded. Thus, I found myself, at age fifty, unemployed.

Unexpectedly, I was presented with an opportunity to provide two weeks of temporary coverage for a surgeon in Alaska. That first assignment was a joy. I was in a place where I was both welcomed and needed by the other physicians in town. My wife, Betty, and I made friends with the local residents. We were able to see and experience sights that the average tourist, herded around in tour buses, would miss.

We decided to give *locum tenens* surgery a trial for a "year or so." Within that time, I would surely find a multispecialty group that I could permanently join. Long story short, what we thought would be a year of travel while I provided temporary coverage turned out to be a seventeen-year adventure. As our experience evolved, we purchased and refurbished a used fifth-wheel RV so that we had a home away from home. When we decided that it would be pleasant to permanently move south to avoid the harsh Iowa winter months, we were completely free to decide just where we wanted to live. Most people have to relocate based on where a job is available. Living in Florida merely made my "commute" to work a bit more lengthy. Since most of my assignments lasted several weeks, this "inconvenience" scarcely mattered.

Aviation has been one of my obsessions. I have been fortunate enough to earn both single- and multi-engine commercial and instrument ratings. Aviation, it turns out, dovetails very nicely with a career in *locum tenens* medicine. During much of my *locum tenens* career, we owned a twin-engine Piper Seneca, which we used on many of our short-term assignments, all at the client's expense!

Following graduation from medical school in 1971, I entered a surgical training program at Geisinger Medical Center in Danville, Pennsylvania, ultimately becoming board certified in general surgery. Surgical training necessarily depends on the number and type of patients available. In the early 1970s, Geisinger Medical Center, which is located in rural central Pennsylvania, had a paucity of trauma patients, as compared to larger inner-city hospitals. Thus, when I had completed my surgical training, I had not seen enough severely injured patients to be entirely comfortable with trauma surgery. In no way should I be considered to be a trauma surgeon.

A surgeon caring for trauma patients in an isolated small rural hospital must often make the best of a difficult situation. Sometimes he or she can stabilize a severely injured patient before transferring them to a larger center. In other cases, the patient might be so critical that the only chance for survival is for the local surgeon to attempt surgical intervention locally. It's better to go down fighting than just to give up and quit.

These stories reveal the anxieties, doubts, and turmoil that can go through the average, run-of-the-mill surgeon's mind when facing a difficult situation, no matter how calm he or she may appear on the surface. The stories range from tragedies to triumphs, to humorous human foibles, and to uplifting happy endings.

The stories in this book also illustrate that the practice of surgery is not a simple algorithm. We do not always reach our diagnoses based on a laboratory or X-ray test. Many of these stories took place thirty years ago—a time when CT scans with clear diagnostic information were not commonplace. In many cases, to even reach a diagnosis, we surgeons have to balance a complex array of often conflicting data, some of which is, at times, erroneous. This calls for increased reliance on one's instincts as tempered by his or her previous experience. Then after a tentative diagnosis has been adopted, it does not automatically dictate a fixed treatment plan. The pros and cons of alternative possible courses of action have to be carefully considered. Perhaps worst of all, in many instances, all these decisions have to be made in a few hectic minutes in the face of a deteriorating situation.

It goes without saying that all patient names in this book have been changed. Furthermore, all the events in this book took place more than twenty years ago in towns that I often refer to vaguely as "somewhere in _____." For the most part, physicians in these stories are also not named.

I hope the stories are enjoyable and educational both to members of the medical profession and the general public.

Peter G. Roode, MD, FACS

Debacle in the Desert

The phone call came at 2 a.m. The emergency room of the small Arizona hospital for which I was providing temporary surgical coverage informed me that an even smaller neighboring hospital was sending us a young man who had been stabbed in his abdomen during a domestic dispute. It seemed that he was having an argument with his wife. Unfortunately for him, she was holding a large butcher knife at the time and used it freely on his abdomen. The referring hospital, having no surgeon on staff, was forced to transfer the patient. They told our ER that the victim had a blood pressure of only forty and they were starting two large-bore IV lines before sending him to us.

The person calling me then politely asked the routine question: "Will you accept him in transfer?"

Bureaucratic rules and regulations require that a patient may not be transferred from one hospital to another without documentation that the receiving hospital has accepted the patient. In this instance, that was a moot point. The patient was already on his way to us. It sounded to me that what this severely injured patient really needed was to be cared for in a much larger and better-equipped hospital than the remote one I was covering. However, it also seemed unlikely that he could survive such a transfer, considering the distances involved. Thus, his only chance for survival depended on what we could accomplish locally.

And so I told the Emergency Room nurse to immediately call the OR crew and anesthesia and have them come in STAT. The X-ray technician and lab should be standing by in the ER. I then hustled on in, arriving well before our critically injured patient.

Upon my arrival at the ER, I rehearsed just what we were going to do. The OR was set up with instruments selected and laid out. The portable X-ray machine was rolled down to the ER and made ready. Checking with the lab, I made sure that we had blood immediately available.

It was then that I discovered to my horror that there was nobody available to assist me at surgery! Sometimes you need more than two hands to do surgery. The assistant, holding retractors, gives you the exposure you need to see and make repairs. But that night, there was nobody available, not even an extra scrub nurse.

I grumbled anxiously to myself, "Why me? I didn't ask this guy to argue with his wife. I must work under this stressful situation with inadequate help, and even if I am perfectly successful and save his life, which is doubtful, they will all just take it for granted. On the other hand, if, perchance, surgery is not successful, it will be obvious to any number of after-the-fact observers just what should have been done. There must be an easier way to make a living."

Presently, the ambulance from the other hospital roared up to our ER, lights flashing and siren wailing. Our victim was rolled out. He turned out to be a young man in his midtwenties. He was conscious, but lethargic. His blood pressure had risen to eighty from the copious IV solutions given during his ambulance ride to our ER. No need to waste time taking a complete history or doing a detailed physical examination. Just the heart and lungs—key items—then off to the OR. A quick glance at his abdomen showed his stab wound was right in the middle of a long, wide, and old midline surgical scar. Evidently he had had previous surgery. This was not going to be a picnic. I'd have to go through that existing surgical incision. Surgery often results in adhesions—scar tissue that can cause the abdominal organs to adhere to each other. Surgical reexploration in the presence of adhesions can easily result in damage to the bowel. In such cases, we have to proceed cautiously. However, with trauma cases, we often don't have the time for a slow, methodical exploration. I asked him what kind of surgery he'd had, but he either didn't know or was incapable of answering.[1]

A portable chest X-ray was obtained. We needed this film to be sure the knife had not penetrated his diaphragm and collapsed a lung. If so, I would need to place a chest tube prior to exploring his abdomen. The chest X-ray was normal, so we then rushed our patient directly to the OR. I glanced at the clock; he was on our OR table precisely eighteen minutes after he had been wheeled through the doors of the ER! Now *that* is better than many hospitals can do.

We added blood to his IVs as I quickly scrubbed. Despite the IVs and transfusion, his blood pressure was now back down in the 40s. He was slipping away and clearly would not have survived any attempted transfer to a larger hospital.

I thought, *I have to quickly get into that tense abdomen with its ugly, mocking scar staring at me. If I can't pull this one off, he's a dead man.*

I quickly applied the sterile sheets and drapes and held out my hand. The scrub nurse pressed the scalpel into it, and I began hurriedly but with care because of the likely adhesions, which can stick a loop of bowel right up there on the inside of the abdomen, just waiting for the careless surgeon to be a wee bit too vigorous.

As expected, the abdomen was full of blood. And yes, there were numerous adhesions from his previous surgery. The blood poured out of the incision, obscuring my view. I tried to sop it up with large gauze lap pads and then asked for the self-retaining retractor. To my further horror, I discovered that they didn't have one.

My god, what else can go wrong?

The lack of an assistant meant that I was going to have to do this operation with only a lone scrub nurse holding a piddly little retractor in one hand as she also tried to hand me instruments from the sterile tray with the other. She couldn't even efficiently hand me the lap pads to soak up the blood so I could see what and where the

---

[1]   Only later, after surgery, did I learn that the young man had had a hard life. This was his third serious abdominal injury. At this age of seventeen, he was shot in the abdomen and had surgery. Then at age twenty-one, he needed a second operation after he was stabbed in the abdomen. And now this.

injuries were. The blood continued to well up out of the incision, obscuring the adhesions as well as the injuries. I removed the little handheld retractor and asked for a suction.

"Pool tip," I requested.

But no, they didn't even have that item on the instrument trays beside the table. The circulating nurse, a temporary stand-in, rushed around the OR, trying to find one, asking the scrub nurse for directions. Trauma surgery is hard enough even in a well-equipped large hospital, but this was just ridiculous!

I glanced at the monitors at the head of the bed and saw that the blood pressure was back in the 40s. So far, I'd made no progress at all. I was getting desperate. We were pumping in blood as fast as we could get it from the lab—O negative at first and then type-specific when it was available.

I gave up on the pool suction, and finally, after what seemed like an eternity to me, I was able to get the abdomen open and then pack all four quadrants with large gauze lap packs.

As I had suspected, the adhesions from his previous surgery allowed his assailant's knife to slice through several loops of small bowel. Ordinarily, if you are lucky, the soft, squishy, mobile bowel can sometimes move aside as a knife plunges inward. Not this time. I would have to patiently repair each laceration to the bowel.

But first I had to locate and control the source of blood loss, which was the immediate threat to his life. I removed the lap pads one quadrant at a time, carefully assessing the damage, finding that the assailant's knife had severed several branches of his mesenteric artery. These were clamped and ligated. I also discovered a puncture wound in his colon, as well as a deep wound in his retro-peritoneum just to the left of his aorta.

After I had the hemorrhage under control, I was able to then return to the bowel lacerations. Each was carefully repaired. His abdomen was then copiously washed with saline to remove fecal contamination. The blood pressure slowly crept up. I inquired about the Foley.[2]

"He's still making urine," said the circulating nurse.

---

[2]   The catheter in his bladder to monitor how well the kidneys are functioning.

Thank God for young kidneys. It was now 5 a.m., and we were finally done. Our patient's blood pressure was comfortably in the 120s. We had used 8 units of blood as well as several thousand cc's of crystalloid (IV solution). I estimated his blood loss at roughly 4,200 cc. Yes, that was almost his total blood volume, but he had continued to bleed massively well after we had begun his transfusions.

In the ICU, I finally sat down. The sun was just coming up. I had not been aware of the passage of time, only of the terrible feeling that if I failed, this young man would have died. Forever. I was his only chance, and I felt only lucky that morning. Not skillful, just lucky.

They must do ten of these a night in Detroit, I thought to myself. *What's the big deal out here in the Arizona desert? Why was it so damned hard? I've done equally difficult cases before. Why do I feel only lucky on this one?* I sat there in the alcove after dictating my operative report and wondered, *How often am I going to face debacles like this in inadequately equipped and poorly staffed hospitals? Maybe I need to rethink my recent decision about* locum tenens *surgery as a career choice.*

But the very next month, while attending the annual American College of Surgeons Clinical Congress in San Francisco, the answer came to me. I was wandering through the exhibit hall admiring all the surgical instruments on display for sale. Of course! Buy your own self-retaining retractor and take it along with you on assignment. You need to get caught only once in the desert with a gut-stabbed victim in a poorly equipped hospital to learn what you need.

One last note: After surgery, when I talked to this patient's mother, I mentioned the huge blood loss. Yes, I was rather pleased that, despite the odds, we'd gotten him through surgery with such a huge blood loss. She just took it for granted that all would be well. And so I told her that during surgery, he needed 8 units of blood.

"More than 4 quarts," I added for clarification.

Still she looked at me blankly, not comprehending.

Hmm. I'll have to translate this into terms she will understand. Lessee now, a can of beer is 380 cc. Divide that into 4,200 cc (mumble, mumble).

"Ma'am, your son lost about eleven beer cans full of blood."

Her response: "Wow, that is almost a twelve-pack!"

CHAPTER 2

A Trial Run in Ketchikan (My First *Locum* Experience)

There I was, sitting on a mooring bollard, down on the dock in Ketchikan, Alaska. It was a sunny and warm day in July 1990. I was watching the tourists come and go, forcing myself to just sit still. This was a novel experience for me. What was I, a general surgeon from Iowa, doing here? Basically, just trying to sit still! That's what.

Two weeks ago, Ketchikan was only a name to me. Indeed, all of Alaska was merely a name to me. Now I was licensed in this state and the only surgeon within three hundred miles! How had all this transpired?

As usual with many major events in our lives, it was largely without planning. I had been the sole general surgeon for a multispecialty medical center in eastern Iowa. It began to disintegrate, and nobody really knew why—incessant bickering among the physicians, high overhead, poor administration, suspicions of embezzlement, defection of some physicians, an ill-advised lawsuit, more defections... Finally, there were simply no more referrals.

And so, at age fifty, I was out of work. What to do? Move? Interview with another group? How does one find a quality, stable medical group to join? Who is lying to you? What do you *really* learn during a site visit and interviews anyway?

At first I did nothing. I'd toyed with the idea of temporary (*locum tenens*) work but had contacted only one agency and what I learned was discouraging. Only later did I learn that it just happened to be one of the least productive agencies in the country. So nothing developed from that, and I continued to procrastinate day after day, but not without stewing. Hey! Surgeons aren't supposed to be unemployed! I had put out feelers, but the phone stayed quiet, and as one day rolled into the next, I found myself simply hiking along the banks of the Mississippi, looking at birds (a new hobby). And worrying.

Soon the bank account reached the condition of "red alert." Then, fortuitously, I heard from a different *locum* agency offering me a short-term assignment in Alaska.

"Yes, thank you. I'll take that assignment!"

Whew!

And soon I was on a plane...

And so, on this Saturday morning, my eighth day of basically not doing too much, I was sitting on that mooring bollard at the dock and watching tourists come and go. For me, all this was a brand-new experience—this relaxation stuff. I had no idea if one could make a living doing temporary *locum* surgery, and I wasn't sure if I'd enjoy it or not. In any case, I'd come to the dock this Saturday morning to force myself to sit and watch and absorb and memorize the sights, sounds, and smells. My self-imposed assignment was to see if I could actually do this for a whole three hours. It was harder than I anticipated.

Ketchikan is a stop on the Alaskan Marine Highway. Indeed, there are only two ways to get to Ketchikan—either by air or water. There are no roads connecting it to the mainland. During the nights, the cruise ships proceed up or down the Inside Passage, the Alaska Marine Highway, to their next stop. Upon awakening, tourists are greeted with new sights in a new town. They make a frontal assault on the tourist shops. (The shops always win.) And there are side tours for those who wish to pay extra.

Thus, I could watch tourists coming and going, back and forth, from the downtown shops to the cruise ships. One interesting observation was that no tourist ever went into a restaurant in Ketchikan. After all, they had paid for their food on the cruise ship, so come noon, everybody traipsed back to the ship for lunch.

A *locum* physician is paid whether working or sitting. It's not as much as most other surgeons earn, but it's possibly enough to make a living. Having no overhead, no office, no employees, and no malpractice insurance premiums certainly helps. Yes, there was a smattering of patients to see, a few patients in the ER, and I even performed a couple surgeries, but it had been a far cry from the usual hectic life of a general surgeon.

I had filled in the extra time available to me by exploring the town and as much of the island as one could, which wasn't much, considering the road only went eleven miles in one direction and thirteen in the other. But there were interesting side roads to drive, mountain trails to hike, new places to explore, and new birds to see.

One day, I amused myself by following a busload of tourists from the cruise ship that happened to be in town. It was headed a few miles north to Totem Bight State Park. The tourists paid a hefty fee for this "extra" to their cruise ticket. They were going to see totem poles being made and would tour a replica Native Alaskan village. Nobody noticed when I joined the group and followed along, enjoying the tour guide's spiel. Suddenly, my beeper went off.

There was an awkward silence, and I felt them all staring at me. "Hey! He's not one of us!"

From this, my first taste of the *locum tenens* world, I recollect two memorable patients.

Harold Singleton

My beeper went off on a Tuesday afternoon. It was the hospital wanting to connect me to a British physician working on one of the cruise ships. She described her patient as having abdominal pain "for no good reason." She felt he needed to be seen and also warned me that the ship was to leave that night. She did not think it safe to allow him to remain on board as they sailed to their next destination. Well, of course, I agreed.

By and by, the hospital called me to let me know that my patient was ready to be seen. The ER physician had seen him and started with lab tests and X-rays. I found a sixty-five-year-old gentleman with RUQ[1] pain, an elevated white count, and a positive ultrasound. The diagnosis was obvious: acute cholecystitis.[2] Indeed, a probable gangrenous gallbladder. And so it was that I proposed surgery to Harold and his wife. I was not surprised at their anxious suspicions.

What kind of surgeon is this guy? How risky is the proposed surgery? Do we have any other options? Can't we just go home? Oh, why couldn't this have happened back in Texas so that we could be seen by our regular doctor!

I patiently went over the situation again. They really had no choice, so reluctantly, they agreed to surgery.

My next stop was to stroll over to the OR. By now, it was nearly 5 p.m., and everybody was getting ready to go home.

I said to the OR supervisor, "I'm sorry, but we are going to have to add a case tonight—exploratory and probable chole.[3]

"Oh, Dr. Roode! Where did you dig this patient up?"

"He is from one of the cruise ships."

"Well, is he one of the newlyweds or nearly deads?"

Thus, I learned how the locals divide the source of much of their economy into two classes of tourists.

It turned out that Harold did indeed have a gangrenous gall-bladder, and after surgery, he made a gratifying recovery. The case was not that unusual. It was an incident in the postoperative recovery period that qualified Harold for entry into my "memorable patient" files.

Their cruise ship had long since departed. So their dream vacation was destroyed. Worse, the cruise line refused to refund their ticket price. After all, it wasn't the cruise line's fault that Harold became ill. The Singletons should have purchased trip insurance. Not only were the Singletons out of their vacation and money, but now they were stranded in a strange town in Alaska with no way to

---

[1]   Right Upper Quadrant of the abdomen.
[2]   Infection of his gallbladder.
[3]   Surgical slang for removal of the gallbladder.

get home. Airline tickets would cost them more of their dwindling funds. Clearly, money was now a much bigger factor in their lives.

Mrs. Singleton approached me after a few days.

"Doc, we plan to sue the cruise line."

"Oh. Okay. Whatever. What are you suing them for?"

"It was their fault that Harold became ill. They should pay for the canceled vacation, for the hospital bill, and for us to get home again."

"How so?"

"Well, you see, it all happened on the first night of the cruise. There was an orientation meeting. Now mind you, Harold didn't want to go up on stage. They made him."

"And?"

She explained, "Well, they played this skit. Harold didn't want to participate, but they made him. In the skit, he had to kneel down on all fours and a fat lady sat on him!"

I exclaimed, "Oh my!"

"Yes! He was the couch in their living room, and the fat lady sat on him."

"Well, I still don't get it. What does that have to do with his gallbladder attack?"

"I think that her sitting on him knocked his gallbladder loose and caused it to get infected."

"I think you are gonna have a hard time proving that in a courtroom. It was probably his preexisting gallbladder disease that triggered the attack."

A Drunk in the ER

The hospital called one evening, asking me to see a woman injured in a motor-vehicle accident. Upon walking into the ER, I saw the usual pandemonium—except for one striking difference that caught my attention. A man was handcuffed around a metal pillar, drunk and loudly abusing everybody. He was not my patient. It was his wife that I was called in to see. She was the passenger in the car he was driving and had a large facial laceration that the ER doctor wanted me to suture. I obliged, and upon completion, I inquired of the policeman about the drunk handcuffed to the pillar.

It turned out that Mr. and Mrs. Rubio were having marital difficulties and had decided to consult the local marriage counselor (aka bartender). They discussed and tried to settle their differences at the local bar, but as the evening progressed, they made no progress. Eventually, it was time to go home.

Now José knew he had way too much to drink, so he concentrated on his driving. Slow and easy. Right down the middle of his lane. All of his attention was on the road ahead of him. Meanwhile, his wife evidently was not finished trying to hash out whatever marital problems they were facing. Her husband, concentrating intensely on his driving, was not saying a thing.

This annoyed his wife, and so she grabbed the steering wheel and yanked on it while screaming, "Hey, Buster! I'm talking to *you*!"

And that was how they ended up in the ditch. By and by, their car was noticed in the ditch. The police were summoned. Officer Dudley walked down into the ditch and rapped on the window. José obligingly rolled it down.

Officer Dudley said, "You seem to be having a problem!"

José replied, "Offishure, shheee did it!"

This was basically true. What angered him was that *he* was the one who was arrested, not her. Having limited resources, the police brought him along with her to the ER, and when he continued to be obnoxious, they simply handcuffed him to the nearest pillar and ignored him.

My two weeks in Ketchikan flew by. My brief introduction to Alaska and to the world of *locum tenens* surgery had been so satisfying that I arranged for an airline ticket to appear in Moline, Illinois, for my wife, Betty. Yes, it's true. In those pre-TSA days, anybody could purchase an airline ticket for anybody else. And so after this assignment was over, I flew to Juneau, where I met Betty arriving on Alaska Airlines. I had signed us up for a Glacier Bay tour. We followed this with a trip to Skagway, where we explored the area where the Klondike Gold Rush stories had taken place. A rental car took us up the Klondike Highway, through the White Pass, and into the Yukon. We arrived at Whitehorse just in time to observe the celebration of Canada Day (July 1) before wending our way home to Iowa. The net result of my first *locum* experience was that it seemed we had spent the entire amount I'd earned at Ketchikan touring around Alaska and Canada. Our bank accounts were still in condition red alert.

Not to worry. Just a few weeks later, I was called back to Ketchikan for another assignment. When that was over, we decided we'd give the *locum* lifestyle a try but only for a year at the most. Surely during that year we'd come across the perfect location with the perfect medical group and we could resettle. That trial period of a single year somehow stretched out to 17 years filled with 244 different assignments in 74 different hospitals. The stories in this book have been gleaned from notes I made at the time the events took place.

CHAPTER 3

Crew Cut Porcupines

After our initial, encouraging experiences with the two trips to Alaska, Betty and I decided to continue to explore this *locum* lifestyle. Was it really for us? And so I accepted an offer to work in a small desert hospital in Arizona located about a hundred miles from Phoenix. Thus a warm and sunny Thursday afternoon found me driving a rental car down a gently sloping, open desert valley in Arizona. The twin lanes of asphalt curved between the low, almost-rolling hills, which were studded with outcrops of decaying granite rocks, various shrubs, and cacti. Lots of cacti.

I have got to learn them, I thought to myself.

The windows of the car were open. The afternoon breeze felt good. There was no need for the air conditioner. I was relishing my newfound freedom in the *locum* lifestyle, drinking in the sights, sounds, and smells. Imagine driving into the desert on a *Thursday*, no less! Where had I been all my life, and what had I been doing that it was such a novelty to drive off without a care on a Thursday afternoon? Man, it was time I started to enjoy life a little more!

Strange as it seemed to me, I was technically "at work," as the beeper and cellular phone on the empty seat beside me reminded me. I picked up the strangely silent beeper, held it to my ear, and pushed the little button. It emitted a comforting *hsss…*

Yup, it's still working. Guess they don't need me.

An inviting odd-shaped hill to the left ahead beckoned. A rancher had obligingly left me a wide area next to his barbed-wire gate. Luckily, nobody was behind me as I jammed on the brakes, grabbed the beeper, and hastily got out of the car. I hadn't climbed through a barbed-wire fence since I was a kid.

I started walking up a dusty ravine, occasionally testing the beeper to be sure it still was alive.

I can't get used to hiking instead of doing surgery, I mused. At my feet, a striking piece of pink conglomerate rock grabbed my attention. *Hmmm. Wonder if I can trace it back to its origin.*

That's what early prospectors had done when they found gold. I walked up the ravine till I found a seemingly suitable place to begin the climb of the small odd-shaped hill. It was rough going.

I must get a pair of hiking shoes, I thought.

Sure enough, near the top of the hill was the same distinctive rock lying there in a thick band. Obviously, it was the source of the small pieces that had eroded into the valley below.

I paused, sitting on a rocky outcrop, enjoying the scenery. I wanted to etch it into my mind. Below me, I saw a hawk gliding over the valley. *Below me!* How many times can one look down on a hawk? After all those years of working within confining schedules, either of my own making or somebody else's, this freedom was heady stuff indeed. And such a simple thing! A hike in the desert on a Thursday afternoon!

I was enjoying this *locum* assignment every bit as much as I'd enjoyed those in Alaska. The *locum* lifestyle can be addicting. The collapse of my former multispecialty group in Iowa, which had seemed like such a catastrophe at the time, was evolving into an amazing new lifestyle, one that I had never envisioned. I was discovering that there was more to life than doing three gallbladder operations and a colon resection in a day. Now there was time to enjoy the world around me.

I clambered down from "my" hill. It would be forever mine now, at least in my mind. Returning to my car, I tested the beeper along the way. Old habits are hard to break. I continued driving down the road, feeling guilty, like the proverbial kid in an unattended candy store. Deep down inside me, I "knew" that hiking in the desert on a weekday afternoon was somehow secretly wrong. I'd surely be "caught" and made to pay. I pushed those thoughts away as I marveled at my newfound freedom and happiness.

This assignment had started when a physician recruiting agency in New York called and asked me if I would consider relocating to a hospital in rural Arizona.

"Well, no. Not really."

The recruiter slickly shifted gears and asked, "Would you be willing to provide temporary surgical coverage for them until such time as we can find them a permanent surgeon?"

Now *that* I could agree to. The hospital arranged the flights from Iowa, and a rental car was waiting for me in Phoenix. I checked in at the local Best Western.

The following morning, I awakened early. Force of habit. It was too early to go to the hospital and make my introduction. Wandering outside into the warm morning sun, I decided to explore the abandoned field that lay behind the motel. There on the ground sat a bird I'd never seen before. Hurrying back to the car, I dug through my suitcase and hauled out my somewhat battered bird book and binoculars.

Doves. Hmm. There! A scaled dove!

It was a new one for me. I supposed I ought to get really organized someday and start keeping one of those Life Lists that serious birders do. I wandered between the scrubby bushes standing apart on the sandy soil. In the distance, a small bird with a chirping call that was neatly synchronized with its undulating flight reminded me of goldfinches. I followed its flight to a tree and approached carefully. Lifting my binoculars, I saw to my delight that it was indeed a goldfinch. When I had first suspected that it was goldfinch, it was much too far away to see any colors. I'd recognized it by what experienced birders call its "jizz."

Say, I'm getting the hang of this new hobby! I thought. *How can such a simple thing as seeing a new bird give such pleasure?*

Breakfast was soon over, and it was time to report to the hospital and introduce myself. The town was so small that I didn't bother asking directions. I just drove around, looking for the blue signs with the white "H." It turned out to be a one-story building at the edge of town, next to a shipping firm's truck parking lot, up against a low hill and surrounded by the ever-present sagebrush and cacti. I parked in the visitors' lot and walked in the front door.

Lessee now… Where is administration?

"Can I help you, sir?"

"I'm Dr. Roode."

Blank stare.

"I'm the new surgeon. I'm supposed to work here for the next couple of months."

"Oh, of course! Right this way." And she showed me to the administrator's office.

The administrator turned out to be a lady. Yes, I was to hear some tales of her toughness, but later, Betty and I were to be warmly welcomed into her home at Christmastime. But at first, it was all stiffness and formality. Introductions all around the office—names and faces that I would forget within two minutes. The next order of business was a tour of the hospital. I was handed off to the head nurse for that chore, and off we went, dashing through the building.

"Wait a minute! Stop and draw me a map of this place so I can put things in place," I cried.

The OR proved to be pedestrian. The hospital actually boasted two operating rooms no less, but then they had only one crew—so there might as well have been only one. Everybody was pleasant, smiling, but still uneasy. They were all wondering what the new guy would *really* be like.

Will he throw things? Will he yell? Will he be aloof or can we actually relax around him or even joke a little? Wish we had good old Dr. M. back…

I was smiling and bobbing my head and trying to be both pleasant and reassuring to an uncertain OR staff while still projecting an aura of confidence that not only do I know what I am doing but that I will, after all, be in charge here. They showed off their OR rooms proudly and began with the hesitant questions…

"What do you like to use to close with all we have is chromic for the peritoneum that's all that Dr. M. used." The words rush out of Angie (the head OR nurse) both anxiously and apologetically.

"That will be fine," I responded. Only later would I streamline this whole process by writing a personal manual of OR procedures that I could give to a new crew so that they would know how I did things.

Then we were off to see the apartment that the hospital had rented. I was to learn that this apartment was used by the hospital on a more or less permanent basis. I was only the latest in a succession of *locum* surgeons who had come and gone.

Hmm...

This was a small point that the recruiting agency had conveniently neglected to mention when they painted such a rosy picture of this job opportunity.

What are the real problems here? I wondered.

Ever since Dr. M. had left for "greener pastures," the hospital had been looking for a surgeon but, so far, to no avail. And so for the next several months, I was the only surgeon there. Yes, they did invite Betty and me to relocate there, but by then, we were becoming thoroughly addicted to the *locum* lifestyle.

The apartment was clean and modern, located at the very top of the highest bit of land in the city. From its balcony, I could look down to the hospital in the valley below. Directly behind it, in the distance, was a distinctive mountain. In this part of the world, the timberline is reversed. The trees grow from the timberline on up; the lower slopes are too hot and arid.

In the days that followed, when I'd finished seeing the few patients they had for me, I was free to roam. My binoculars had revealed an inviting dirt road winding up the side of that solitary mountain behind the hospital. I headed out the south end of town, past some run-down shacks and an empty corral, then up the eroded and eroding dirt road. Here one could see geology in action. I hiked up an inviting arroyo. People have drowned in these arroyos, I have read, on clear and cloudless days. Now I could understand why.

The walls were vertical in places. If one were to imagine a cloud-burst over the horizon, the water wouldn't soak into the hardpan desert floor. Flash flood! I could imagine a rumbling noise, then turning in panic to run but easily being outpaced by the roiling brown water. I set my camera on a nearby rock and took a picture of myself. Who of my friends or former patients in Iowa would believe what had become of their surgeon! With a battered hat, blue jeans, and a sweaty T-shirt, I didn't look the part.

Over and over again, I marveled to myself, *People will actually pay me to live like this!*

My enthusiasm for my Arizona surroundings was a source of continual amusement for the nurses. One day, I discovered a tarantula walking down the hospital corridor. The nurse calmly used a dustpan to put it outside. (They are much too large to squash.) On another day, it was a scorpion that I discovered in the hospital. The next day, one of the nurses gleefully handed me a brown paper package. Inside was a whole jar full of living scorpions she'd captured at home. They were all amazed at my childish delight, for I knew exactly what to do. I went straight to the local drugstore and bought a pint of rubbing alcohol, which I poured over them. The largest was then fished out, and carefully mounted on a 3 × 5 card with dabs of airplane glue.

"Boy, will Betty be surprised when she gets *this* in the mail!" I chortled.

I carefully set him out in the air on the apartment balcony, only to find that after a day or so, he was getting a mite soft in the middle.

What he needs is more sunlight, I thought.

So on one of my daily jaunts up the dirt road south of town, I took him along and carefully set him out on a rock, weighed down with a couple of little stones.

Just then, my beeper went off.

Uh-oh.

I'd left my cellular phone at the apartment. There was only one thing to do—dash back to the hospital. I was asked to see a patient in the ER. When I was done, it was dark. The next day, I checked on my scorpion, only to find eight small scorpion feet still glued to the 3 × 5 card was all that remained. I supposed there was a drunk roadrunner somewhere that night in the Arizona desert! So much for my plans for mailing scorpions back to Iowa.

On one of my explorations, I came across a visitor center and gift shop! A cactus book lured me. I parted with a buck and a half and had this marvelous little pocket field guide. Now I could learn about the cacti that fill the landscape. Only thirty pages long, it was organized in a logical fashion that appealed to my scientific instinct.

You start at page 1 and answer the first question: "Does the cactus have branches? If yes, go to page 6. If no, go to page 4. If you continued through the book, it would lead you to the name of the cactus that you happened to be standing in front of.

Late that afternoon, on my way back to the apartment, I pulled off into an abandoned dirt road for the umpteenth time and hiked out into the desert at the base of a hill covered with silvery, soft-looking cacti. I tried my new little cactus identification book. Following the questions and directions, I concluded that it was one of the cholla cactus species.

But the question on page 11 intrigued me. It invited me to strike the cactus with a pencil. If it falls apart, I have a "teddy bear" cholla. If not, then it will be another kind. I have no pencil handy, but there is a stick. And lo! The branches break off with barely a nudge. They break into segments. And then I saw that the ground was strewn with these segments that I hadn't noticed before. I was fascinated. So this is how this plant propagates. A wandering and perhaps indiscreet animal would bump it or maybe just the wind, and voila!

I wandered through the cactus field, randomly knocking off branches. The book cautioned against trying to pick up any of the segments. But one had attached itself to my shoelace. I reached down tentatively and gently nudged it with my finger. Suddenly, it was attached to me! These things were sharper than a scalpel. And barbed! Now the segment was painfully attached to my hand. I had to approach this problem carefully, or things would get a lot worse. I walked around with a cholla segment attached to my left hand, looking for a suitable implement for its removal. Finally, somewhat uncomfortably, I scraped it off with a nearby stick. The broken-off spines were not deeply embedded. I could pick them out with my teeth.

It nevertheless occurred to me that a cowboy could have a very unpleasant ride through a cactus field. I mean, just lightly brushing up against one of them could lead to all sorts of problems that we never read about in dime-store novels. No wonder they invented chaps! But what if you happened to be thrown from your horse and actually landed on one of these? What did they do in the days before hospitals? I presumed one should be able to pick all the spines out of such a victim, but if it were a child, he might need anesthesia.

The sun was sinking low, and it was time to return to my apartment. I checked in at the hospital upon my return, and no, nobody was looking for me. Good. It was a freebie. I had a beautiful afternoon to myself, saw new things, learned new things, wasn't missed, and got paid for it to boot.

It was a week later, in the early evening while it was still light, that I learned what happens to cowboys who are thrown into Teddy Bear Cholla cacti. My beeper went off. It was the hospital operator, who informed me that the ER would like to talk to me.

Soon the ER doctor was on the line. "I've got a man here who was in a motor vehicle accident and is going to need a chest tube."

To the uninitiated, this means that he has as a minimum some broken ribs, one of which has punctured his lung. I was being requested to insert a tube between his collapsed lung and the chest wall for the purpose of re-expanding his lung.

"Okay, I'll be right in."

When I walked into the ER, I found the usual bustle of activity. No, it wasn't the pandemonium of trauma, just the usual quiet hum of a busy ER. Patients with colds, fevers, and the flu were sitting patiently on the chairs that lined the hallway, waiting their turn to be seen. The exam rooms were all full. I went into the trauma bay and found things quiet. Indeed, the nurse had stepped out to tend to something else. At first, the room seemed empty.

I thought there was an accident victim here! Then I noticed the unshaven man lying there on the gurney with an IV running. *Evidently the victim*, I thought as I wandered over to see. I was greeted by the familiar odor of stale alcohol and vomitus. *Hmm… He appears to be sleeping peacefully. There are abrasions on his face, so he must be the accident victim. But man, look at all those cholla spines!*

He was covered with them. There must be hundreds of them, each embedded to a different depth, each protruding at a different angle, some broken off at skin level, some sticking out. Now I was to find out what happens to a cowboy who falls into a Teddy Bear

Cholla. Well, what was the story here? Things seemed stable, so I left in search for the nurse, finding her coming down the hall.

"What's going on?" I ask.

"Well, we have a motor vehicle accident with two victims. Manuel Garcia, the driver, rolled his jeep down an embankment. They were both thrown clear and tumbled to the bottom." Then she adds, somewhat unnecessarily, "They were drinking."

"When did this happen?" is my next question, as we both walk back into the examining room.

"We don't know. Sometime earlier today, they were both unconscious for an unknown period of time, but eventually, Manuel came to and crawled back up the ravine and hailed a passing car."

And then I notice the other victim—a youngish woman who is also completely covered with teddy bear cholla spines. She, too, is lying quietly, but at least she isn't asleep. It is Manuel, however, who needs the chest tube. The chest X-ray on the wall viewer shows that his left lung is, perhaps, 50 percent collapsed. Broken ribs, no doubt. But also there is no doubt in my mind that he isn't seriously hurt.

Anytime you have a patient who was in an accident several hours ago, lays unconscious at the bottom of a ravine in the desert with no medical attention, then crawls back up the embankment, and finally arrives in the ER with stable vital signs…well, you simply don't have a life-threatening condition. By definition. Period. This case is gonna be a "freebie" for me; a simple chest tube and an admission. Then paperwork. This is not gonna be mad, life-and-death rush to the OR to save an accident victim from bleeding to death.

I turn my attention to Manuel. I don't know about the woman. I am not even asked to see her, so she must be even less injured than Manuel. His wife, no doubt. I'll be glad to see her if the ER doctor wants me to; otherwise, I'll let him handle her disposition. And so I nudge Manuel. He grunts and goes back to sleep. Certainly, the collapsed lung isn't giving him any breathing difficulties. I nudge him again, harder. He wakes up and stares bleary-eyed at me.

"What's your name?" I yell.

"Garcia," he mumbles and then falls back to sleep.

"Do you hurt anywhere?"

"Grunt."

He had walked up the embankment, so I presume he doesn't have any broken bones in his legs. While he could have a head injury, probably all we have is a man who is pretty well anesthetized by his "drug of choice." I'll have to keep him overnight for observation to be sure and X-ray every place where there is a bruise.

But look at those cholla spines! There must be hundreds of them. How are we going to get them all out?

I am interrupted by the nurse asking me what size of chest tube I want to put in.

"Oh, 28 should be okay. And do you use Pleur-evacs here?"

"Yes, I'll get it ready."

I turn back to Manuel and complete his physical exam. Those hundreds of cholla spines continue to intrigue me. Manuel and the woman are both covered with them. Later, I described the couple to Betty as looking like porcupines with crew cuts! It was only last week that I even learned the name of the pretty silvery cactus that covers so many of the hills. And even then I didn't know how to properly pronounce it. One of the doctors in the hospital, with only a slightly pained expression on his face, had corrected me, pronouncing it slowly, "C-H-O-Y-Y-A."

Last week, on one of my idyllic exploration rides, I had wondered what would have happened to a cowboy who was accidentally thrown into such a beast. Now Manuel had obligingly gotten himself thrown from his modern-day horse. *I wonder if it was a Bronco?*

I rummage through a drawer against the wall, finding a sterile hemostat.[1] I rip the package open and use it to grasp one of the spines. It comes out easily enough, and Manuel says "grunt." I pull out another. And another. And another...

Well, no mystery here, but he is, after all, well anesthetized. But it quickly becomes boring, you know. Who has the patience to sit here and tease out hundreds of cholla spines? Then I notice that a nurse's aide was washing the woman and is in the process of pulling

---

[1] It's a small pliers-like surgical instrument ordinarily used to clamp blood vessels.

out her cactus spines. It is all quite routine. This isn't a strange or unusual occurrence to her—just to the new guy from Iowa.

The nurse is finally ready with the chest tube. This, at least, is familiar. I prep Manuel's skin and carefully place the drapes around the selected spot on his left chest. Manuel sleeps peacefully.

"Be a little pinch here!" I yell.

Nothing. He doesn't seem to mind the Novocain.

Why do we still call it Novocain when all that we use nowadays is Xylocaine? I wonder.

The chest tube insertion proceeds uneventfully, with Manuel coughing repeatedly as his lung re-expands. After inserting the chest tube, I place the dressings. I always like to do that myself so that I know that the tube is securely both stitched and taped in place. It saves phone calls at 3 a.m., saying, "Doctor, I don't know how this happened, but we just found so-and-so's chest tube *lying* on the floor. We were just in there..."

At this juncture, I become aware that the room is suddenly and strangely quiet. Nobody is talking. All are looking—no, staring—at this older woman standing in the doorway.

"What's going on?" she loudly demands.

Who is this lady? Who let her in here anyhow? We're taking care of trauma victims. What is this, visiting hours? Somebody throw her out.

"Doctor, this is *Missus* Manuel Garcia," says the ER secretary, who had accompanied her into the trauma room.

Stunned silence. *Of course! The other victim is much younger than Manuel. Why am I so dense? Manuel was out drinking with his girl-friend. Now we have this touchy threesome on our hands.*

"Well, ma'am, your husband has a collapsed lung, and I just put a chest tube in to re-expand it. He'll be fine."

But I shall never forget the marvelous mixture of emotions on her face. Anger. Concern. Disgust. Anxiety. And yes, smug satisfaction that he'd been "caught." She didn't know whether to be angry with him or not. Then her questions kept tumbling out.

"Who are you?"

"I'm Dr. Roode, and I'm filling in here temporarily till they get a permanent surgeon."

"Where did this happen?"

"I don't know. You'll have to ask the police."

"Does he have any broken bones?"

"No."

"How are you going to get all those spines out?"

"We'll pull them all out." I still have the hemostat handy, and to demonstrate, I pull one out.

"Grunt," says Manuel.

"Is he gonna be all right?"

"Yes." I pull out another spine. Another grunt from Manuel.

"Are you sure? Have you taken care of things like this before?"

Finally I decide that I can no longer reassure her. Besides, she is starting to get on everybody's nerves.

"Look, lady. Do you want to do something nice for your husband?"

"Uh. I guess so…"

"Okay. Here's this thing." I hand her the hemostat. "*You* pull out the spines."

She tentatively grasps one, and pulls.

"Harder," I say.

After the spine comes out, she pulls another. I leave to check on the lab work. The vital signs are still stable. I am not needed in the trauma bay any longer. I have paperwork to do. I write up his admission orders in an alcove and dictate the H&P.[2]

Fifteen minutes later, I return to the trauma room. What a transformation has taken place in the real Mrs. Garcia! She is industriously pulling out spines and has even enlisted the aid of their ten-year-old son.

She looks up and grins broadly. "Doctor, I'm going to charge him a dollar for each one!" she proudly announces, pointing to the row of spines neatly lined up on the counter behind her.

---

[2] The History and Physical exam report that must be filed on every patient's chart.

CHAPTER 4

The Adventure Continues

My evolution as a *locum* surgeon continued in Arizona. I purchased a small word processor to carry with me. In it were placed all of my postoperative instructions so that I could print them out on the local hospital's stationery. At the end of each day, I recalled the patients I'd seen. Were any of them particularly outstanding, unusual, illustrative of human nature, or otherwise memorable? If so, their stories made it into that word processor. Without those original, contemporaneous notes, this book would have been impossible.

My first word processor was a little affair that I could simply carry with me on the airlines. This later evolved to become an "oak office,"[1] in which I placed other office essentials. I also began carrying with me special surgical instruments that I found necessary, those that the host hospital might not have. After a year of *locum tenens* surgery, we graduated into using a fifth-wheel RV for both travel and lodging. It was then easy to carry additional essentials, such as my operating room headlight, which was especially valuable when I was working through a small incision. Many times I found myself alone in a small hospital without the usual specialty backup. And so I began carrying with me a large number of medical textbooks in CD format.

---

[1]   A "suitcase" I made of oak, with compartments in which I carried not only my computer but all manner of office supplies. I was able to check this in with the airlines.

The following are a few of the patients from early in my *locum* career, ranging from those with trivial conditions to those facing life-threatening situations. They all took place in Arizona, within roughly a hundred miles of Phoenix.

Rachel Freemantle

I received a call from a doctor at a nearby hospital, asking me if I could stand by while he attempted a VBAC.[2] Alas, I had no surgical privileges at his hospital, and so I demurred. Although a physician may possess a valid state medical license, he or she must still be credentialed by each hospital before actually seeing any patients there. As a result, the doctor in question wound up admitting the patient to the hospital that I was covering. Eventually, I would have to perform a C-section on her—but for fetal distress, not a ruptured uterus. This was my first C-section at this hospital. I pulled out all the stops and got the baby out in just over three minutes by the clock. There was a hushed silence, and I wondered where I'd gone wrong. It was later confided to me that I'd just beaten Dr. M.'s all-time record. What better way to start off in a new hospital! Word spread all over the hospital that at last they had a surgeon who could operate.[3]

---

[2] VBAC stands for a "Vaginal Birth After a C-section." The fear in the 1990s was that, for a woman who has had a prior C-section, the uterine scar, which is potentially a weak point, could rupture during labor, creating a life-threatening emergency. So for a long time, the mandate was "once a C-section, always a C-section." Those who tried a VBAC had to ensure they had plenty of backup immediately available in case the uterus did indeed rupture. However, nowadays, a low-transverse uterine incision is used, and this greatly reduces any chance of a uterine rupture.

[3] Dr. M was the respected surgeon who'd left this hospital. This was the reason they were forced to use *locum tenens* surgeons. They had been disappointed with a series of academic, research surgeons they had hired who were not used to actually doing surgery. Their latest *locum* surgeon was a "world-renowned" surgeon from Boston. It turned out that he was world-renowned for his research but hadn't done any actual surgery for two decades! A small hospital in the Arizona desert is *not* the place to get back into the swing of things!

Little did I realize at the time that my ability to perform a C-section was to be a big factor in being able to actually make a living doing *locum* surgery. If the lone surgeon in a small town is the only one who can do this operation and if he leaves town, not only must the surgery department close but also the OB department. If fetal distress should develop and there is no way to rescue the baby, well, that is an open-and-shut million-dollar lawsuit that is quietly settled out of court. Incidentally, most general surgeons are not comfortable performing a C-section due in part to limited exposure during training coupled with the fact that they rarely, if ever, do this operation. The *locum* agencies often have to hunt far and wide for those few who can.

Carl Reid (An Unexpected Colon Cancer)

A delightful seventy-nine-year-old man was sent over by Dr. C, who had discovered a left inguinal hernia. My physical exam, however, revealed a mass in the lower left quadrant of his abdomen. I scheduled him for an endoscopic examination, and that was how we diagnosed his rectosigmoid colon cancer. His operation was therefore a colon resection rather than a simple hernia repair. Once again, Pete Roode stock around the hospital rose. Many times, Betty and I were asked to move here permanently, but by now, we had become thoroughly enamored with the *locum* lifestyle.

Beverly Lawson (Medical Imponderables)

There are patients with medical problems that trap health-care providers into uncomfortable situations with no easy solutions. The case of Beverly Lawson illustrates how we struggle with such issues as patients without resources or patients with difficult medical conditions beyond local ability—all in an environment rife with bureaucratic rules and regulations. I am no politician. I have no snappy answers. All I can do is describe the situation Beverly presented.

Society has struggled with these problems, but evidently, it still has a ways to go.

I was out jogging one pleasant afternoon when my beeper went off. It repeated in two to three minutes, so I knew it was something urgent. I hightailed it back to the apartment, and once I was on the phone, I was informed by the ER physician that they had a lady in labor with a transverse lie[4] and would I please come in and do a C-section! I inquired as to who was the patient's physician and was informed that she had none. A midwife had driven out from the Phoenix area in an attempt to deliver this patient at home.

Oh, how people like to imagine and long for the "good old days" with "natural" home deliveries. Who wants to go to the nasty, expensive hospital with its uncaring doctors and nurses? Who would want to be treated like a number? How much nicer to deliver at home, eh?

It was the midwife who recognized the transverse lie. She made the long-distance call to her supervisor, asking for advice. It was suggested to her that she take her patient to the nearest hospital for delivery. I informed the ER physician that I was not an obstetrician and wouldn't recognize a transverse lie if I fell over one. I suggested that he should get one of the family physicians with obstetrical privileges into the hospital. The enormity of my predicament was then brought home to me with the next bit of information. They were all away, and the only physician with any knowledge of obstetrics was *me*.

So I dashed to the ER and found the situation as described. Somebody was hooking up a fetal monitor, and everybody looked to me to solve this problem. At least I knew that treatment of a transverse lie is *not* an automatic C-section. There are ways to externally rotate the fetus so that it can deliver vaginally. Not being an obstetrician, I hadn't the faintest idea of how one should go about perform-

---

4   The fetus is lying horizontally in the uterus. Normally, they are either vertex (head down) or breech (head up). A transverse lying fetus cannot be delivered. One's choice is to somehow manipulate the uterus to rotate the fetus into either vertex or breech. Only when such a version maneuver fails is one forced to do a C-section.

ing these maneuvers. She needed to be under the care of somebody with obstetrical knowledge and skills, but no one was available.

We now entered a world of medical care imponderables, of problems without easy solutions. Hospitals hold themselves forth to the public as providing health care. Consequently, the public expects (demands?) that this service is available 24/7. Emergency rooms, for example, are not open only during daylight hours. You are pretty much assured that a physician will somehow be available anytime you need emergency care. Are exceptions made for other areas of service the hospital provides? How can it be that no physician was available for someone in need of emergency obstetrical care?

This in turn gets into the matter of how health care is provided in this country. Is it a right or a privilege? What about those who have no insurance and who lack the means to pay for their care? Must hospitals and health-care providers provide the service gratis? Well, yes, there are governmental programs to pay for a part of their care, but that still leaves the hospitals coming up short. And you'd be surprised at how many people have not availed themselves of these services. Independent physicians are still free to accept or refuse to see nonemergency patients without insurance.

I, being a *locum* surgeon, am lucky… I receive a salary just for being available. So the insurance status or ability of a patient to pay matters not one whit to me. This is one of the attractive features of this lifestyle. I can provide care to all without fretting about any economic consequences.

Back to the case in hand—Beverly. She had an obstetrical problem that nobody present knew how to deal with. Worse, she was in active labor, and it was physically impossible for her to deliver the infant. The problem could not be "shelved" until somebody with that knowledge returned to town. What to do? One obvious solution would be to simply transfer her to another hospital that had the capability of dealing with a transverse lie. But that was easier said than done, for there are rules against transferring patients in active labor. Never mind the fact that this rule could very well harm Beverly, the rule stands. (An aside: I must make it clear that this episode took place more than twenty-five years ago. In what follows, I describe the then-current rules and regulations. For all I know, they may have changed since then.)

Now why would there be governmental regulations against the transfer of a patient in active labor? Here's the explanation. In the past, there have been cases of indigent patients in uncomplicated labor who present to a hospital just like Beverly has presented here to us. And in those cases, some hospitals have chosen to transfer said patient to another hospital. Laboring patients have been loaded into ambulances that set out for a distant hospital. This is called "patient dumping," and there have been instances of a woman delivering the child in the moving ambulance. All in all, not a desirable situation, eh! And so our all-knowing, wise government has "solved" this problem by making it illegal to transfer a woman in labor. Thus, Beverly, with her very real problem, is trapped in a place that cannot care for her.

My immediate problem, of course, was what I was supposed to do? Should I try to take care of a woman with a condition for which I have no experience only because I was the only physician available? If something went wrong, I could easily be blamed in any resulting medical malpractice lawsuit. Or should I transfer her to another hospital where there was somebody who could take care of her and, in the process, risk a $50,000 fine from the government? Nice choices.

I called a medical center in Phoenix and asked for advice on what to do and whether they could accept her in transfer even though she was in active labor? I was instructed in the dose of terbutaline.[5] Glory be, it worked! Her labor stopped. Since we still had no physician who knew how to rotate a fetus, our only option was that she still needed to be transferred, rules or not. And so the helicopter was called. She remained stable, and it seemed like a reasonable course of action. After conferring with the nurse on the helicopter and calling Phoenix once more, we swallowed hard, took a deep breath, and broke the law. We transferred her to Phoenix.

---

[5]   This is a drug to stop labor and thus buy time for solution of the problem at hand.

She arrived safely. An obstetrician did a manual external version, and she ultimately delivered vaginally. There was no need for a C-section. So all was well that ended well.

Later, as my education progressed, I learned that a transverse lie is one of the few remaining absolute indications for an old-fashioned classical uterine incision.[6] If you try the popular low-segment transverse uterine incision, you are rewarded with a 50 percent fetal mortality rate! Why is that? Well, chances are that there is usually a definite reason for the transverse lie, some anomaly, perhaps an abnormally short umbilical cord that you can't deal with through the low transverse uterine incision. You wind up tearing the cord and risk losing the infant. So had I been stampeded into doing a C-section or had the terbutaline not worked, I would have used the only uterine incision I was familiar with, and there is every reason to expect that I might well be poring over legal briefs rather than contentedly writing these lines on my new word processor in the hospital apartment.

Now what was my thanks for all this? The patient was unaware that there was even a problem. All she wanted was for her labor pains to stop. Furthermore, she never received a bill from the hospital. Her father-in-law, however, wrote an irate letter to the hospital administrator, complaining about our treatment of his daughter-in-law. He was particularly incensed that I "didn't even examine" her.

Jeff King (A Cardiac Arrest in the Desert)

We now come to my most memorable, most difficult, and most educational case of this assignment. On a rainy afternoon (yes, it does rain in Arizona!), about three blocks from the hospital, Jeff King pulled out in front of another car. The windows of his car were steamed up, and he didn't bother to roll them down to see if anybody was coming. Unfortunately for him, somebody was.

---

[6]   A large vertical incision is made into the uterus. The low transverse incision that is so popular, the only one I knew at the time, heals much better.

When I saw him in the ER, he had a left flail chest.[7] For this, I placed a chest tube, which stabilized his condition. However, a flail chest—and the likely underlying pulmonary contusion—was clearly something that we were not equipped to handle in this small isolated hospital. Alas, due to the foggy weather, I was unable to arrange for a rapid (helicopter) transfer to a trauma center. A transfer via ambulance would take much longer. I had to be sure he was not hemorrhaging internally.

If you try to transfer a hemorrhaging patient, via ambulance, to a distant hospital, he or she will surely deteriorate. And so I performed a peritoneal lavage,[8] which has the advantage of being quick and easy to do as compared to a CT scan. Well, my peritoneal lavage returned gross blood, mandating an immediate dash to the OR. His pre-op hemoglobin was 7.8 grams, and I carelessly wrote that off as "lab error."[9] It seemed the thing to do at the time, but my error was to come back to haunt me a few hours later. Things are always so much clearer in retrospect.

Yes, I was still covering the hospital where I had struggled with the abdominal stabbing related in Chapter 1. As much as I wanted to avoid any more trauma surgery in this poorly equipped hospital, it was forced on me. No other possible choice.

At surgery, I discovered he was bleeding from a ruptured spleen, but before I could remove it, Jeff developed an even more life-threatening condition—a tension pneumothorax.[10] Now how could that

---

[7] Ribs broken in two places so that the section of the chest wall between the breaks flops up and down. A patient cannot breathe efficiently with a flail chest.

[8] A small tube is inserted into the abdomen to see if there is any free blood there, indicating an injury to one of the internal organs.

[9] Why a lab error? Normal hemoglobin is twelve to fourteen grams. If you are bleeding to death, your blood is running out, and the last drop before you die will have the normal value of twelve to fourteen grams. The hemoglobin level only drops if you have had a slow, chronic blood loss and your body has replaced the lost blood with serum, diluting your blood and lowering the measured hemoglobin level.

[10] In this situation, not only was the lung collapsed but the surrounding pleural space was somehow under increased pressure forcing the heart over to the opposite side of the chest, compressing that lung as well.

have happened after I had placed a chest tube? Well, the hospital's suction pump had failed. A blood clot then formed in his chest tube. The result was that his injured lung not only collapsed but pressure then built up in his left chest, pushing the heart to the right and compressing his right lung. And as per usual in this hospital, there was nobody else available to replace the chest tube. I had to break scrub (stop surgery in his bleeding abdomen) and place a second chest tube.

After placing the second chest tube, I returned to controlling the situation in the abdomen. Fortunately, we lost only 1,500 cc of blood in surgery. We replaced his blood loss with 2 units of packed red blood cells and 2,000 cc of Ringer's.[11] It was then off to the ICU. Another successful case. Or so I thought.

It was at this point that things began to unravel. When I first saw Jeff's face after surgery, I was shocked to see how white it was. I inquired about his blood pressure (which had been stable during surgery), only to find that it had since dropped down into the 60s. Now what the hell was going on? Had a tie let loose? Was he bleeding again in the abdomen? Should I take him back to surgery? Had he developed another tension pneumothorax? I ordered more lab work, a chest X-ray, and began transfusions. I also placed a third chest tube, and did another peritoneal lavage. There was no blood in the abdomen. The chest X-ray did not show another pneumothorax. The CBC came back with a hemoglobin of only 6! Where could the blood be going?

Later, too much later, it dawned on me that he was not bleeding at all, that what I had here was a chronically ill old man driving a car around town with a hemoglobin of less than eight *before the accident*. I should not have carelessly discarded the initial blood test as erroneous.

Meanwhile, I was still most anxious to get Jeff into a trauma center where they could care for his chest injuries. The weather remained way too foggy for a helicopter. Now the rules are such that you simply cannot transfer anybody without having some physician

---

[11] It's an IV solution, basically distilled water with some chemicals added.

accept him on the other end of the line. So I was simultaneously try-ing to talk to physicians in Phoenix (the first one I talked to refused to take him), trying to figure out why Jeff was doing so poorly and continuing to monitor and optimize his care. It was a most hectic time.

While more blood was being transfused, our nurse anesthetist, quite unbeknownst to me, gave Jeff 1 milligram of Neo-Synephrine.[12] He did it because Jeff's blood pressure was so low, and he told me what he'd done *after he'd done it.* Now I knew that this was not the right thing to do when treating hypovolemia[13] and had never done it myself. But what I didn't know was how god-awful bad that is for the patient. We are taught to treat hypovolemia with volume,[14] not vasoconstrictors like Neo-Synephrine. I asked for an arterial blood gas, and it came back with unbelievable numbers: pH = 6.8 and pCO_2 = 135! What to make of this new information? He was on the ventilator. His chest X-ray was reasonable. He was obviously still in shock but was receiving blood. So for the second time in the day, I discarded a lab data as erroneous. What this lab test was trying to tell me was that his heart was unable to pump sufficient blood through his constricted blood vessels.

While all this was going on, I had finally been able to arrange for his transfer to Phoenix. A fixed-wing aircraft was at the nearest airport, several miles away. In general, fixed-wing air ambulances can fly and land in much worse weather than helicopters. I called for the ambulance, gave Jeff two ampoules of bicarbonate, grabbed two bags of blood, and rode with him to the airport. It was now 9 p.m., and the air evacuation team at the airport was furious with me because they had been kept waiting half an hour at the airport. Ordinarily, such a team expects to be met at the airport, be taken to the hospital

---

[12] This is a drug that causes blood vessels to constrict. When they do, the blood pressure comes up. But the patient is *not* improved because it is harder for the heart to pump blood through constricted blood vessels. The rise in the blood pressure caused by Neo-Synephrine merely makes some of the attending medical personnel feel better.

[13] Low blood volume caused by bleeding.

[14] Blood transfusions and IV solutions.

where they can (*plod, plod, plod*) evaluate the patient. But I had taken Jeff out to the airport to shorten the transfer time. This did not please them one little bit. When the ambulance backed up to the airplane and opened the doors, they were horrified that we had the patient right there with us.

"WHAT! You have the patient here!" they exclaimed.

"Damn right I do."

We loaded old Jeff into the air ambulance. The doors were shut. The pilot started the turboprop engines. Suddenly, there were two gushes of flames from the exhaust pipes, and the engines stopped.

Great! I thought. *Engine trouble.*

But no, the aircraft door was flung open, and the nurse yelled, "Get in here, Doc! He's having a code!"[15]

So there I was running a cardiac arrest code in a darkened airplane at the end of a dark runway in the middle of the dark Arizona desert. How do I get into these situations? And why was I doing this to this poor old man? He was surely going to die. His bradycardia[16] progressed to asystole.[17] I resorted to the outmoded intracardiac epinephrine,[18] with a gratifying return of his heartbeat. For his bradycardia, I gave him atropine,[19] and then, not knowing what else to do, I gave him what in retrospect probably saved his life—two more ampoules of bicarbonate.

His cardiac rhythm returned. He stabilized. The air ambulance took off. When he arrived in Phoenix, he was in stable condition. He was not in shock. As a matter of fact, the physicians in Phoenix had a hard time understanding just what all the excitement at our hospital had been about. To them, it was a simple case of an old man with a flail chest and a ruptured spleen, who was properly treated with a chest tube and splenectomy. They must see hundreds of such cases a year. So what was the big deal?

---

[15] Cardiac arrest.

[16] Slow heart rate.

[17] Cardiac arrest. His heart was no longer beating.

[18] I injected adrenaline through his chest wall and directly into his heart.

[19] A drug to speed up the heartbeat.

I went home to try to put it all together in my mind. The next day, as I was reading an old (1983) issue of *Surgical Clinics of North America*, a sentence on pulmonary physiologic dead space leaped out of the page at me. The only way to raise pCO_2—the amount of CO_2 in the blood—is to either increase CO_2 generation or increase the physiologic dead space. This happens in low flow states and with the administration of vasoconstrictor drugs. Of course! The damned Neo-Synephrine! The anemia! It all made sense to me now after the fact. I had operated on a chronically ill, anemic old man and had not given him enough blood during surgery. His vital signs were stable up till the end as they so often are. I should not have discarded the pre-op hemoglobin determination. What we had was a classic low-flow postoperative state and made it hugely worse by giving him the Neo-Synephrine. His cardiac output must have been zilch. The blood gasses were essentially correct, but I wasn't smart enough to interpret them.

The bicarbonate saved Jeff's life while the Neo-Synephrine was wearing off. Oh, yes, I did check the half-life of the Neo-Synephrine. Its effect is gone in about fifty-five minutes, almost the exact amount of time it took us to get him from our hospital to Phoenix via that darkened airstrip in the desert! No wonder the physicians in Phoenix found him to be stable and rather unremarkable. Both our anesthetist and I were sadder and wiser after this case, and fortunately, Jeff was none the worse for wear.

CHAPTER 5

Tales of Sitting Bull

Mobridge, a pleasant town of roughly 3,500 pleasant people, right on the Missouri River, was the site of my next *locum* assignment. The call from Mobridge came after its beloved surgeon, Dr. Lawrence, relocated south. I had known him way back in the 1970s at Geisinger Medical Center in Pennsylvania, where we both received our surgery training. And so 1991 found me trying to fill his shoes. At least the townspeople were pleased to have a classmate of Dr. Lawrence's available.

Betty and I were both cordially welcomed into town. After three months, a permanent replacement for Dr. Lawrence was hired, and we were then off to new adventures elsewhere. Several years later, that replacement also relocated, and we were called back. In all, I served the good people of Mobridge during six different time periods. Betty and I are still in touch with friends we made there.

Nonmedical Reminiscences of Mobridge

Mobridge is the westernmost town in South Dakota still in the Central Time Zone. Drive across the bridge over the Missouri River, and you are on Mountain Time. If you get off work at 5 p.m. in Mobridge and live across the river, you arrive at home shortly after 4 p.m. Years ago, the railroad bridge was simply known as the Missouri Bridge. Abbreviate the names, and the railroad siding became known as the "Mo-bridge." As people settled and a town grew, the name stuck—Mobridge, South Dakota.

Mobridge's annual rodeo is called the Sitting Bull Stampede, fittingly named after the nineteenth-century Indian (er, Native American...er, Early American) chief who either was or was not (depending on whom you listen to) at the Battle of Little Big Horn, who either personally did or did not defeat (depending on whom you listen to) General Custer, and who either is or is not (depending on whom you listen to) buried at Mobridge. On the other hand, perhaps he is or is not (depending on whom you listen to) buried at Ft. Yates, *North* Dakota.

And thereby hangs an interesting tale.

Back in April 1953, some Mobridge residents made a midnight raid to Ft. Yates, dug into Sitting Bull's supposed grave, and recovered fragments of a human skull, which they then returned to Mobridge. Those fragments were then buried in a suitable location on a bluff overlooking the Missouri River just opposite the town of Mobridge. And to ensure that nobody from Ft. Yates would ever try to return those fragments to their "rightful" location, some twenty tons of cement were then poured over his grave. The reaction of Ft. Yates people?

"*Nah-uh.* You got the wrong human remains. Sitting Bull is still at Ft. Yates."

Being neophytes, Betty and I were fascinated at some of the trivia associated with the annual rodeo that we attended. For example, not one single contestant comes from Mobridge. The Mobridge citizens are 100 percent spectators. Naturally, I asked the OR crew to explain all this to me.

"Doc, they are all professionals."

"You mean riding bucking broncos is a profession?"

"Yup. Some of 'em make good money."

"Oh."

We were to learn more, much more. The various professional contestants participate in twenty to thirty rodeos per season. There is a complexity to this that we had not appreciated—various circuits, levels of entry, levels of contestants. Points are kept all season long. The contestants travel from town to town. Each week, they see the same familiar faces that they have competed against the week before. Making their lives more complex is the fact that the various towns do not collaborate with one another on the matter of scheduling. There might be two profitable rodeos that the professional riders very much want to register for taking place on the same day. The best riders find it worthwhile to actually rent an airplane. That way, they can ride a bucking bronco in Mobridge and then dash out to the airport and be flown over to Spearfish to ride again!

The record this year for a top contestant, who rented an airplane and judiciously using the time zone difference, was to participate in four rodeos in a single day. He caught the early performance in an eastern town, flew west (gaining an hour), did another rodeo, flew back east for a late show, and finished the day to the west.

But that is not all. Not only are all the contestants from out of town, but so are the animals! I thought they just rounded up local mean animals and rode 'em. Hardly! There are people who specially breed and raise horses and bulls to be rodeo contestants. Those animals also travel from town to town and see the same familiar animal faces in their fellow bulls and horses from week to week!

Not only are the animals considered professional participants, but the whole business is a two-layered affair. There are judges for the riders and other judges for the animals. The animals, like the riders, accumulated points, becoming more and more valuable to their owners. Rodeos then pay more and more for their services. The penalty for a human rider with a poor score is a polite round of tepid applause. But a bull that begins to turn in poor performances is soon converted into chuck steaks.

The day after the Sitting Bull Stampede, many a nurse in the hospital came up to me asking if we had enjoyed the rodeo. They then stood back to carefully evaluate my response. If I said it was okay, they shrugged and went on their way. But when I grinned and said "Sure thing!" or "Oh, boy!" they broke out into happy choruses of "Isn't it *great?*" Turning the tables on them, I asked *them* what *they* thought of it. The most common response is "The problem with this year's rodeo, Doc, is that the clown show was too long." Skip the clowns. They didn't come to see clowns. They came to see the bull riding.

One last point about the rodeo: During the bull riding, sometimes the bull gets it in his head to stomp the life out of the rider. For this, they have clowns to distract the bull as well as a barrel for the bull rider to jump into. And one last prop—a straw man that looks like a real person for the bull to charge and trample. What was the likeness of this year's straw man's face? Bill Clinton.

No Secrets in a Small Town

We have been amused in our various experiences over the years that there simply are no secrets in small towns. Here are illustrative examples from Mobridge.

On the first day of my first trip to Mobridge, I stopped in to the local barber shop. I had been too busy to have a haircut in Iowa before my departure. I quietly took a seat to wait my turn.

The barber, without looking up, said, "Hello, Doc."

I had been in town less than twenty-four hours and had never met the barber, but he and everybody else in town evidently knew who I was and what I was doing in town.

The day after the Sitting Bull Stampede, Betty and I were fifty miles away, nearing the town of Pollock, when we decided to stop for lunch in the local café. As we were munching our fish sandwiches and fries, a rancher who was leaving drawled, "Enjoy the rodeo, Doc?" as he walked past our table. We had no idea who he was.

Later, during idle banter in the OR, I asked the scrub nurse how people went about having affairs out here since we were spotted together fifty miles away in a cafe.

She said, "Well, you simply don't. And if you do, everybody knows about it instantly. There are even people who drive around the town at night, checking to see whose car is parked where…"

Jeremy Benson (Resourcefulness of Rural Doctors)

Jeremy, aged three, had a red raw perianal area that would occasionally bleed. He was seen by the town's beloved family physician

(Dr. Linde) and was referred to a pediatrician in Bismark, who determined that the child needed a colonoscopy. Alas, there was no *pediatric gastroenterologist* in Bismark, and you just have to see a pediatric gastroenterologist, don't you? He therefore suggested a referral to one in Fargo, North Dakota, some 270 miles to the east. Jeremy's parents refused to do this. What to do?

Dr. Linde asked me to see him. "Could you work something out?"

Hmm… He needed a colonoscopy. Yes, I'd done about a thousand of them, but the Mobridge Hospital did not have a pediatric-sized scope. *Hmm…* But we did have a gastroscope, which has a smaller diameter than a colonoscope and is plenty long enough. *So yes, let's do it!*

The "gastro-colono-scopic" exam ruled out any other conditions. The appearance of his perianal inflammation, coupled with a medical report I'd recently read, allowed me to suggest a diagnosis of perianal streptococcal infection. A simple penicillin prescription was all it took to cure the little tyke, but my using a gastroscope at the other end of the human alimentary canal led to endless hospital jokes and queries as to how well we cleaned it afterward.

Helen Berger (On Dumb Luck in Medicine)

Sometimes, for obscure reasons, the gods smile on you. There is no other way to explain this lady's good fortune.

I was asked to see ninety-one-year-old Helen because of an anemia. Part of my workup was a colonoscopy. I had successfully maneuvered the flexible fiber-optic examining scope to the right side and hadn't found a thing. It looked like it would be an entirely normal colon. But just as I was starting to withdraw from the cecum, a peculiar fold of tissue whipped across the monitor. I was the only one in the room to notice it, and I'd like to think that the reason I noticed it was because, at that time, I'd done nearly a thousand colonoscopies. But no matter how I maneuvered the scope, I was not able to see the entire lesion, just the edge of it. I was not able to even position the biopsy forceps to perform a biopsy so that we could have a tissue diagnosis.

Nevertheless, based on its appearance alone, I recommended that we do surgery despite her age and frail heart. I made a little five-inch incision right over the tumor, removed it in an hour, closed the bowel with running 4-0 PDS,[1] and was done before her heart knew we were messing around in her abdomen. This was the first time that anybody in Mobridge had seen such a small transverse incision for colon cancer using 4-0 PDS with no nasogastric tube and the patient being fed the next day.

Helen was lucky. That was all. I just chanced to see the lesion. What about other patients in whom I had not seen anything amiss? Have I missed a tumor in them? I worry about these things. Am I now growing a colon cancer as I type these words despite my own normal colonoscopy last year? I dunno. Sometimes life isn't fair. We don't always get what we deserve. There is ancient wisdom in that oddball biblical book of Ecclesiastes: "The race is not to the swift, nor the battle to the strong, neither does bread come to the wise, nor riches to men of understanding, nor favor to men of skill; *time and chance happens to them all*" (Ecclesiastes 9:11; emphasis mine).

Faith in the Practice of Medicine

Faith can be defined as a strong belief that you know what is going on. It can exist in the absence of evidence, or, worse, even in the presence of conflicting evidence. Faith is a key component in religion, but it is also occasionally needed in medicine. What follows is an illustrative story of inner doubts that can be running through a doctor's mind despite his external appearance of unperturbed confidence and calm. Faith that all is well is sometimes needed in caring for your patients. On the other hand, one must not allow misplaced faith to interfere with the safe practice of surgery. It is all such a delicate balance.

Mr. Chait, a semiretired grocer in Mobridge, had heart disease that eventually led to a quadruple coronary artery bypass graft done

---

[1]   A type of suture material.

a month before in Bismarck, North Dakota. On Friday, he came to see his Mobridge internist because he was short of breath. A chest X-ray revealed the problem—the left side of his chest was filled with fluid, compressing his lung. This can be easily remedied. You simply insert a needle or a tube into the chest cavity under local anesthesia and draw the fluid off. I've done it hundreds of times for heart failure or cancer. The internist called me over to his area of the clinic and introduced me to Mr. Chait. We then repaired to the ER, where this little drama was to unfold.

I carefully choose a spot on his back, about six inches to the left of his spine, and sufficiently high enough that I am sure will be safe. There is nothing on the inside of his chest at that location for me to hit with the needle. Besides, the needle only goes in a quarter of an inch or so before a thin, soft plastic tube is threaded through it. That plastic tube can't hurt a thing. All these articles of faith are buoyed by my having done this countless times. But nonetheless it remains faith, because I am unable to see through skin and ribs.

I had expected the fluid to be thin and bloody, as is usually the case. But what comes out of my soft, plastic tube is thick, dark blood. *Hmm… Unusual.*

Things seem to be going on smoothly enough, and so I chalk the thickness of the fluid up to my inexperience. I've never drained fluid out of a post-op heart surgery chest before. Heart surgeons always care for any complications in their patients. Maybe this kind of a complication is different than the cancer or heart failure patients I am familiar with?

We drain a liter. Then 500 more cc's. Then Mr. Chait says he feels dizzy. The nurse nudges me, nodding her head to the blood pressure gauge.

Holy cow! His blood pressure is down to 80! Is Mr. Chait going into shock? Can it be that this thick fluid is his actual blood? Could I have inadvertently placed the thin tube into his heart or a great vessel and even now am slowly but surely bleeding poor Mr. Chait to death? Oh my god!

But I know that the tip of the needle is in a safe place. The soft plastic tube had slid in through the needle so easily. I just can't be anywhere else than safely in his pleural space. However I can't actually see inside his chest, so it is not unlike a religious faith, eh? Could Chait have some peculiar anatomic variation? Or could it be something related to his surgery?

As another 300 cc of that thick red fluid comes out, I find my "faith" rapidly deteriorating. I force myself to be still, to try to quell my growing doubt. Mr. Chait is feeling worse and worse. I disconnect the tube from the suction. If it really is in a great vessel, then the blood should spurt out. It doesn't. It merely tidals up and down, back and forth, evenly with his breathing, like it should. That means the tube is just where it is supposed to be. My wavering faith is restored and I resume draining the red fluid. Mr. Chait, however becomes chalky white. My faith wavers again. Still his pulse is reassuringly slow. If he really is in shock, it would be sky high. So he is not in shock. But then why is his blood pressure dropping even lower? What the hell is going on?! My mind tells me that he is just fainting, and that it is safe to continue draining the fluid. But my heart mutters: "Are you so damned sure of yourself that you'll just let that tube stay there while you suck out all of his blood out?!"

And so at just over two liters of bloody fluid, I call it quits and yank the tube out. Mr. Chait is laid flat. He still looks awful. I obtain a chest X-ray, hoping to see that the fluid level in his chest is diminished. To my horror, the chest X-ray is substantially unchanged! I can't see any improvement at all. So where did all that fluid come from if it didn't come from his chest? Can it be that I had not drawn any fluid from his chest after all? Did I have the tip of that tube in some large vessel? Good thing I removed it!

In the end, I admitted Mr. Chait to the hospital, started an IV, and watched him. His blood pressure slowly returned to normal. He became pink. His pulse remained still nice and slow. So it must have been chest fluid after all. *Maybe I worry too much.* He must have just been fainting. But if that is so, then why did the X-ray fail to show that any of the fluid had been removed?

The next morning, his blood count was down by 2 whole grams. Dang! Maybe it was blood after all. I repeated his chest X-ray, and it still showed no substantial improvement. All the fluid seemed to still be present. I repeated the blood test, and it contradicted the first test. One test said 10.3 grams; the other one said 11.8 grams. Which should I believe?

Decision time: I put on my best calm exterior demeanor and continued to treat Mr. Chait. This time, I chose yet another, different, guaranteed (for sure, for sure) safe location on his chest, and, bolstering my faith factor, reinserted the needle-and-tube affair. More "blood" came out. I drained off 2 more liters, and then the tube clogged. But at least this time, he did not get pale nor go into "shock." And a repeat chest X-ray finally showed that the fluid level was down.

Mr. Chait is fine. None of this was an error of technique. All of the fluid really was post-op chest fluid that had to come out. The day before, Mr. Chait was nauseated and pale because he doesn't like needles. Chait had no idea of what went through my mind yesterday and today.

And yes, I did talk with his cardiac surgeon in Bismarck, who sheepishly said, "Guess I pulled his chest tube out too soon, eh?" But he saw no reason to have his patient drive two hours north just to have a needle inserted there when we were perfectly capable of doing the job locally.

Well, it's a pointless little tale, isn't it? It merely illustrates that we doctors are also human and suffer the same anxieties everybody else has.

Alex Evans (Strange and Wonderful Are the Ways of Coincidence)

The year was 1964, and a young engineer at the Naval Reactors Branch of the Atomic Energy Commission had been assigned to the sea trials of a brand-new class of fleet ballistic missile nuclear submarines—the USS *Lafayette* (SSBN 616). I was working for Admiral Rickover, the father of the nuclear navy. It was his practice to have one of his engineers present on sea trials. Everybody knew that said engineer would be reporting directly back to Rickover, so I was treated "gingerly." After a long day, I was "hot-bunking" it (sleeping in the still-warm bed of another who had just gone on duty). At some time during the night, I was awakened by an announcement over the loudspeakers: "We are now at test depth. All personnel, check for any additional leaks and call control."

Holy cow! We are leaking at test depth. As it turned out, there were only minor leaks, but I'll never forget that day.

Now on the same ship, at that same time, back in the storeroom, was a sailor. Let's say his name was Alex Evans. He was in charge of supplies. He, too, was on that test dive, and he, too, remembered that ominous midnight announcement. No, we never met. Years went by—thirty-six of them. We had both gone our separate ways. Each of us individually had many experiences and many adventures.

He went to business school, eventually moved to Mobridge as the business manager of the local elementary school and one of the banks. His wife came down with colon cancer and was operated upon by Dr. H. (the surgeon I was replacing at the time). She was then in chemotherapy. Alex was very devoted to her.

I, too, had left the nuclear navy and was luckily able to obtain one of the coveted slots in medical school. Penn State College of Medicine at Hershey accepted only 40 of over 1,600 applicants that year. My four years at Penn State were followed by a surgery residency and then a surgical practice in Pennsylvania, followed by one in Iowa. And now I was giving the world of *locum tenens* surgery a trial.

Fate decreed that it was now time for our destinies to intersect again. We were both in Mobridge, South Dakota, at the same time.

Alex experienced just one episode of rectal bleeding. He was talked into going to the hospital by one of his friends. I just happened to be working in Mobridge and did the colonoscopy,[2] which revealed that he shared everything with his wife, up to and including colon cancer!

And so the next day, I did a right hemicolectomy.[3] All his lymph nodes were negative. Hopefully, he was cured. My assignment was coming to an end. Three days later, I had to leave town. My replacement surgeon was now in Mobridge and assumed his care.

---

[2] Examination of his colon (large intestine) with a lighted fiberoptic scope.

[3] Surgical removal of the right side of his large intestine.

CHAPTER 6

A Naked Artery in Alaska

Kodiak, a sleepy little fishing town, is on an island in the Gulf of Alaska, some 260-odd miles southwest of Anchorage. When I worked there, the total population of the entire island was somewhere south of 6,000 people. It didn't take me long to explore the island; the longest road (which led to essentially nowhere) was only 38 miles long, while the north shore was reachable by a shorter 14-mile road.

I was there to cover the hospital during the absence of the regular surgeon, who was away, taking his vascular board exams. I provided coverage to this hospital on two occasions, separated by about a year. Due to the time zone change from Iowa to Alaska, I awakened at 3 a.m. My body, still on Iowa time, thought it was 7 a.m. Looking out the hill-top motel window on my first trip there, I was startled to see much traffic in the street below. Yes, most of it was taxi cabs, but why were there so many of them? Naturally, I inquired of the OR crew at the first opportunity.

"The bars had just closed."

"But why so many taxi cabs? Don't people drive drunk in Kodiak?"

"Doc, they don't have cars. They work on the fishing boats."

"Oh."

I saw only four patients in my first trip to Kodiak, yet half of them made a memorable impression on me.

Otto Robbins

As I stepped off the day's first flight and strolled into Kodiak's small air terminal, heading for the luggage area, I was met by a lady who turned out to be the hospital administrator's secretary.

"Are you Dr. Roode?"

"Why, yes, ma'am. I am."

"Quickly come with me. They need you badly in the ER."

The ER physician (a family practitioner) had seen a patient at 4 a.m. who had suffered a spontaneous tension pneumothorax. For the uninitiated, a short detour into how the lungs work is in order. The lungs are not physically attached to the inside of the chest. Rather, they are held up against the inner chest wall by a slight vacuum. That way they passively inflate and deflate as the chest expands and contracts when we breathe. Anything that destroys this slight vacuum causes the lungs to gently deflate. One of the most common causes of a spontaneous pneumothorax is the rupture of a bleb (blister) on the lung's surface. When this happens, air leaks out of the lung and destroys the vacuum between the lung and the inner chest wall. The lung quietly collapses.

Ordinarily, a person can tolerate a simple pneumothorax fairly well, inasmuch as he or she has lost the function of only one lung. Otto's situation was different. In his case, the ruptured bleb had a flap over it such that air would leak out but could not flow the other way. As air pressure built up in the pleural space, it not only collapsed the lung but also pushed the rest of his chest contents to the opposite side, where that lung, too, began to collapse. This is called a tension pneumothorax.

And so the ER doctor had a serious problem to deal with. Now came the tough part. The treatment for a pneumothorax is simple enough. A plastic tube is inserted into the space between the lung and the chest wall. This chest tube then sucks out the air in the pleural space so that the lung can re-expand. However, this particular ER doctor had never actually inserted a chest tube. Thus, he was in the ER with a man terribly short of breath, needing a treatment he was unfamiliar with. It did not appear to him that he could safely wait until my scheduled midmorning arrival.

Something had to be done immediately, so he called the hospital in Anchorage, asking the physician there what should be done. He was instructed to insert a 14-gauge angiocath[1] into the second intercostal space anteriorly. Once he removed the central needle, there would be this nice (if tiny) plastic sheath left behind to vent all that high-pressure air out of the pleural space. He did, and the angiocath whistled as the air came out. Otto felt better immediately. Now it would be safe to wait for my arrival.

Alas, Otto's shortness of breath returned, hence my being rushed from the airport to the ER by the administrative secretary.

After I examined the patient, the reason for his deterioration was evident. That little angiocath that the ER doctor had inserted was bent over, lying flat against his chest and obviously blocked. More puzzling to me was his chest X-ray. Yes, there was air in the pleural space but also a lot of "fluid" as well. I could even make out an air-fluid level, meaning that this fluid was freely sloshing around in his chest. So this was more than a simple pneumothorax.

Was this fluid there to start with before Otto developed his tension pneumothorax? One of my worries was that somehow the ER doctor's angiocath might have hit a large blood vessel. But then I noticed that even the first X-ray that was taken at 4 a.m. showed the presence of fluid. So the fluid might have nothing to do with the pneumothorax at all. Well, no matter, this man obviously needed a chest tube. The only size available was a size 20; somewhat small, but it ought to do the job. I inserted it and sucked out the air from the pleural space, as well as over a liter of nonclotting blood. He was then admitted and observed. But he continued to bleed into his chest. We began to transfuse him. By evening, we had drained nearly two liters of bloody fluid. Worse, his chest X-ray had "whited out" (become opaque). Something more, much more, was going on. Evidently, he somehow had developed a spontaneous tension hemopneumotho-

---

[1]   A needle sheathed inside a plastic tube that is normally inserted in a vein to start an intravenous.

rax,[2] and it was not resolving with our chest tube. It was clearly time to call for the air ambulance from Anchorage.

Later, I received a phone call from the chest surgeon in Anchorage. He had done surgery on Otto that evening. An additional 3,000 cc of fluid was found in his left chest. All they could find was the expected, severe bullous parenchymal[3] lung disease. No, they were unable to find a definite cause of the bleeding. Sometimes I am secretly relieved when the big city hospital can't solve a problem any better than I can. And just to make things interesting, during his postoperative period in Anchorage, he blew out another bleb (this one on the right) and developed a tension pneumothorax on that side as well!

Paul Perron (A Naked Artery)

Paul was brought to us from a fishing boat shortly after it had docked. I was told that he had "passed out." However, the story is much more interesting, which is why it made it into these notes. Paul, a laborer, had been hired as crew on one of the local fishing boats. He had a vague history of an "ulcer." His family doctor had given him a prescription for Tagamet[4] just prior to his departure on the fishing boat.

While on this fishing trip, Paul vomited blood. Perhaps he didn't feel that he was all that sick. He certainly didn't complain. He vomited again, and again it was bright red blood. The fishing vessel captain dealt with the situation by ordering him to stop vomiting. There is a great reluctance for a commercial fishing vessel to make the long return trip to port prior to the official close of the short, tightly regulated commercial fishing season. The boat's owner would stand to lose considerable income. So when Paul persisted with his

---

[2] Spontaneous bleeding into the chest. Air leaks? Yes, I see them all the time. Fluid? Yes, quite often. But blood? Yes, after trauma but never spontaneously.

[3] The source of the "bubbles" on the lung surface that burst and caused his collapsed lung.

[4] An anti-ulcer medicine.

vomiting, grew even weaker, and felt the world beginning (in his words) "to spin around," he was sent to his bunk below.

At last the fishing season was over, and they headed back to port. After they docked, Paul was found to be unconscious. It looked like they ought to take him to the hospital. There he was found to have a hemoglobin of only four![5]

The ER doctor called me and said that he had a "big-time" bleeder on his hands. I thought not. After all, Paul had been sick for 17 days and was still alive with a hemoglobin of 4. He had to be bleeding slowly, allowing for his body to adjust to the situation. Nonetheless, he certainly needed admission and blood transfusions. I inserted a nasogastric tube, and it showed only coffee-grounds material (old blood). This proved my assessment that he had chronic (not acute) bleeding, so there was no need for a mad dash to the OR. Instead, we should run the IVs, give him blood transfusions, monitor the situation, and evaluate what was going on.

My first clue that things weren't going to be as advertised (a chronic bleed) was the fact that Paul nearly passed out after having received four units of blood. I put the nasogastric tube back down, and lo! Now bright red blood was in his stomach. I irrigated his stomach with iced saline, but it would not clear, indicating ongoing bleeding. Should I head directly to the OR or perhaps do a diagnostic exam via an endoscope? I chose the latter, and it showed a channel ulcer[6] with a so-called naked artery[7] in the middle of it. But it wasn't bleeding.

Hmm… Surgery is necessary, but when? Should I operate now or take a chance with him—as in waiting for the morning in order to save the OR crew from coming in at 3 a.m.? Stop and think, Pete! We are on

---

[5] Normal is around twelve to fourteen, so this means that Paul had lost two-thirds of his blood volume.

[6] This ulcer was in the pyloric channel between the stomach and duodenum.

[7] These are particularly dangerous. The ulcer has eaten away the normal tissue, leaving a clotted artery alone, out in the pyloric channel where acids can eat it away, causing massive bleeding. The denuded artery is unable to constrict and stop bleeding.

a small island in Alaska with a limited supply of blood. So, no, don't take a chance. Operate right now while he is stable, not when he is in shock.

At surgery I oversewed the ulcer. I then performed the appropriate anti-ulcer surgery (vagotomy and drainage) since he had developed this condition while on good medical therapy. He made an uneventful recovery.

On a second visit to Kodiak a year later, I can relate this amusing incident. After I'd been there a day or two, one of the secretaries from the administration office came to me hesitantly and humbly apologetic.

"Dr. Roode, I know you were here last year, but I cannot find your file anywhere. I know you had surgical privileges, but I need to update them for coverage this year."

"Okay…"

"Could I ask you if you wouldn't mind filling out the application for surgical privileges a second time? We are so sorry to bother you. I simply do not understand how we could have lost your papers."

"Well. Uh, I can tell you why you don't have any files on me. You never gave me any forms to fill out last year."

"Oh."

My visit the year previously had started off with that mad dash to the ER to see Otto with the collapsed lung and hemorrhage into his chest. In that excitement, somehow they seemed to have forgotten to give me the necessary forms to fill out to obtain surgical privileges. Apparently, I had even done five operations without ever having been officially granted hospital privileges.

Toying with the RV Idea

A small town in West Virginia was the site of an early assignment when we were beginning to think of purchasing an RV to live in when "on the road." To try this idea out, we rented an RV and parked it right beside the hospital. It seemed to work out just fine, which then led us to purchase a fifth-wheel RV that we used for several years all across the upper Midwest and even back to Alaska.

Evidently we made a sufficiently good impression on the nice folks in this town in that they invited me back on no less than six additional occasions. And here is the interesting part: on most of these trips I was asked to provide coverage for (get this!) just one single day. It was the case of a lone surgeon in town, the only one who could perform a C-section, if needed, to rescue a fetus in distress. When I had first started doing *locum tenens* surgery, I had no idea what a powerful drawing attraction my ability to do a C-section would prove to be. If a hospital lacks ability to perform an emergency C-section, it must close the entire OB department. The loss of a baby caught in arrested labor would instantly translate into a million-dollar lawsuit that could only be settled out of court.

Once when I was working in Fargo, North Dakota, this West Virginia hospital called, saying it desperately needed weekend coverage. No, I was not on call that weekend but was reluctant to agree. "But why?" they asked me. I told them I was on assignment in Fargo and that I was not about to fly halfway across the country, leaving Betty alone in a strange city. Their counteroffer was to fly *both* of us to their hospital, just so that I could provide them with a single day's worth of coverage for their OB department.

The funny thing is, despite all those trips to that hospital in West Virginia, I was never once called upon to actually do a C-section there. Nonetheless, I still had a couple of "memorable" patients.

Kenneth Collins (The Heretic and the True Believer)

This beloved hospital employee was using his chainsaw the day after Christmas. It was getting late, and he was in a hurry. The task at hand was to saw up some old pallets in his backyard for kindling. He "revved" up the chainsaw so it would cut the last remaining wood faster, thus setting up the classic "kickback" accident. The chainsaw flew out of the wood and into his face. These were the days before the automatic anti-kickback safety feature for chainsaws had been invented. My first involvement was when my beeper went off at dusk. The ER doctor didn't want to tackle the quarter-inch-wide facial laceration that just barely (by less than the proverbial silly little millimeter) missed Ken's left eye. Had it hit the eye, he'd have been treated to a ride to a larger hospital to see a plastic surgeon and/or ophthalmologist. As it was, this laceration was well within my capabilities as a general surgeon.

But for maximum cosmetic benefit, I decided to perform the repair of the injury in the OR. There, under intravenous sedation, I could vigorously scrub out all dirt and debris, trim the edges of the laceration perfectly straight, and exactly re-approximate the edges. And so it was proposed to the patient. And so it was agreed upon.

All was going well in the OR as preparations were being made for his anesthetic sedation. I'd scrubbed, gowned, and gloved, and was sitting at the patient's head. Overhearing the light banter between patient and nurse anesthetist, I noticed that there were frequent and fervent expressions of "Praise God" and "Praise the Lord." It seemed that Ken had the conviction that the chainsaw was, in fact, headed directly for his left eye when, at the last minute, the Creator of the

74

Entire Universe had swooped down and, with His finger, actually pushed the whirling blade a bit to the left so that it missed his eye and merely lacerated his cheek.

Almost involuntarily I muttered, "Pity He didn't shove a bit harder. Then it would have missed your face entirely."

Instantly I knew I'd erred. The OR suddenly became deathly quiet. All eyes were on me, then quickly averted. They now knew that they had a blasphemous unbeliever in their midst. Slowly the conversations started up again—on a different topic. I valiantly tried to remedy the situation by quietly humming hymns during the repair. I don't think I succeeded.

Billy Williams

If you are in the mood to contemplate one of life's pointless tragedies, read on. Shortly after I had checked into the motel, my beeper went off. It was the hospital informing me that a surgical consultation had just been requested. The problem was a bowel obstruction of four days' duration. Well, I was already suspicious that there was more to this problem than met the eye. Most family practitioners don't wait four days to get a surgical consultation if the X-rays are indicative of a possible bowel obstruction. When I came to the hospital, another clue greeted me. Billy turned out to be a resident of a nearby nursing home. Moreover, he was still in the nursing home rather than in the hospital with IVs and all.

A short while later, I was in the nursing home with Billy's chart in hand. It turned out that Billy was only fifty. What was a fifty-year-old man doing in a nursing home, surrounded by eighty-year-olds? Further perusal of the chart provided the answer. It seemed that, in 1988, Billy had been involved in a three-wheeler[1] accident and suffered severe brain injuries. He was now bed fast, unable to speak,

---

[1]   Over the years I've taken care of a number of people who have come to grief on these most unstable of recreational vehicles. They have since been outlawed, being replaced by 4-wheel, all-terrain vehicles.

fed through a tube in his abdomen, and perhaps only dimly aware of his surroundings. The chart further revealed that, five years ago, he'd developed a gangrenous gallbladder and survived surgery for that, although his convalescence was complicated by a prolonged ileus.[2] The purpose of my consult, far from treating a bowel obstruction, was to reassure the family practitioner that this was merely another ileus.

Well, after examining Billy and reviewing his X-rays, I came to the same conclusion. It was indeed an ileus and Dr. J was doing everything quite properly. So this is not a tale of treating an ileus or an operation for a small bowel obstruction. The question I had was why the family practitioner felt it so important to obtain a surgical consult. Me, the pragmatic and ruthless surgeon, would simply have written Billy off as one of life's far too many pointless tragedies.

It was not so for Billy's seventy-ish mother. The complexities of the family dynamics began to reveal themselves. Billy's mother visits every day. She feeds him. She changes his diapers. He has returned to his babyhood and she to her motherhood. Now both are frozen in time. She talks to him as if the accident had never happened, telling him the news of the town, as if only his body was harmed, not his brain. He is really "in there," just isn't able to communicate. All this is profoundly depressing, but there is not a thing you can do to change the situation. There is no hope for Billy, nor can you change his mother. Each has found their place in life.

---

[2] Paralysis of bowels, necessitating prolonged intravenous feeding.

CHAPTER 8

Into the "Big Time"

Locum tenens surgery was proving to be so rewarding that Betty and I decided to continue. Our initial doubts that you could actually make a living doing this had been allayed. And so the next step in our evolution was to purchase and upgrade a used fifth-wheel RV that would serve as our home away from home. The cheap built-in dinette table that folded into a bed was scrapped and was replaced by a nice homemade oak table with an included offset to maximize use of available space. The flimsy living room sofa bed was replaced with two reclining chairs that were carefully fixed in location so as not to move when we were on the road. Space was made for Betty to have room for her sewing machine. Eventually, I built a custom oak desk with a built-in filing cabinet to serve as my office.

On a cold and snowy day in February, while we were in the midst of this refurbishing activity, the phone rang. It turned out to be Dr. Howell, the chief of surgery at Meritcare Clinic and St. Luke's Hospital in Fargo, North Dakota. He was inviting us to work for them. And why was a four-hundred-bed major medical center needing a *locum* surgeon? Well, their normal surgical staff had been unexpectedly reduced to three through a combination of an unexpected death, a retirement, and relocations to other medical centers. But Fargo? In North DaColda? In February! We didn't think so... However, we agreed to talk again perhaps in the spring or summer.

What Dr. Howell didn't know was that, at the time, we were hoping for a return trip to Alaska in the summer. What an adventure it would be to drive our RV up the AlCan Highway and live in it while working in Alaska! Eventually, we talked again, and we agreed to work at Fargo after all. During this assignment, we fell in love with both Fargo and its hospital.

The months spent in Fargo turned out to be quite unlike the typical *locum* assignment. Usually, we find ourselves in small towns with equally small hospitals (twenty to fifty beds). We rarely get called to larger towns because large multispecialty medical groups can more easily absorb the temporary absence of one physician. Now, despite its size, with its normal complement of eight surgeons reduced to three, they were desperate for help.

Fargo turned out to be a delightful town to live and work in. In fact, it would be perfect were it not for its fierce winters. It was with mixed feelings that we turned down their offer for permanent employment there. Over the ensuing years, I continued to work for them from time to time, covering smaller outlying hospitals affiliated with them, especially in the summer months. One of the attractions of the *locum* lifestyle is that one can choose not only *where* to work but *when*.

This assignment in Fargo proved to be very challenging. The on-call surgeon was the only surgeon available at night. We never received routine, low-stress referrals. Since Fargo was the largest medical center between Minneapolis and the West Coast, the idea of sending a really sick patient to a "larger hospital" made no sense. I had sent many a very sick, complex patient from smaller hospitals to major medical centers. Now the shoe was on the other foot. If Fargo couldn't take care of the situation, then apparently nobody else could either. So while I was stressed that summer, I also grew both medically and surgically.

Harry McClain (Initial Trauma Code)

What could be more fitting than a trauma code on my very first night on call in this major medical center? I was well aware that I was the only surgeon available in this four-hundred-bed tertiary health-care facility. Sometime after midnight, my beeper went off. I called in on my cell phone and was told that a trauma code had been called.

Only later was it explained to me that they used a special number for trauma codes and that it was unnecessary for me to waste time calling in to ask what was going on. I was just to get to the ER as fast as possible.

Heart thumping, wondering if I could remember all that I'd learned over the years about trauma, I quickly dressed and drove to St. Luke's.

What if the man is in shock and needs immediate heroic surgery on some god-forsaken part of his liver, say, the retro-hepatic veins? What have I gotten myself into?

The ER was in the expected state of usual pandemonium when I arrived. The accident victim was a twenty-some-year-old graduate microbiology student who had been out drinking rather than back in his apartment, studying for his finals. He was on his way home on his motorcycle when he lost control and flipped himself into the median strip. Fortunately, all he had was multiple abrasions (road rash), contusions, and a significant facial laceration.

It was only later, upon reflection, that it occurred to me how different things were at Fargo. Trauma was very well organized. Dr. Brent Krantz, the trauma guru who had written the ATLS[1] textbook, was on the staff and had organized the trauma service extremely well. At the smaller hospitals I'd previously worked in, when I was called into an ER to see a trauma victim, everybody stood around, looking to me, asking, "What do you want us to do?" This meant what labs, what X-rays, what people, what operation, etc. Here, the pandemonium was still present, but everything was oh so much better organized. This was, after all, a Level II Trauma Center. The ER doctor was running the trauma code,[2] and I was content to stand quietly in the background and observe the action.

It quickly became apparent to me that Harry's injuries were not serious. I could relax a trifle. Then came something that was a first for me after all these years of handling trauma patients in

---

[1]   Advanced Trauma Life Support—an intensive course that all medical personnel caring for trauma victims must take.

[2]   Ordering labs, X-rays, getting the IVs started, and determining how fast to run them.

smaller hospitals—people began handing me things, things that I hadn't requested: a blood gas report, an amylase. X-rays were about to be done, they assured me. They had the whole process automated. When a trauma code was called, all manner of people would rush to the ER—anesthetists, lab technicians, X-ray personnel, aides, and orderlies. Somebody would bring a cooler full of O-negative blood. Even the hospital chaplain would come and sit with family in the waiting room. Each person had an assigned task, and so there was order underlying the seeming pandemonium.

Before I knew it, a picture of his injuries began to emerge. And following the Fargo modus operandi, the plastic surgeon could now be consulted to tend to the facial laceration, which would best be done in the OR inasmuch as it was quite extensive. Yes, the trauma code went well, but I felt that I was merely lucky to have had an easy first one. What would the next one be like? Would I be able to handle it? What would I miss? Would I be able to perform at the expected MeritCare level?

What follows is by no means a complete listing of my trauma code patients, merely the interesting ones that made it into my "memorable patient" files. It was with a degree of pride that when I left Fargo several months later, I reflected that I had indeed been able to handle everything that was thrown at me, without either getting into trouble or having to call one of the other surgeons in. During those months, I was to care for trauma more severe than I'd ever seen before. Being at a regional center, I did not have the escape valve available to me in a smaller hospital: transfer it away. Fargo enjoyed its reputation of being able to handle any situation. Sometimes I'd wryly think that it was like the popular song "Hotel California": "We are programmed to receive." And always, in the back of my mind was the uncomfortable knowledge that if I couldn't handle it, then it was just going to be too bad for the patient.

Elizabeth Hardy (Weekend Call)

After I had a couple of trauma codes under my belt and although still not by any means comfortable with them, I felt that I could at least handle them. Friday was the start of my first full weekend on call in Fargo. What was a weekend on call at St. Luke's like? Well, in addition to being on call for the ER, I had to make rounds on all the other surgeons' patients. They worked hard enough during the week, and on weekends, by common agreement, the surgeon on call made rounds for them.

When I was a surgeon in Iowa, I might have had five or six patients to see in the hospital. At St. Luke's, it turned out that I had thirty-three patients to see! And these were not just the ordinary post-op patients that I was accustomed to. These were *sick* patients—a post-op aortic aneurysm patient in renal failure on TPN[3] with questionably viable feet, a patient with necrotizing pancreatitis, three patients who had gastric surgery for bleeding ulcers, a renal transplant patient. All told, some six or seven patients were on TPN. It took me eight hours just to make rounds. I'd have to determine the diagnosis. What had transpired in the hospital, and what needed to be done? Temperature? Intake and output status? When was the last blood gas? Then if an emergency came into the ER, everything was dropped, and I had to rush down there and tend to that patient. When that was done, I would then resume my rounds.

Well, God smiled on me, for I didn't have to do any emergency surgery at all on Saturday, just rounds on thirty-three patients, two consults, three or four ER patients, and one trauma code. I was aware that, during the previous weekend, the on-call surgeon had to perform no less than five operations on Saturday alone in addition to rounds. No wonder surgeons have a reputation among the internists for writing short "sloppy" progress notes on the charts.

My Saturday trauma code was a two-year-old with a fractured skull from being hit by a truck. But of course, you must go through the entire "drill" and rule out all the other possible injuries. How nice it is to have all the specialists that you can think of at your beck and call. You want to talk to a neurosurgeon? No problem. How about a

---

[3]   Total Parenteral Nutrition. Ordinary IVs provide few calories… Basically, a patient on IVs who cannot eat is starving. TPN patients are given sufficient calories to even gain weight on occasion. But it requires a whole lot more care than a patient with a simple IV.

pediatric neurologist? No problem. Well, in any case, my little tyke did well in the pediatric ICU. By the way, there were four ICUs in this hospital—neonatal, pediatric, neurosurgery, med/surg—all in addition to the coronary care unit.

What I was doing that summer was turning this *locum* assignment into a fellowship, one for which I was well paid… I found myself doing surgery that I hadn't done in years and all while surrounded by specialists who knew ever so much more than I did about any single area.[4] I bought a critical care textbook, studied it, and with exposure to badly injured patients and the rest of the MeritCare team, every day I engaged in an orgy of learning. When I returned to working in small isolated hospitals, I was more competent and confident.

Now as to the patient Elizabeth, I was seeing patients in the clinic when the ER called and told me about a woman who'd been a passenger in a car that had been struck by a train. She was in another hospital and was in shock. Their surgeon had put in a chest tube. That was all they knew. That local doctor was doing what I had so often done in the past—sending a desperately ill or badly injured patient to the larger hospital. Now I was on the receiving end rather than the sending end. The helicopter was on its way out to that hospital to retrieve the patient.

My immediate concern was the shock. What was causing that? One simply shouldn't transfer a patient in shock. I had never done that in the past. I would always resuscitate the patient sufficiently so that I was sure he or she would survive the transfer process. Say, who had agreed to this transfer in the first place? Well, it was the ER. What had been done to stabilize the patient, to reverse the shock? Nobody knew.

As I asked these questions, it dawned on me that the Fargo ER had a very liberal policy on accepting trauma victims. It adhered to the "scoop and run" philosophy. The trauma surgeon was not even

---

[4] I was somewhat flattered when one of the general surgeons told me that he'd be terrified having to take care of trauma in a small hospital without the support of the various specialists.

involved in decisions to send the helicopter. The ER would accept anything on the assumption that our trauma surgeon could handle it, and if he could not, well then, nobody could either. This was in sharp contrast to other trauma centers I had dealt with in the past. When I had my surgical practice in Iowa and needed to transfer an injured patient to Iowa City, I'd have to convince the University Hospital's surgeon that the patient was no longer in shock and could safely withstand the transfer.

Trying to obtain a little more information on my soon-to-be patient, I called the hospital that was sending Elizabeth to us. No physicians were even in the ER! The surgeon who had seen her had gone back to his office and this despite her being in shock. Nobody knew the results of any X-rays that might have done. Elizabeth seemed to be stable, and once Fargo had accepted her in transfer, there was nothing more for them to do. Everybody went back to what they were doing before her accident. And so all I could do was sit and await her arrival. When that occurred, it turned out that her injury was primarily fractured ribs (on the right) and an underlying pulmonary contusion.[5] I did a peritoneal lavage[6] to be sure that there was no occult abdominal trauma might have caused her shock. Perhaps my examination of her abdomen could have been rendered problematic by her lower chest pain.

Learning point here: Before, in smaller hospitals, when I had to evaluate patients with abdominal trauma, I found peritoneal lavage to be a quick and simple way to rule in or rule out significant abdominal organ injury. If it was negative, you could transfer the patient to a larger hospital with a clear conscience. But when you got a positive result, then you had a problem that must be dealt with locally before any transfer could be done safely. One reason that I favored the quick and easy peritoneal lavage in smaller hospitals was that they tended

---

[5]   Bruised lung. Why this is important is that the lung is a light, airy organ and, if bruised, can fill with blood and interfere with respiration.

[6]   A small plastic catheter is threaded into the abdominal cavity to see if there is any blood there.

not to have good CT[7] capability. Even if they did, often they were not used to rapidly performing CT scans on badly injured patients, especially at inconvenient times, such as the middle of the night. A peritoneal lavage was a neat way to get an instant answer, when a decision about transfer had to be made quickly.

Now, however, I was in a medical center with top-of-the-line CT capability. As a consequence, the Fargo trauma surgeons didn't do many peritoneal lavages. Instead, they sent the patient to the X-ray department for a quick CT. That way they obtain information not only whether there was any injury but, if so, what and where it was. It was a good learning point for me, and I was to change my approach to abdominal trauma, at least until I returned to working in small hospitals with marginal or no CT capability.

Elizabeth was also interesting because she did well for about a week in the ICU. Her pulmonary contusion resolved nicely without any heroic measures. However, the day after she was transferred out to the intermediate care unit, she rapidly deteriorated. She went into respiratory failure and required mechanical ventilation for eight or ten days. The cause? Staph septicemia from an infected IV line! Here was a perfectly routine case by Fargo standards that would have given me the willies back in Iowa. What a comfort to have any number of critical care specialists available for consultation.

And Elizabeth? Well, she survived to go home and live happily ever after...

Baby Boy Lee

This 500 gm infant, born 17 weeks prematurely, was a real nightmare for the entire neonatal ICU staff. The mother was a schizophrenic who threatened to kill nurses and doctors. The infant, besides being severely premature, had bled into his cerebral ventri-

---

[7]   Computed Tomography—an X-ray machine that is much more sensitive than "old-fashioned" simple X-rays.

cles[8] and was probably blind from oxygen toxicity. And now he had the temerity to develop free intra-abdominal air! Evidently, he had also developed neonatal NEC.[9] The only treatment for that is surgery to remove the dead bowel. I found it interesting that here I was in Fargo, a major medical center, which at that time was temporarily without a bona fide full-time pediatric surgeon. But their operating policy, that virtually nobody is referred away, seemed to be still in effect. Presto! I was now a pediatric surgeon. Yes, I'd done plenty of pediatric surgery but never regarded myself as a pediatric surgeon.

And so it was with considerable trepidation that I looked at the ominous X-rays showing the free air on this Sunday morning before going to see and examine the patient. Scarcely eight inches long by three inches wide. Yes, I had seen cases like this before, even assisting a pediatric surgeon (Dr. Konvolinka) at Geisinger back in 1975. And I had performed much bowel surgery (albeit in adults) in the intervening years, so it wasn't as if I had no idea what to do. I merely lacked experience in this particular type of case since I had always worked in smaller hospitals. Heretofore, when I encountered such a case, I would refer it to the nearest large medical center. Gulp. This *is* the medical center, and I was expected to be the expert pediatric surgeon.

The surgery was done at noon in the neonatal ICU, in the special procedures room. I opened transversely and found large amounts of dead small bowel, which was removed, leaving him with a jejunostomy and a terminal ileal mucous fistula.[10] I did this because it looked like he had a nonsurvivable condition, secondary to extensive necrosis elsewhere in the abdomen. I did take a few moments to remove an obviously gangrenous gallbladder, then closed. He lin-

---

8   Chambers inside the brain.

9   Necrotizing enterocolitis, a condition in a premature infant in which a portion of the intestines dies and becomes gangrenous. When this happens, air leaks out of the dead intestines and is "free" to move around inside the abdomen. Hence the ominous finding of "free air" on X-rays of the abdomen.

10   After all the dead bowel was removed, rather than risk joining the two ends together where they might not heal, I brought them to the surface of the abdomen.

gered for several more days but ultimately died of his other medical problems.

Owen Newbanks (A Need for Boldness)

Tonight's excitement commenced at 10 p.m. Why do these cases always seem to happen late at night? The trauma code beeper went off, and so I hustled right in, actually arriving before the ambulance because it took a while for the first responders to extract the victims from a motor vehicle that had been involved in a collision with a train, right in downtown Fargo.

There were three patients. One was essentially DOA. Another was a young girl who didn't seem to be badly hurt. She was screaming bloody murder, but otherwise was medically stable. It turned out that she was suffering only from a cerebral concussion.

The third patient, a seventeen-year-old boy had been intubated[11] in the field. He was deep in shock, turning blue, and with a falling blood pressure was obviously in the process of dying right in front of our eyes. We had no labs. We had no X-rays. What was causing the shock? What could be done about it? A quick exam showed his trachea was midline, but I could hear no breath sounds on his right side. Yes, yes, I know. All the books all say that a pneumothorax[12] can be diagnosed by stethoscope alone, but in some twenty years of doing this, I have never seen a case that really could be.

Were there really breath sounds there, or was I simply unable to hear them in the very noisy ER? We, all of us, always obtain an X-ray to confirm or refute our suspicions of a pneumothorax. But if ever there was a case that that needed to be diagnosed with stethoscope

---

[11]   He was not breathing at the accident scene, so a plastic tube was inserted through his mouth into his trachea. The ambulance crew could then breathe for him during the ride to the hospital.

[12]   Collapsed lung due to broken ribs that pierce the lung and allow an air leak. A "tension" pneumothorax means that pressure builds up in the chest cavity, pushing the heart over to the other side and compressing the other lung. A true emergency that is solved by inserting a chest tube.

alone, this was it. Owen was so close to death that I did not believe I had even the short time needed for a confirmatory chest X-ray. There is a time for bold action. I simply grabbed a scalpel and, based on my suspicions alone, cut right into his chest. I was greeted by a gratifying rush of air. With the pressure relieved, his heart returned to the midline, and his left lung re-expanded. He quickly improved. I then had the time to place a chest tube to treat the underlying lung air leak.

HA! I thought to myself. *Small-town surgeon from Iowa makes good in the big city.* Or maybe it was… *At least I haven't screwed up yet.*

However, since Owen was still in shock, I next performed a quick (it only takes a minute or two) peritoneal lavage (rather than a trip to the CT scanner) and was greeted by gross blood. So he needed to be rushed to surgery. One entire surgery crew stays in the hospital twenty-four hours a day as do anesthetists. Thus, surgery at night could quickly be arranged.

Before heading off to the OR, I noticed that the chest tube kept on leaking, leaking, leaking… And not a small amount either. That was most unusual. *What the hell is going on? What am I missing? What should I be doing?* (My usual worries.) *It must not be just a simple little pulmonary laceration. Could he have a ruptured bronchus?* (I'd never even seen one of those; I had only read about it.) *What to do?* Despite the fact that it was now 2 a.m., based only on my suspicions, I contacted the on-call chest surgeon and told him I had a guy with a belly full of blood that I needed to operate on but was worried because I had a high air leak on the chest tube. He agreed to come in. When he got to the hospital, I already had the patient in the OR. Naturally, the first thing he did was rip off my dressings around the chest tube to see if I'd improperly sutured it in place.

Amused, I said, "I'm glad you're checking that, but the problem won't go away so easily."

So he decided to bronchoscope[13] the patient, and while he was fiddling around with that, the patient turned blue again. What to do first—chest or abdomen? These are such difficult decisions, always

---

[13]   A flexible examining scope is inserted through the patient's trachea, into the bronchus, to assess the nature of the injury.

open to second-guessing by critics after the fact. Basically, the problem is, What is killing the patient the fastest? We opted for the chest, opening it immediately. Sure enough, a ruptured bronchus! Double HA! Small-town Iowa surgeon makes good *twice* in one evening! The injury was so bad that it could not be repaired, and so the chest surgeon had to remove the lung. I then did the exploratory laparotomy, where I found and repaired a lacerated omentum[14] and mesentery.[15] It was just plain dumb luck that he did not have a ruptured spleen or badly lacerated liver. If so, he would have bled to death while we were dealing with in his chest injury.

Gratifyingly, Owen did quite well. He recovered and left the hospital with one lung. We had made all the right decisions.

At the end of having dodged all the bullets on this, my first full weekend on call, I was tickled to overhear one of the regular staff surgeons talking to another about the case. He said, "I wonder if I'd have made that diagnosis without an X-ray." So maybe there was hope for this old geezer after all… At least I was accepted here. (And that, somehow, amazed me…)

Jeff Porter

Another train wreck! This forty-five-year-old truck driver didn't look both ways at the railroad crossing, no doubt to his brief horror and regret as the train plowed into the eighteen-wheeler he was driving. He was brought in, probably brain dead, and when the trauma code was over, the rest of him was dead as well.

What was so special about him? Well I've read that people have bled to death from scalp lacerations, and over the years, I have seen a lot of people lose a lot of blood from them. This, however, was the first time I'd seen somebody actually bleed so badly from a scalp laceration. All told, we poured twenty-three units of blood into this

---

[14]   A fatty apron of tissue that drapes down from the transverse colon.
[15]   Base of the small bowel.

man! He bled from his nose and ears and facial lacerations and, most of all, from his scalp lacerations. It just wouldn't stop.

Three of us—Drs. March, Brody, and myself—were running the code, and each of us thought of something else to add to our collective efforts. It's so nice to have all this intellectual help with tough cases. Take, for example, the matter of fluids. We were getting further and further behind, and Dr. S (anesthesiology) came down and said, "Well shit! You guys need *big* IVs." And with that, he slipped in a subclavian[16] access line normally used for hemodialysis, containing two 12-gauge and one 16-gauge lines in it. He then went upstairs and came down with a hydraulic clamshell device that squeezes a unit of packed red blood cells into the patient in only a couple minutes or so. And that was how we gave twenty-three units of blood in the ER. Alas! We were unable to save Jeff.

Brian Hearn

Brian was a patient I almost lost. And if I had, there would have been countless wiser souls that could have easily told me (after the fact) just exactly where I had gone wrong. But we didn't lose him, and so his splenectomy[17] was then considered merely routine by the other surgeons. Ho-hmm. Patients with ruptured spleens are *supposed* to survive, aren't they?

It all started when this nineteen-year-old youth was not watching where he was going. He ran his car head-on into an 18-wheeler and was taken to a small hospital with all four of his extremities broken.

They put in two small bore IV lines and called for the helicopter. As far as I could tell, they did not bother to evaluate his abdomen (for which I fault their general surgeon), and so when he "arrove," he

---

[16] The subclavian vein, which is right under the collarbone, leads directly to the heart.

[17] Removal of the spleen, a fragile organ in the left upper quadrant of the abdomen, easily ruptured or torn in trauma. When so injured, the patient can easily bleed to death unless surgery is performed.

was in not only in shock but also had a distended, tender abdomen. We quickly determined that it was full of blood, and he'd need emergency surgery.

But here's the twist—he also had a "blown" left pupil[18] and wasn't moving his right arm or leg. So clinically he had an epidural hematoma[19] and would need both abdominal and neurosurgery. Now what tests should I obtain prior to going to the OR? He seemed stable after appropriate fluid resuscitation, and so I opted for a quick brain CT[20] scan on the way to the OR to repair whatever was hemorrhaging within his abdomen. I was sure that the neurosurgeon would need that information.

Yes, the abdominal surgery had precedence over neurosurgery, for he could easily bleed to death during neurosurgery. Because he was in shock, I could not wait for a neurosurgeon to come in and examine the patient. So he would first see this patient in the OR under anesthesia. Thus, a CT would be essential information for him to relieve the epidural hematoma. Besides, a CT would only take fifteen to twenty minutes to do. Was I not in a major medical center? Were they not used to doing emergency CT scans expeditiously? And so I decided to take the chance, delaying our rush to the OR by only a few minutes.

Well, things went to pot in the CT scanner. For one thing, his blood pressure began to fall. CT scans never take 15 to 20 minutes. And in the midst of things, the nurse who was helping hold Brian still for his head CT scan swung her ample "rear end" around and accidentally hit the emergency power cut-off switch. The entire CT scanner and computer crashed! Brian's blood pressure was now falling into the 70s, with a pulse over 140. I desperately needed to be in the OR with this kid. *Now!*

So there we all were, standing around this multimillion-dollar CT scanner that had just crashed. You wanna know how they start

---

[18]   Meaning the pupil was "fixed and dilated"; in other words, it would not contract when a light was shone in.

[19]   Blood clot within his skull but outside the brain itself. When it enlarges, it compresses the brain, which is a neurosurgical emergency.

[20]   Computed tomography X-ray.

that thing up? The tech takes a paper clip, bends it straight, and sticks it in a little hole in the back of the keyboard and jiggles it!

Wonder of wonders, the head CT scan was normal. He didn't need neurosurgery, and nobody to this day can explain to me how the supposedly sure clinical sign of the blown pupil meant nothing. And we did get him to the OR in time. It was a ruptured spleen, and I got it out quickly. He lived and did well. But just suppose he'd died in the CT scanner or died post-op from the shock. Any fool could have told me I was simply wasting time in the CT scanner.

Lucas Dahlman (A Desperately Ill Three-Year-Old)

This is another surgical horror story. As Dr. Brent Krantz was leaving Fargo on yet another one of his interminable lecture tours, he turned over to my care a three-year-old patient that he was "sitting on" because telephone conferences he had with a pediatric surgeon in Omaha had assured him that kids with hemolytic, uremic syndrome[21] do not develop toxic megacolons.[22] They might appear to, but it always "blows over" if you are patient. That might be true. After all, who was I to disagree? I had never even seen a case of hemolytic, uremic syndrome and could only vaguely recall having read about such a condition.

My usual luck resulted in a page to the pediatric ICU not ten minutes after Dr. Krantz, probably the most experienced surgeon in Fargo, left the building. Lucas was perfectly healthy one short month ago, but out of the blue, probably as the result of an infection, he developed hemolytic, uremic syndrome. When I first met Lucas, he

---

[21] Hemolytic uremic syndrome is a condition that destroys red blood cells, which then clog the kidneys, resulting in renal failure.

[22] A condition in which the large intestine is paralyzed, then swells. Toxins can kill the lining of the colon, which can then rupture, leading to peritonitis.

was in the ICU, on the ventilator, and receiving hyperalimentation.[23] He was also on renal dialysis.

Unfortunately for both of us, he was also now bleeding from his rectum. And bleeding a lot, enough to require transfusions, and there was no sign of it stopping.

The pediatrician wanted me to operate. "Just go in and take out the bleeding segment."

How easy it was for the well-intentioned expert (an expert in all things *not* surgical) to make what seemed to him to be a simple request. All I had to do was "go in there and stop the bleeding." Well, you can open the abdomen and look at the blood-filled intestines from the outside, and I promise you, you will not be able to tell where the bleeding point might be. Nor can you just open the colon willy-nilly to hunt for a bleeding point without spreading contamination and infection widely. You have to know the exact location of the bleeding point ahead of time in order to safely stop it.

And so I countered the pediatrician's request with one of my own. "How about endoscopy[24] to determine the bleeding point?"

So they called Dr. K, the pediatric gastroenterologist, and proposed that. To my astonishment, he declined, saying it was too risky for the patient! For crying out loud! How safe did they think surgery was going to be! Endoscopy is a much more minor procedure compared to opening the abdominal cavity. So I refused to operate without endoscopy. Telephone conferences were then held with that same guru in Omaha. He agreed that massive bleeding from the colon in hemolytic uremic syndrome was 'unusual, but at least he backed my position on the need for endoscopy. The impasse continued until the pediatrician managed to talk Dr. S, the adult gastroenterologist, into scoping this kid.

The colonoscopy was to take place in the OR, under general anesthesia, in case surgery was indicated. It went without a hitch and showed a complete loss of mucosa starting just above the peritoneal

---

[23] Very concentrated IV solutions that can completely support a patient who cannot eat for a prolonged time.

[24] A lighted scope is inserted into the colon so it can be examined from end to end.

reflection. The entire lining of the colon was dead and gone. All that was left of Lucas's colon was a raw, bleeding muscular tube.

There is no repairing, no healing of a colon that has lost *all* of its lining. And there is no one single isolated point of bleeding that can be stopped. No, what remains of the colon—what used to be the colon—has to be entirely removed. Surgery was his only chance. And so I reluctantly opened his abdomen and was horrified at the number of adhesions I saw. The colon was nowhere visible. It was surrounded by a mosaic of small bowel, each loop densely adherent to a patch of his colon. The colon had obviously broken down and leaked contamination at many points; each one was then sealed off by a bit of small bowel. There were no tissue planes for dissection. Trying to free the adherent loops of small bowel off the colon risked perforating it and spilling its toxic contents all over the place.

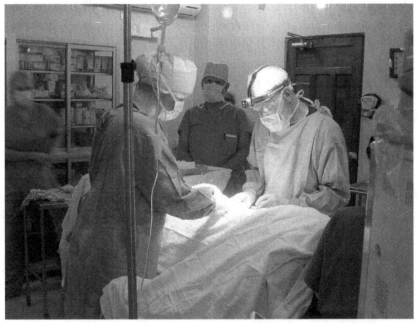

At work in the OR

But I had no choice. I began in the most superficially available location, the transverse colon, and immediately found myself inside the colon. The wall was virtually nonexistent. I spent four hours gently dissecting and losing in the process some 1,100 cc of blood (89 percent of his total blood volume), and all I had managed to do was free up and remove the transverse colon. I had no idea how I would be able to take down the hepatic flexure (ordinarily quite easy), and any imagining of how to deal with the even more remote and difficult splenic flexure quickly deteriorated into the fantasy world. As near as I could tell, he'd sloughed his entire colon lining some weeks before, and it was all sealed by loops of small bowel, which now were arranged in a tubular fashion. His colon was now composed of a tubular array of small bowel adhesions with little if any colon remaining. I never did see his left colon, nor could I enter his pelvis.

At this point, I began having visions of losing Lucas. It seemed to me that the wisest course of action was for me to quit while I was ahead. And so I placed Foley catheters[25] in the hepatic and splenic flexures and closed. I was frank in telling the pediatricians that he needed a transfer to a major *pediatric* surgical center, but they refused,[26] hoping that I'd done enough. I knew better. Finally, three days later, when he further deteriorated and after I wrote a suitably gloomy progress note on the chart that would be damning if seen by a lawyer, they relented and sent him to Minneapolis.

Later, I learned that the pediatric surgeons in Minneapolis put barium through the Foleys that I had placed and found that there were, in addition to the total colon slough, fistulae (abnormal channels) from the cecum to a pelvic abscess and thence over to the sigmoid colon. They did operate, and after four hours and another 1,000 cc of blood loss, they managed to remove the left colon. As of this writing, he seems to be doing better. In retrospect, what Lucas needed was an 8-hour, 2,000 cc blood-loss operation. I did half, and Minneapolis did the second half. What a scary case!

---

[25] These are normally placed in a patient's bladder to drain urine.

[26] That damnable Fargo policy again.

CHAPTER 9

Carpentry in Illinois

This assignment, in a small town in north-central Illinois, started, as they usually did, with a call from a *locum* agency. We were in the Grand Tetons, on our way home after our Fargo, North Dakota, assignment was completed. (Hey! Aren't Yellowstone and the Grand Tetons on a direct route home to Iowa from North Dakota?)

"Would you be interested in an assignment in Illinois?" was the query.

"Well, not really."

"Why not?"

"I got things to do," was my reply.

"What sort of things?" persisted the agency recruiter.

I explained to him that we were now using a fifth-wheel RV to live in during my *locum* assignments. We had refurbished much of it, and I was planning to construct a built-in desk and file cabinet, made of oak, to serve as my office.

"Sure you won't change your mind?"

"Yup."

To my surprise, he was back on the phone the next day with. "Do I have a deal for you!"

"What kinda deal?"

"Doc, you won't believe this, but this hospital's former CEO was an avid woodworker. He managed to convince the Board of Directors that the hospital needed a really good woodworking shop. And if you agree to provide surgical coverage for this hospital, you can have free rein of their complete woodworking shop."

Now how could I refuse that offer? So our travel plans were changed, and we found ourselves on I-80, heading for a small town in Illinois. The woodworking shop was everything they advertised it to be. Thus, this assignment found me spending a good part of the next two weeks doing surgery on oak boards, not human beings. A small oak desk for our fifth-wheel was completed during our stay at this hospital, between calls to the ER.

New office desk in the RV

Here are my memorable patients for this assignment

Charles Lambert (Brightening a Policeman's Evening)

At about 11:30 on a Friday night, my beeper went off. It was the ER, wanting me to see a fellow named Charles Lambert. He had come out second best in a barroom brawl. It had been a long, hot week on the construction job, and Charlie was just relaxin', minding his own business, drinking a beer, when along about ten or eleven o'clock, a disagreement apparently broke out nearby. Over a girl, I believe, but we'll never know for sure. In any case, he noticed that it was, as he later put it, "three against one." This aroused a dormant sense of chivalry in him, and he intervened. The three ruffians who were beating up on the one victim took Charles's intervention in stride and obligingly beat him up as well.

Of course, I knew none of this as I walked across the parking lot and wandered into the ER. Charlie was lying there, peacefully snoozing on the examining gurney. The combined effects of an evening's worth of booze, plus assorted blows to his head and elsewhere, had put him into a state he didn't seem to mind at all. When he didn't respond to questions, I applied a noxious stimulus.[1] This had the effect of rousing him enough to greet his surroundings with a curse. And his movements were purposeful.[2] He then drifted back to sleep. Well, at least I knew he wasn't comatose.

His stupor was, of course, the reason that the ER doctor had called me. Were we dealing with a simple drunk? Or a concussion? Or worse? It is notoriously difficult to diagnose a subdural hematoma (blood clot pressing on the brain) in the inebriated. That's one of the reasons why they invented the CT scanner. And he did have some facial lacerations that would need suturing. All in all, it was a nifty reason to call the surgeon "on call," let him worry about all the tricky details, and quietly retire to wherever ER doctors retire to when things are under control.

I proceeded with my examination of Charles, satisfying myself during the process that most of what I was seeing was the booze. Of

---

[1]   This is a euphemism for a painful stimulus. Generally, it is done by firmly pressing one's knuckle into a stuporous patient's breast bone and carefully observing his response.

[2]   It is amazing what one can learn by observing the result of the "noxious stimulus." If a patient tries to move your hand away, the motion is termed "purposeful," which, in general, is a hopeful sign. If, on the other hand, he withdraws or curls his arm and hand into a peculiar extended outward position (a.k.a. decerebrate posturing), why, then you have just learned a world of information on how the brain has become "unglued."

course, I'd still have to keep him overnight for observation. And I'd have to get the CT scan to "cover my butt."[3]

As I set about sewing up one of his facial lacerations, I casually asked the nearby ER nurse, "Say, did anybody report this to the police?"

Well, it seemed that they hadn't.

"Don't you think we should?" I asked. "I mean, this isn't exactly an accident, you know."

"We were about to do that when you showed up. We're not used to having the surgeon appear so quickly." (Our fifth-wheel was parked right across the street, on a bit of grass, in the employees' picnic area really, so commuting was not one of my problems.)

By and by, a uniformed officer appeared, none too pleased, judging from his demeanor. But you've got to look at things from his perspective. How many drunks do you need to investigate before you get bored? How many barroom brawls till you get irritated? And the later at night, probably the worse the mood. While the events of the evening were of immense significance to Charles, to our Officer Dudley, they were just one more annoyance—more paperwork to fill out, more reports to file, papers that would be shuffled and stored but would probably never amount to anything. Yup, to the policeman this evening, Charles was just a pain in the neck, pure and simple.

By and by, the policeman tore himself away from the attractive nurse at the desk and wandered over to see Charles. I was making steady progress on his facial lacerations, and Charles was still peacefully snoozing.

"HEY! BUD! Where did this happen?" inquired Officer Dudley at high volume.

After several attempts, Charlie was eventually aroused to mumble something like "Eekrz."

"How's that again, Bud? Was it Sneakers?" yelled the officer in a louder voice. He was still obviously bored and annoyed, merely at a higher volume.

"Yeah," mumbled Charles.

---

[3]   Protect myself from the usual riffraff lawyers and lawsuits.

Sneakers was the name of the bar that Charles had been patronizing. I was following this conversation, only half listening, but then I noticed an amazing transformation in Officer Dudley. He now had a sudden interest in his client. The next question was totally unexpected.

"Charles!" He used the man's actual name for the first time. "Where exactly did this fight occur? Was it inside Sneakers or out in the parking lot?"

Charlie needed to be roused a couple of times to concentrate because this was obviously a much tougher question. Finally, he mumbled "Parkin' lot" and went back to his blissful sleep.

"Aha!" cried our policeman, who now instantly lost any semblance of interest in Charles. He walked back to the reception desk with a new bounce in his step. "Since this happened out in Sneakers's *parking lot*," he informed the nurse, "then it would be across the city line. That would make it the county's jurisdiction. You'll have to call the sheriff on this one." And with that, he bounced out the door and back to whatever policemen do to at night when they aren't enforcing the law.

"Why, Man, Yo Jes Shet Yo Eyes"

While driving around town, we noticed that some of the roads had signs posting a three-ton weight limit. That had caused us to pause when we made our arrival to the hospital. Our RV tipped the scales at nearly ten tons. But I saw no other route to the hospital.

Still, I wondered, *How do the really heavy trucks get to the hospital?*

One day, I noticed a fully loaded eighteen-wheeler making a delivery of heavy equipment to the hospital. They were in the midst of an expansion project. And so I inquired of the big, burly black driver how he managed to get his truck into the hospital.

"Down that road there."

"Is there a route in here without the three-ton load limit?"

"Nope."

"Well, how do you do it then with the three-ton weight limit?"

He gave me a look that one might give a child and responded, "Why, man, yo jes shet yo eyes."

CHAPTER 10

Fate Is the Hunter

Many *locum* assignments resulted in invitations to return. Once the client was satisfied with my performance, I became an unofficial member of their medical staff, to be called upon again and again when the regular surgeon was out of town. The stories in this chapter took place over a period of eight years in a small (population four thousand or so) town in Wisconsin. Sometimes Betty and I lived in our fifth-wheel RV, and sometimes I'd catch a flight to Minneapolis and drive over in a rental car. A unique feature of this hospital was that sometimes we'd be put up in the nursing home across the highway.

"Eh-eh-eh-ay. Lookit that. A really young one," said one resident to another.

There are some interesting things you learn when living in a nursing home. For example, if you want a warm shower, don't even *think* of touching the "cold" faucet. Turn the hot water on full blast. The water is only going to be lukewarm so that the residents don't accidentally scald themselves. And whatever you do, *don't* touch that switch on the wall in the bathroom, the one with the string tied to it. If that is activated, a three-hundred-pound orderly is sure to burst into the room and lift you off the commode, whether you want him to or not.

Fate Is the Hunter (The Tragedy of Stan Creel)

Above all the other patients I saw and cared for over the years in this small Wisconsin town, this one, for some reason, sticks in my mind, somehow emblematic of the blind fate that all of us are subject to.

This Saturday in September started so beautifully. It was warm and sunny. I was at peace with the world. So, too, undoubtedly was Stan, but for him, that would soon change, though he'd only appreciate the first two or three minutes of this particular tragedy.

Morning hospital rounds were soon over. I had time on my hands, and with nothing else to do, I drove out to the local airport to check on our beloved Seneca, which had been my transportation for this very short assignment. What better way to kill time than going to the airport to chat with the local pilots? But the airport was quiet, and shortly after one in the afternoon, I returned to town. A speeding ambulance passed me in the opposite lane, lights flashing and siren wailing.

The twin engined Seneca aircraft that we owned and used for many of our shorter assignments

Uh-oh, I thought. *I hope it isn't heading to an accident.*

But shortly thereafter, my beeper went off. It was the ER. It seemed that a patient with a gunshot was being brought in. Upon my arrival to the ER, I found the entire crew assembled and ready to go. Everybody was there—anesthesia, respiratory therapy, X-ray, operating room crew. They don't get many cases like this in this sleepy little Wisconsin town, so everybody was ready to do the "big city thing." As usual, there was a paucity of information. Nothing more than that an accident which had happened at the local shooting range (located some eight miles east of town). The ambulance crew had radioed in that the victim had no blood pressure.

Not a good sign, I thought, *especially in view of the distance (and time) between the accident site and the ER.*

Presently, the ambulance roared up, and Stan's limp, unconscious body was unloaded. Sure enough, his pupils were fixed and dilated.[1] But he was brought here to see if we could help. Two IVs were started. He was given massive amounts of crystalloid.[2] Un-crossmatched "O" negative blood was ordered from the blood bank and run in. And lo, to my astonishment (and anxiety), Stan's heart commenced to beat. My examination had revealed an entrance wound in Stan's back, about three inches to the right of his spine. Ominously, the exit wound was on the left side, meaning the trajectory crossed his midline, just in front of his spinal column. The aorta lives there. And a bullet through the aorta is rapidly fatal, virtually anywhere in this country.

Now what to do? In a sense, I was secretly dismayed that we now had his heart beating again. (Yes, I know that is a selfish reaction, and I hate to admit it.) But now everybody was looking to me to save Stan. How was I to repair his aortic injury? I had never done vascular surgery, and the hospital's little OR had no vascular instruments. Such surgery is done in larger, better-equipped hospitals. Any heroic surgery would be far, far more difficult than what we had accomplished so far. All we had done was start a couple of IVs and run in fluids. Like the proverbial man grasping a tiger's tail, we couldn't let go. We couldn't stop. All we had done was to buy some small amount of time—time that must promptly be used wisely.

---

[1]   A bad sign. Pupils become fixed and dilated at the time of brain death.
[2]   IV fluid.

For one brief instant, I entertained the insane notion of rushing Stan to the OR. Maybe I could get some type of cross clamp on his aorta to stop the fearful hemorrhage and thereby purchase additional time, time that could then be used to effect a transfer to a larger hospital that could repair the damage. But then reason returned. Even if I could get some type of unorthodox, nonvascular clamp across that vessel, in all probability, he'd still die. Indeed, even if this gruesome accident had taken place in the parking lot of a larger hospital, the outcome would still, in all probability, have been negative. Furthermore, in Stan's case his precious brain had now been much, much too long without oxygen. A technical "triumph" all too often is nothing more than a tragedy in disguise.

Wanna know what else deterred me from heroics? The omnipresent threat of a lawsuit. A lawyer could now blame me: "Doctor, you had your patient stabilized enough to take him to an inadequately equipped OR. If instead you'd used that valuable time to transfer him to a larger, better-equipped hospital rather than engaging in foolish heroics in a small hospital, my client would have survived." And so Mayo One (Mayo Clinic's Helicopter Ambulance) was summoned. Had I just refused Stan that one tiny chance of survival for the sake of my own skin? Not in this instance, but there are instances in which doctors hesitate to take chances because of the malpractice pall. The public pays a price (hidden but nonetheless paid) for our medical legal climate.

While we awaited the helicopter's arrival, I went out to the ER waiting room to meet and speak with the family and friends. I was greeted with the usual expressions of disbelief and horror that events of this type generate.

"No! It can't be! Please, God, don't let it happen! He can't die!"

And I learned a little more of what happened out at the firing range. It seemed that Stan and his best friend had gone out there to do a little target shooting with Stan's new 9 mm handgun. Neither one was drinking. Both were very careful, safety-conscious handgun aficionados. After shooting a few rounds, Stan gave the gun to his friend (the weeping youth who told me all this) and became engaged in a conversation with friends twenty or thirty feet away. A cartridge jammed in the gun. In attempting to free it, the gun discharged. The bullet struck

Stan in the back. These were the days before cell phones, so somebody had to drive several miles to summon an ambulance. Meanwhile, Stan lost consciousness. All in all, it was a stupid, pointless accident.

Presently, the helicopter arrived, and thank goodness it was Mayo One. The Mayo Health System helicopter service has two outstanding features. First, it often launches on the request of even a nurse. They must figure that the lone physician may be busy with the patient, and if he said he needed air care, then it must be true! In sharp contrast, in Tennessee, I had seen it take two lengthy phone calls from the ER physician to the tertiary care center just to get the helicopter launched. This necessarily detracted from the care of a critically injured victim. In one hospital, I witnessed a fifty-four-year-old man bleed to death from a leaking aneurysm due to the combination of a faulty beeper, an answering service operator who simply didn't have any idea of the urgency such a situation required, and hospital policies requiring independent verification with a physician who agreed to accept the transfer and care for the patient. Conversely, I have seen lives saved by prompt dispatch of air care.

Mayo One's second outstanding feature is alacrity. Less than ten minutes after landing, they were airborne again. I've seen similar helicopters in Iowa take nearly an hour to get a patient airborne. And once in Arizona, to shorten the pickup time for a desperately ill patient, I took the unorthodox step of actually taking the patient out to the airport so that the rescue crew, though frustrated and quite angry with me, had no choice but to pack him aboard and head home as fast as possible.

Anxiously, we waited for word on Stan. Finally, in the early evening, we called the receiving hospital and learned that Stan Creel, twenty-eight years old, had died in the elevator taking him up to their OR.

Now what to make of this whole sorry tale? In my youth, I wasted time pondering the meaning of senseless accidents. Now I think that "why" questions are simply inadmissible, meaningless, in the same category as questions such as "To whom is that bachelor married?" or "What does blue smell like?" Meaningful answers to invalid questions are not possible, even in principle. Switch the channel. Go on to doing something productive.

It so happens that I had recently reread Ernest K. Gann's classic book *Fate Is the Hunter*. Gann, an early airline pilot who flew all over the globe during World War II, found himself having to live with many senseless accidents that befell his friends. He imagined there was a genie somewhere out there remorselessly stalking and ambushing its victims. *Fate*[3]. Gann would simply conclude that Fate (for unknown and unknowable reasons) had simply placed Stan Creel at exactly the wrong place and at exactly the wrong time so that his aorta intersected the trajectory of a few grams of lead traveling some six hundred miles an hour. It's as good an explanation as any. I later calculated, for my idle curiosity, just how accurately Fate had to position Stan. If he had been only an inch to one side or another, which works out to somewhat less than two-tenths of one degree to the left or right, then I could have saved him.

Bummer…

Another Late-Night Tragedy

"And all your wealth won't buy your health." So goes the line from the old Simon and Garfunkel song.

There was a poster on the wall outside this hospital's sleepy little ER that showed a sleek car next to a wheelchair and asked which "set of wheels would you like to drive?" And under that was the caption "DON'T DRINK AND DRIVE."

There is nothing profound to report on this, my last day on this particular assignment. This story is really nothing more than an incident report, an incident that took place the night before.

---

[3]   Quoting from Gann's book: "Tell me now…since you are older and wiser than me, by what ends does a man ever partially control his fate? It is obvious that favorites are played, but if this is so, then how do you account for those who are ill-treated? The worship of pagan gods, which once answered all this, is no longer fashionable. Modern religions ignore the matter of fate. So we are left confused and without direction."

The morning dawned bright and sunny, with the townsfolk rousing themselves and planning their routine activities. Most of them were quite unaware that, the evening before, a youngster, a recent high school graduate with his entire promising life stretching out in front of him, had tragically illustrated the consequences of drinking and driving. Indeed, he illustrates it far more graphically than a poster on the wall. No doubt he is in a very, very deep depression (now that he has sobered up). You see, he'll never walk again.

He graduated from high school a week or so ago. His family had bought him a brand-new Cavalier. He was often seen around town, bragging about his $500/month car payments. Late last night, after considerable alcohol intake, he failed to negotiate a curve on the highway. His precious new car rolled end over end. He was brought to the ER paralyzed from the mid-abdomen down. This netted him a helicopter ride, which he probably didn't enjoy that much, to a nearby tertiary care center. He greets this morning, the first one for the rest of his paralyzed life, from a hospital bed.

It is all the talk of the hospital. It is all the talk of the town. In a small town, everybody knows everybody else, and their family is wealthy. That is how he could afford his car payments.

But all their wealth cannot buy his health.

The Subtleties of Diagnosis

As all of us in the medical field know, a good 80–90 percent of our diagnoses are handed to us by the patient. This may not be appreciated by the general public, which is impressed by laboratory tests and X-rays. Yup, our patients give us the diagnoses when we take the time to talk to them. It's called the medical history, and if you take your time and conduct your interview properly, more often than not, you come away with a pretty good idea of what is going on. And this, by the way, remains an attraction of *locum tenens* medicine. I have few patients. I can take the time. My pay is not determined by how many patients I can "crank" through the system. Harried physicians, employed by HMOs that mandate X number of patients per hour, have a much harder time doing this.

The case of Marie illustrates this well. She was a nineteen-year-old girl with abdominal pain sent to me by an internist who characterized it as nonspecific. It turned out that she had a diseased gallbladder, which indeed was one of the diagnostic possibilities the internist had considered. What threw him off was the lack of the expected history. People with gallbladder attacks usually have pain in the right upper quadrant of their abdomen, and it is usually brought on by eating fatty foods. "Fatty food intolerance" is how the medical books put it. Marie had neither. She maintained that she hurt all the time, that no food aggravated her pain, and that she hurt all over her abdomen. She would have made an ideal sample patient used to teach medical students how to conduct an interview.

It turned out that she did indeed have fatty food intolerance, but it took subtle questioning to tease that history from her. It took me considerable time to phrase and rephrase my questions (a luxury the busy internist did not have). Stumped by the lack of food intolerance, I chanced to ask her just what it was that she ate. It turned out that *all she ate* was fatty food. No wonder she couldn't say what types of food aggravated the pain. She was continually eating greasy food and therefore had continual abdominal pain.

And, oh yes, she also had pain in the right upper quadrant of her abdomen. But that, too, was subtle.

"Where do you hurt?" I asked.

"All over."

"Any one spot worse than another?"

"No."

"Hmm. Are you hurting right now?"

"Yes."

"Good. Lie right down there and feel around your tummy. Find the worst spot."

Well, it turned out that after she took the time to poke around, she hurt in the right upper part of the abdomen and nowhere else. She just didn't know where she hurt. She hadn't bothered to notice. Yes, you guessed it. She was not rocket scientist material. And so a

HIDA scan was ordered, which confirmed my hunch. It was abnormal. A laparoscopic chole (removal of gallbladder) was done, and Marie was a new person.

Conversation with a Lawyer

Here is a snippet of a conversation I had with a lawyer shortly after arriving on one of my many trips to this town. He was recovering from a bilateral inguinal hernia repair, which had been done a week before by Dr. P, whom I was replacing.

"Well, things seem to be progressing satisfactorily," I commented.

"Yes, I am having surprisingly little pain."

"Say, you didn't drive to the clinic today, did you?"

"Well, as a matter of fact, I did."

"Umm. You realize, of course, that if you were involved in an accident, even one beyond your control, that one of your professional colleagues would be able to prove that no matter what the circumstances were, it was your fault because you drove so soon after a major operation."

The lawyer responded with a laugh, "Yes, I'm sure they could."

"Indeed, surgeons have been successfully sued when one of their patients was involved in an automobile accident and the patient claimed that he was never told not to drive."

More laughter from the lawyer as he said, "Yes, I'm sure it's true."

I continued. "Which is why I am going to write on your chart that I told you not to drive for two more weeks."

"Hey, that's terrible! Don't do that."

CHAPTER 11

Back to Alaska

Back to Alaska, this time in style. By now I had been providing *locum tenens* surgical coverage for some three years. We had upgraded our on-the-road living quarters to a fifth-wheel RV. Betty and I had long imagined the adventure of driving it clear up to Alaska. And if we were responding to a call for *locum tenens* surgical coverage, why, the hospital would pay all our expenses for the trip! Finally, we received a suitable invitation and happily began planning for our big adventure.

June 15 found us bound for Fairbanks, Alaska. We had plotted a route across Canada and up the AlCan highway, some four thousand miles in all. With two whole weeks to make this trip, we had plenty of time for sightseeing along the way. Our stops included hiking, riding our folding bikes, watching birds, and enjoying the magnificent scenery of the Rocky Mountains. At last, on June 29, a Tuesday afternoon, and just one day ahead of schedule, we pulled into Fairbanks and parked our RV at a choice site on the banks of the Chena River.

This two-month *locum* assignment quickly flew by. We had free weekends to travel and visit local tourist attractions (AlaskaLand) as well as other nearby attractions: Manley Hot Springs, the town of Circle, the Yukon River, and abandoned gold dredges. Fairbanks seemed to have hundreds of miles of paved bike trails for us to explore on our little folding bikes. As a matter of fact, I used to regularly ride my bike to work at Fairbanks Memorial Hospital and, for a while, became a fixture around town. Tour buses would stop and call their passengers' attention to their "traveling surgeon" as I rode by. We invited relatives to make a trip to Fairbanks, and then leaving me behind to cover the hospital, Betty took them on tours to Denali, Prince William Sound, Whittier, Valdez, etc.

Commuting to work at the Fairbanks Memorial Hospital

Alaskan Surgeons

General surgeons seem to be a different breed in Alaska, far more diverse than those in the Lower 48. I've watched one of them (Dr. G.) perform a total gastrectomy[1] for widespread stomach cancer (*linitus plastica*) using a thoraco-abdominal approach in only one and a half hours! He was partnered with another general surgeon (Dr. H.), though only one would be in their office at any given time. When one of them was working, the other would be hunting, fishing, flying, or camping somewhere out in the Alaskan bush. One apocryphal tale related to me by the staff was that once, upon returning from his bush activities, Dr. G. showed up in the OR lounge unshaven and in dirty blue jeans. One of the temporary *locum* sur-

---

[1]   Removal of the entire stomach.

geons at that time (not me!) called security to report a "vagrant" in the doctor's lounge.

Nonetheless, Dr. G. is an extremely competent and talented surgeon, one whom I would allow to operate on me. He and his partner are a dying breed, one of the last of the old-time general surgeons who can seemingly do anything. They have been known to turn a flap to decompress an epidural hematoma, repair hip fractures, perform vascular surgery, and of course, perform any kind of abdominal or chest surgery.

One day, upon his return to active surgical duty, Dr. H. related to me an almost unbelievable tale. He was on a fishing trip, flying his pontoon float plane hundreds of miles to the north, beyond any civilization. He landed on a likely lake. Unfortunately, one of his pontoons struck a submerged log and was damaged beyond repair. He was outside radio range of any town.

"My god!" I exclaimed when he told me this. "What did you ever do?"

"Oh, no problem," he replied. "I just waited till I saw the contrails of a transpolar airliner overhead, called them on 121.5,[2] and explained my situation."

They in turn relayed the problem back to Fairbanks. A new aircraft pontoon was strapped to the exterior of a float plane and was flown up to his location. Makeshift repairs were made, and he flew home in time to meet his scheduled "change of shift" with Dr. G.

Eric Bremer

Eric, a twenty-three-year-old professional guide from Cody, Wyoming, was in Alaska for the summer, working for one of the more "colorful" local Alaskans, the owner of a resort and guide business, who had been involved in many affairs, including threatening the life of the local surgeon Dr. G. for allegedly hunting on "his"

---

[2]   The international aviation emergency frequency.

land. (It was public land, by the way.) He had also, once, actually buried a competitor's Piper Cub with a bulldozer.

He owned a small aircraft, a single-engine Piper Super Cub, complete with a three-bladed prop and tundra tires. On the day he came to grief, he was hauling feed to his horses and showing his new guide (Eric) around. While landing on a sand bar, he got into a dangerous situation, one characterized by pilots as "low and slow." The wind unexpectedly shifted direction. The Super Cub lost lift and stalled. Eric distinctly remembered his last words as "Oh, shit!" There was also in this small aircraft some hay, groceries, camping equipment, and Eric's faithful dog. It is, therefore, likely that it was being flown over its maximum gross-weight.

A Piper Super Cub holds only two passengers, seated one in front of the other. When an aircraft stalls, typically the nose drops sharply. It then loses altitude and rapidly gains speed. This is fine if you are high enough to recover, but they were very low, trying to land on that sand bar.

The pilot died instantly. Eric, despite his broken back, dragged himself out of the wreck and, using his elbows, dragged himself away. When it was evident that the plane was not going to burn, he dragged himself back, retrieved his sleeping bag, and crawled inside it for some shelter. In a couple of hours, their absence was noticed, and a search was launched. In due course, the wreck was found, a helicopter was called, and shortly thereafter, Eric "arrove" at Fairbanks Memorial Hospital. Being the only general surgeon available at the time, I was asked to see him.

I found an alert, conscious young man with an acute abdomen and completely numb below the umbilicus (indicative of a serious spinal injury). A diagnostic peritoneal lavage[3] was positive for gross blood, and so it was obvious that a trip to the OR was in order. At this point, one of the regular Fairbanks surgeons, Dr. G., just happened

---

[3]   A small plastic catheter is threaded into a patient's abdomen. Saline solution is injected and then aspirated to see if there is any blood in the abdominal cavity, indicative of serious internal organ injury.

to stroll into the ER, saw what was going on, and then wordlessly came to the OR with me, assisting me with the exploratory surgery.

At surgery, I found a slightly torn spleen. The tear was at the hilum,[4] a classic type of deceleration injury. We used to always, routinely, remove any damaged spleens no matter how slightly damaged. However, the more recent practice of trying to salvage damaged spleens had gained acceptance.

Dr. G. "Here, let me show you how to bag the spleen." This was something that I'd never done.

Dexon, an absorbable mesh, is fashioned into a small bag that can also be lined with clotting agents (Gelfoam soaked in thrombin). The spleen is gently inserted into this "bag," and it is sewn tightly shut. The hope is that clots form, and the spleen will continue its immunological function. After Dr. G. had fashioned the "bag" and sewn it shut, we observed the result. Alas, the spleen continued to bleed at an unacceptable rate, so we had to remove it.

A second injury was the complete avulsion of a portion of the small bowel, which I repaired. A third injury was a large left-sided peri-renal hematoma. Having learned from similar trauma cases involving back injuries, I had obtained a pre-op IVP.[5] The left kidney had failed to visualize, so we knew that it was seriously damaged. Fortunately, in Fairbanks, a urologist was available, and so an intraoperative consult was requested. The urologist felt that the kidney was unsalvageable, and he had to remove it, demonstrating to me the "proper" method of first obtaining vascular control. Now wasn't this a nice coincidence! I had just read an article in *Surgery, Gynecology & Obstetrics*[6] on this subject. And now the Great Surgeon in the Sky had thoughtfully arranged a "practical lab experiment" to cement my heretofore theoretical learning!

Two days later, an orthopedic surgeon fused Eric's spine. Plans were then made for his transfer to the Denver Spinal Center. This was arranged at the request of his insurance company. Initially, the transfer was to be made by Alaska Airlines in a regular passenger jet.

---

[4]   The base of the spleen, where the large blood vessels enter and leave.
[5]   Intravenous Pyelogram, an X-ray showing the function of the kidneys.
[6]   A surgery journal.

In Alaska, they are used to hauling all manner of things even in passenger jets. In this case, nine seats were to be removed to make room for Eric's bed, IVs, and monitoring equipment. But then he began to deteriorate. His bowels quit functioning, and his abdomen turned quiet. I became nervous and insisted on an air ambulance. That was finally arranged, albeit with much difficulty. His insurance company shopped around for the best rate; nevertheless, the final bill for the transfer to Denver was over $44,000!

Much later, I was pleased to learn via very roundabout channels that Eric made almost a complete recovery from his back injury and was able to walk![7]

And oh yes! Eric's dog also survived—with a pneumothorax[8] and a dislocated hip, both treated by a local vet.

---

[7] It is always nice to learn how patients do after being transferred to larger medical centers. Some hospitals are very conscientious about informing the referring physician regarding the status of referred patients. Others are much less so. Maybe they are too busy? Maybe they forget. We referring physicians may be involved with another patient and don't have the time to call for an update. In other cases (such as the case of Stan Creel in the previous chapter), we find the time to call for a report.

[8] Collapsed lung due to a broken rib.

CHAPTER 12

The Loneliness of the Trauma Surgeon

Thursday evening. On call. Again. In Fairbanks, Alaska. Clinic was over, rounds were made, and I was home to Betty by 5 p.m. Would my string of good luck hold? Might I hope for yet another quiet evening? But while we were eating supper, we heard the sirens, shortly followed by my beeper going off.

Uh-oh. Then when I went to dial the phone number indicated on the beeper, it went off again. That is always a bad sign—when they can't wait for me to answer their initial beep. Sure enough, it was the ER frantically telling me they had a car accident and could I please come in? Then when I drove out of the campground, I found the traffic backed up on Airport Way, clear back to and in front of Fred Meyer's store. But I knew of a back way to the hospital.

Must be a bad one, I thought as I cut across two lanes of traffic and was on my way, luckily not becoming an accident statistic myself.

When I got to the ER, there was the usual pandemonium of multiple victims of a motor vehicle accident. All the exam rooms full. Noises and apparent confusion everywhere. Screams or sometimes just moans. I'm always glad to hear the screams. It's the "quiet" patients who are the most seriously hurt. As usual, there seemed to be hundreds of people milling around—nurses, lab and X-ray techs, respiratory therapists, policemen, etc. People rushing to and fro, getting things or bringing things.

"Get X-ray in here!"

"What do you want on this one?"

"I need a syringe!"

"Where is the lab?"

"Come on, come on! Isn't that IV ready yet?"

There were five victims in this accident. Naturally, I always get the worst ones. The ER doctors are very good at stabilizing things, but then they want out because their job is then over.

"Get the surgeon on trauma call in here to take care of these patients!"

So when I wandered in, a nurse spied me and took little time to steer me in the direction of the worst one. The ER crew took care of the rest—though, later on in the evening, I was given another patient to admit for observation. The remaining three were "treated and released," as per the newspapers.

My patient turned out to be a seventy-seven-year-old woman visiting from Idaho. She'd flown into Anchorage and was met by her daughter and son-in-law. They then drove her up to Fairbanks so she could see the scenery, visiting Denali along the way. Just as they were coming into Fairbanks, a car driven by a juvenile suddenly made a turn across traffic and cut directly in front of them. My patient had been sitting in the back seat and had her seat belt on. All quite proper, of course, but it turned out that it was the seat belt that caused some of her major injuries.

When I first saw her, it was obvious that she had extensive facial injuries. Her nose and both maxillary sinuses were smashed. Her eyes were swollen shut and purple. A preliminary X-ray of her C-spine[1] was suggestive of a fracture. Evidently, at the moment of impact, she had snapped forward, and her face had smashed into the head-rest of the seat in front of her. And oh, yes, that wide purple bruise across her abdomen caused by the seat belt. It had perhaps restrained her from even worse injuries, but at a cost of what internal injuries? Shortly after I arrived in the ER, her blood oxygen levels dropped, and she had to be placed on a ventilator. This requires the insertion of a tube into the trachea, which, besides being very uncomfortable, renders it impossible for the patient to speak. She did tell me, before

---

[1]   An X-ray of the bones in her neck.

the endotracheal tube was inserted, that her abdomen hurt. The ER doctor bowed out at that point, and she was all mine.

So now what do I have? A paralyzed[2] patient on the ventilator! In some respect, it has all become strangely dehumanized. A clinical exercise. She can't talk to me, except through the monitors that are connected to her. Some surgeons actually prefer this type of medicine. Well, that's neither here nor there. I have work to do.

Lessee now... What's going on here?

Run through the mental checklist. Blood pressure 134/82. Pulse in the 70s. Fair capillary fill. So at least she isn't in shock (yet), and I am thus spared one of those mad life-and-death dashes to the OR for emergency surgery to keep a patient from bleeding to death from a ruptured spleen or liver. That is such a high tension, anxiety-filled drill that I have gradually come to dread doing trauma surgery, fearing that someday I am going to lose the race. I mean, how long can you continue to bat 1,000? And in this game, you *always* have to bat 1,000.

Thus, it is with considerable relief that I note that she appears to be stable. I have time to think. What is going on inside this older lady? It seems reasonable to investigate the extent of her head injuries. And what about that abnormal C-spine X-ray? Is her neck really broken or not? Will it be safe to send her to the X-ray department for the prolonged time that X-rays always seem to take even in the best hospitals? And the X-ray department—any X-ray department in any hospital anywhere in the country—is always the very worst place for a patient to be when he or she gets into trouble.[3] So I do a quick DPL.[4] The fluid is barely tinged pink, meaning that it should be safe

---

2   She was not paralyzed by the accident but by a drug we gave her prior to inserting the tube in her trachea.

3   Typically, there are not enough nurses or equipment available in an X-ray department to care for a sudden emergency such as a cardiac arrest.

4   Diagnostic Peritoneal Lavage. A tiny tube is inserted into a patient's abdomen and washed with saline. This is a very sensitive test for any blood in the abdomen, which, if present, is a sign that urgent surgery may be needed.

to obtain the additional X-ray studies I need. CT scans[5] of head and neck. And for good measure, I request a CT scan of her abdomen, which is later interpreted by the radiologist as being entirely normal.

Now, it is somewhere around 9 p.m. Nearly three hours have gone by, and we seem to have done nothing! As usual, things always take much longer than it seems they should, but that is another story. I am in the X-ray department with my patient, who remains stable.

"Doctor, she is moving again," the nurse calls out from the CT scanner. This will ruin the CT scans and limit the data that we are trying to obtain.

"Give her another 5 mg of Norcuron."[6]

I keep having to remind myself that this is, after all, somebody's mother in there. (It was only later that I learned that she is, in fact, the mother of a state senator!) My immediate concern is her tender abdomen. Is something going on in there that isn't showing up on the monitors or in the X-rays?

Superman would have made a helluva doctor, I've often thought. All he would have had to do was peer in there and see exactly what is going on. And so I find myself envying a fictional character!

The easy thing to do is simply operate and look inside. "Pete, the toughest decisions you'll ever have to make are those of *not* operating," Harry Klinger, Chief of Surgery at Geisinger, told me way back in 1974, when I was in training under him. Exploratory surgery is often a "cop-out." It is easy to decide to look inside and has the nifty advantage of giving a definite answer, but at what cost to the patient? Unnecessary surgery isn't "free" to the patient. At the very least, it will prolong her recovery, and at the worst, it could lead to a life-threatening complication.

In trauma surgery, what you have to do is prioritize the injuries and treat the most serious ones first. That sounds easy, but how do you do this when you don't know what all the injuries are? Time spent in the OR on a vain hunt for possible internal injuries can

---

[5] Computed tomography, a fancy X-ray but is one that often takes much longer than normal X-rays.

[6] The drug we were using to keep her from moving during the X-rays.

be time wasted, time that perhaps would better be utilized treating another definite injury. The tough thing to do is to be brave, be resolute, trust your monitors and X-rays, and most of all, trust your "gut" instinct. For me, on that first night, it was to *not* operate. I put her in ICU and watched her all night. And worried all night.

That tender abdomen with the seat belt bruise. *What is going on in there?*

The next morning, she is still stable and is still on the ventilator. All labs and monitors are still normal. Normal vital signs. And the abdomen? How do you evaluate it when your patient can't talk because of the ventilator? Time for another tough decision. They are always made with incomplete information, and there seem to be endless people—from nurses, internists, quality assurance committees, and ultimately, lawyers—around to second-guess you after the fact, when they smugly know all the answers. Still, the only one who can actually make that difficult decision is the surgeon, and often he has to decide on the spot—and with *incomplete* information. The public thinks that being a surgeon must surely be glorious. I think that if I have to put it into just one word, that word would be *lonely*.

Should I be bold and continue to watch her? Certainly, the labs and ICU monitor data say it is still safe. The normal abdominal CT scan says it is okay to continue to watch her. But there is also this little nagging worry that I can't explain, can only listen to, that keeps whispering to me, *A mere bruise from the seat belt shouldn't hurt so bad and so long. And why is the abdomen so quiet? The lab tests are lying to you. The X-rays are lying to you. The DPL was falsely negative. Trust your instincts. Trust your fingers.*

So that afternoon, after explaining the pros and cons of exploratory surgery with the family and reminding them that I, too, am human and don't know all the answers, I took her to the OR to explore her abdomen.

After we are in the OR, after the patient is asleep, after her abdomen is scrubbed and prepped, after the drapes are in place, we begin the ritual of surgery. Things fall into their usual rhythm. We have all done this thousands of times. We are once again in control.

The scrub nurse inquires about the location and circumstances of the accident.

"Where did this accident happen?"

"Parks Highway, at the intersection of Geist Road, right where you turn off onto Chena Pump Road."

"That's a bad intersection."

"Why is that?" I ask.

"We get a lot of accidents from that intersection."

"Yes, but why is that? Why is it such a bad intersection?"

"People turn in front of other people."

I protest, "Yes, that may be, but the visibility is so good there. No blind curves. There is even a traffic light, and you can see somebody coming from a quarter of a mile away. Why would somebody turn in front of another?"

"It's a bad intersection. People have accidents there." That last sentence was ended by her with a verbal period. End of discussion.

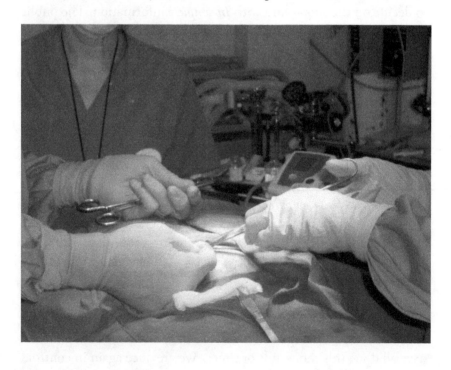

"Give me a pool sucker. Something's going on in here. Look at all that fluid. Brownish… But it doesn't smell bad. Glad we decided to open her."[7]

More exploration. Now I am slowly pulling her intestines out, carefully examining their surfaces. My preoperative diagnosis is small bowel injury, so I look there first. If it was something more major, I'd have diagnosed it sooner. Small bowel injuries can be sneaky, often hiding for several days. More fluid, then some vegetable matter.

There!

A blowout perforation about 15 cm downstream from the Ligament of Treitz.[8] I don't know how a seat belt can make holes in the soft, squishy small bowel. You'd think it would just slip out of the way. The seat belt probably imparts some sort of shock wave that causes a blowout in an area of bowel that is distended or kinked.

Scrub nurse, seemingly bored, "What do you want to fix that with?"

"3-Oh Silk. Pop-off needles." I set about sewing the perforation shut. "Gimme a snap."[9]

"Say," I began again, while sewing on the small bowel, "give me another 3-Oh Silk, and tell me why… I've noticed that, in all the Lower 48 states, when the traffic lights go from green to yellow, it is a signal to slow down, but here in Alaska, the drivers seem to step on the gas instead of the brakes."

"We are all used to it. We don't start up at a green light without checking to see if anybody is rushing through the intersection."

"Yeah," chimes in the anesthesiologist. "My son is learning to drive, and I caught him starting up at a green light the other day without checking to be sure somebody wasn't running the lights."

---

[7]   Peritonitis can smell quite bad, so what I was saying was that while there was an injury, at least it hadn't yet progressed to the point of peritonitis. What I was actually doing at this point was mentally kicking myself for not operating the night before.

[8]   This ligament defines the start of the small bowel. It is located high in the abdomen, right under the infamous seat belt.

[9]   Slang term for a hemostat.

"Yes, but isn't it against the law? I mean, I have a friend back in Iowa, a policeman, whose specialty is picking up drivers running the yellow lights. Why, he gets his whole monthly quota of tickets that way!"

When I am done sewing, I begin carefully examining the rest of the small bowel, a few inches at a time. Hiding under a bit of exudate I find a second smaller perforation and commence to repair that one as well.

"Doc, it comes from the winter driving conditions. Ever hear of *black ice*? You can't always stop at red lights. We call it the controlled skid. We all expect it. If the traffic light turns and you put on the brakes and start skidding through the intersection, what you do is lean on the horn and skid right on through. The others wait for you. We all expect it. We have all done it. It just carries over into summer driving."

"Black ice?"

"That's where the traffic at intersections is so heavy that the cars polish the road surface ice. It's only a thin layer. It's dark outside. You can't see the ice, but it's there. We call it black ice. It's very slippery."

"Well, it's a good thing the tourists are gone!" Much laughter and agreement.

"Yeah, Doc. We'd kill them for sure."

When I was done with the repairs and had explored the rest of the abdomen (it was negative), it was time to begin to lavage all the spilled small bowel contents from the abdomen.

"I'll need at least four liters of warm Ringer's Lactate and one of Good Medicine." The latter request is for a recipe I'd picked up last summer in Fargo, North Dakota.[10] While that is going on, the scrub nurse continues with the conversation.

"That's why we don't allow the Japanese to drive here in the winter. We load them on buses and truck them up to Chena Hot Springs."

---

[10] This is an antibiotic wash solution that I used to cleanse out all the small bowel content from within this lady's abdomen.

Japanese? Tourists? Here? In Fairbanks? In the winter? (We hadn't seen a lot of Asian tourists this summer, just Americanos in their huge motor homes.)

"You mean you have Japanese tourists here in the winter?"

"Oh, lots of them!"

"Why on earth would a tourist—Japanese or otherwise—want to come to Fairbanks in the dead of winter when it is fifty below and dark all the time?"

"Well, Doc, it's like this. The Japanese believe that if a newly-wed couple consummates their marriage when the Northern Lights are glowing, they will have a long and happy marriage. So they come over here to do that."

"Oh."

"I have a friend," she continues, "a musher who makes considerable money off the tourists in the wintertime. He has a dog team and gives rides out along the river. Last year, he was demonstrating how the dogs are hitched to the sled. The Japanese tourists were all bundled up in parkas, like Eskimos, sitting on bleachers, and he was really into giving them their money's worth. He noticed they were staring raptly at him—well, perhaps over his shoulder, really. He thought he was really doing a fantastic job until one couple excused themselves.

"It was then that his assistant pointed overhead. The Northern Lights! He turned back, and the entire group silently, two by two, was going back to their motel rooms. Half an hour later, they all sheepishly reappeared to have their dog sled rides!"

"Hmm... Say, do they have to wait and do it for the first time under the Northern Lights, or is it okay at any old time during the honeymoon?"

"We don't know, but my friend is just waiting for somebody to try it during one of the dog sled rides!"

Mrs. Edwards improved rapidly, and I was able to take her off the ventilator the next morning. That afternoon, on our way home from church, Betty and I stopped by the ICU to see her again. We found that she continued to do very well and now sitting up in a chair and, for the first time, was able to actually smile and talk to us and see her surgeon. Heretofore her face had been so swollen and purple that she couldn't open her eyes. No, her abdomen didn't hurt anymore, and she was grateful that I did the surgery.

With the wisdom of hindsight, it is now obvious that I should have taken the easy route the first night and explored her as soon as I had the "probably normal" neck CT scan. Sometimes you look good in retrospect, and sometimes you don't. So, for a while at least, I'll probably consciously or unconsciously think of this patient and "pull the trigger" a little quicker. The next four or five patients with abdominal tenderness after a car wreck are probably going to get explored, just to be sure I don't miss any more small bowel injuries.[11] Then as the negative surgical explorations pile up, as they have in the past, I'll go back to selective watching and waiting till the next missed injury happens.

In retrospect, it was a simple case after all. An older lady was in a car wreck. She had some facial fractures and a couple of blowout perforations of the small bowel. It was simple to fix. What was all the fuss about, anyway? If, on Monday morning, another surgeon in the locker room were to ask me how my weekend was, I'd have to say, "Well, not bad, really. Had only one case—a lady in a car wreck. But all she had was a couple of small bowel perforations."

Such is the power of "after the fact" knowledge that even I, who has just been through this whole tense scenario, who has just experienced all the doubts and anxieties of half a dozen diagnostic possibilities considered and discarded, even I have a hard time reconstructing my emotions two days later! Had I not written my thoughts down so soon, I'd never have been able to accurately reconstruct them.

Now what of the people who never have to live through one of these experiences, those who *always* have accurate (read: "after the fact") knowledge? This then must be at least a part of the basis for the gulf that exists between lawyers and doctors. How can we doctors ever expect a lawyer to understand the pressures, anxieties, and

---

[11]   It is incredible what goes through a surgeon's mind when he evaluates a patient and decides on treatment. Usually, the patient has no idea of the complex mixture of mental ingredients, which change from time to time in a surgeon's career.

difficulties that trauma surgeons must live with every day when, a day later, even our own perspective is changed by the presence of this hindsight?

CHAPTER 13

IDGAB

Our fabulous summer in Alaska had finally come to an end but not our adventures. How to relate the events, thoughts, and emotions associated with our last week in Alaska? It started with the marvelous weekend in the ghost town of McCarthy. We'd wanted to go there ever since we'd heard about it from Ron Davis, the clinic administrator in Fairbanks.

McCarthy is situated adjacent to the former mining town of Kennecott. Both can only be reached by driving to Chitina and then driving some fifty-odd miles on an old abandoned railroad track right-of-way that ends in a parking lot. From there, you must haul yourself across the Kennecott River on a hand-pulled cable car. You see, the spring floods on the Kennecott washed out every bridge that has ever been built there until finally the townspeople simply rigged a cable across the river, attached a platform to it, and named it the Tram.

Three years ago, while bicycle riding in the Baja, Mexico, in what turned out to be one of those "My, isn't it a small world!" coincidences, we met two delightful retired schoolteachers from Anchorage. They'd described flying their own airplane to an abandoned Alaskan mining town and, finding the empty houses still completely furnished (furniture, dishes, blankets, etc.) as though the people had only just left temporarily, hoping to return someday when the mines opened up again. Sure, there were still a few "inhabitants" there, one of whom had rushed out to meet their plane and implored them to visit: "It's been over a year since my wife has seen another woman!"

They were charmed and had purchased one of the cabins for a few hundred dollars.

It all seemed like such a fairy tale that we'd remembered it over the years. We'd kept in touch with Elaine and Jean, and would you believe it? Their cabin turned out to be in the very same town of McCarthy that we'd learned about from the clinic administrator! Indeed, they offered to fly us to their cabin to be their guests for a weekend.

The infamous Alaska weather refused to cooperate with any flying plans during the various summer weekends that we were free, and so in desperation, we decided that on our final weekend, good weather or not, we'd go—by our truck if necessary. We'd haul ourselves in via the Tram. Then late Friday evening, I called Elaine and Jean to find out that the weather was a go for Saturday, but the forecast for the remainder of the weekend was not good. We might get stuck there Sunday. Well, never mind. I had previously scheduled myself to be off on Monday, so the possibility of us getting stuck in McCarthy wasn't all that bad.

And so it was that Saturday, August 28, found us driving south from Fairbanks, some 200 miles to Glenallen. There is an airport at Glenallen, and soon after our arrival at 1 p.m., a little Cessna 180 daintily touched down and taxied up. Elaine and Jean! Shortly thereafter, we were off for the short hop to McCarthy's dirt strip, with Elaine pointing out the sights along the way. "Over here is a mud volcano. And down there, see that widened area next to the railroad bed? Somebody's got an airstrip there." These Alaskan bush pilots think nothing of landing on sand bars, roads, or even glaciers.

What a couple, these two! Both licensed pilots. They have explored most of Alaska in their Cessna. One year, they did rivers. The next year, it was towns and valleys. We had been saddened last year to learn that Elaine was diagnosed with a horrid adenocarcinoma in her lungs. No, she wasn't a smoker. It was one of those fluke diseases. And almost unbelievably, she'd watched her next-door neighbor slowly choke to death with the same disease the year before! Oh dear! But she'd heard of a new treatment being offered at a medical center in San Antonio, and since conventional therapy seemed powerless, what was there to lose? Now after chemotherapy with a drug based on Taxol (yup, the one derived from the bark of the Pacific Yew Tree), here she is, bald from the treatments, wearing a baseball cap, and otherwise seeming none the worse for wear. After piloting us over some mighty rugged terrain, she set that "taildragger" down on the end of McCarthy's gravel runway, with the stall horn a-wailin' all through the approach, using less than a thousand feet of runway.

After a short drive from the airport in an old friend's old car, we found ourselves back in the 1920s in an Alaska that not too many get to experience in these days of Princess Tours. Their rustic cabin in "downtown" McCarthy lacks the usual amenities, such as running water or electricity. It is heated with wood and sports an outhouse. But there are no pipes to worry about freezing in the winter! On the wall is a 1930 calendar they'd salvaged years ago from what used to be McCarthy's hardware store. Strangely, the paper isn't even yellowed. Elaine and Jean took us on a short guided tour among the tumble-down buildings. Some are abandoned; some are still lived in. One is restored into a lodge that caters to the well-heeled who insist upon the latest in offbeat vacations.

"Just barely making it," commented Elaine.

McCarthy and Kennecott were twin towns. Both abandoned. Kennecott was the company town located five miles up the canyon, perched on the side of a mountain, overlooking the Kennecott Glacier. It consisted solely of the mines, together with associated machinery, dormitories, chow halls, administration buildings, and even a hospital. The copper mines operated from 1911 to 1938.

"Actually the ore ran out in about 1932, but the towns held on while they prospected for more," related Jean.

Ultimately, the company moved to Utah, taking with it only the name. Thus, the huge Kennecott open-pit copper mine outside Salt Lake City, still being operated, has its roots here in Alaska.

Inasmuch as Kennecott was a company town, it was "dry." The miners had to go elsewhere for recreation. That was where McCarthy, down in the valley, on the Kennecott River, at the foot of the glacier, came into the picture. So our tour also includes the remains of several saloons as well as the inevitable red-light district, which was located discreetly down on the river banks. Most of those buildings are now gone, washed away by the Kennecott River, which is constantly changing its course. Not only do buildings age, decay, and collapse, but also the very geography of any given landscape changes. Looking at McCarthy, you'd never realize that part of the town was missing.

During our tour, we were treated to tales of some of the original residents who were still alive in the 1960s, when Elaine and Jean first came here. There were men such as the reclusive old Kennecott Copper Company geologist who "knew" where there was more ore but was waiting for everybody to leave before "finding" it again. McCarthy is *still* occupied by eccentrics and recluses. Some twenty-five to thirty of them are classed as full-time residents, wintering over here.

Jean told us the amusing tale of their first (and only) Thanksgiving dinner. Somebody had the bright idea of getting the whole community together to share a Thanksgiving dinner. And so it was organized, and so it took place. But nobody was having a good time, and presently, they began to ask one another, "Why did we agree to do this thing? We aren't having a good time. We don't even *like* other people. That is why we live here—so we can be alone." And so they finished their meal in silence, went their separate ways, and have never tried to get together again!

From Elaine and Jean's perspective, things have really changed with the influx of tourists. Elder hostels have been held in McCarthy. John Denver taped a video here. We even met a *National Geographic* photographer on our informal tour. On any given summer day, the parking lot the other side of the Kennecott River is full of the omnipresent RVs. But to us, McCarthy is still delightfully primitive. For example, we notice that none of the cars in that town have license plates. Why bother? There are no police here, and anyway, it is all private land. Indeed, the only way to get a car into Kennecott is to wait until winter when it can be driven over the frozen river.

That evening, after a wonderful repast of steak grilled between two old anvils in their front yard, our conversation turns to the observation of how lucky we are to be alive in 1993 and, at the same time, how little of our luckiness seems to be appreciated by people in general. Certainly not by the news media. When was the last time you've heard a politician telling us anything but how bad things are and how he—and he alone—can "fix" them again? We take for granted that two ordinary retired schoolteachers can, for example, save their earnings and actually own their own private airplane and fly into McCarthy. Travel that consumed (until very recently) an entire week is accomplished in an hour or two. Extraordinary? Perhaps, but the RVs parked on the other side of the Kennecott River are as likely to be driven by retired factory workers from Detroit as by company executives.

If you were to propose to any number of eighteenth- or nineteenth-century philosophers the following experiment: Take not one person but an entire country, and make each individual in that country fabulously wealthy, more wealthy than any king who had lived up to that time. A country where each person can not only be fed and be warm but could devote a sizable fraction of his income and time to the pursuit of leisure activities; a country where each family could have a boat, TV, car, home; a country where even the common man could expect and indeed *demand* to recover from such "dreaded" diseases as appendicitis, infections, or a fractured leg.

Betty is reading a history of the Donner Expedition in 1849, and a minor but nonetheless tragic side story relates how one of the men got a splinter in his hand and ultimately died from the ensuing blood poisoning! Now ask our imaginary philosopher, "Would not that country and each of its fabulously wealthy citizens then be happy and content?" What would his answer have been? Haven't we just described for him a sort of heaven on earth, a place of warmth, comfort, and pleasurable activities that we take for granted? But no! All you hear on the radio, in the news, from the self-serving, two-faced politicians, is how terrible our problems are, how bad off we are. Let them live in, say, Somalia for a while and see if they would sing the same tune.

Later that evening, Elaine and Jean haul out some of their treasures from McCarthy's past. When they came here the hospital in Kennecott, although abandoned for some-thirty-odd years, still had the appearance of only a recent, perhaps temporary, departure of its residents. They were able, for example, to find hospital records lying around. We, too, had poked through that building, only to find that everything is gone now, picked bare by tourists. They showed us a few of their precious hospital records dating from 1924. A doctor's order sheet, the sum total of which was "Aspirin, gr. 5," day after day after day. A nurse's notes, each daily entry simply consisting only of "routine care," though once she wrote the word "coffee." What a change from the bureaucracy and paper mills of today's hospitals! But most precious of all to us were the outpatient records. "FB[1] eye" and "Contusion Lt. thigh" were obvious mining injuries, but the long list of names with the diagnosis "urethritis" could only be gonorrhea that the men had picked up in the red-light district down in McCarthy!

The old medical records turn the topic of conversation to the present health-care system, and I am not surprised that the general consensus so widely repeated by the popular press and politicians is also embraced by Elaine and Jean. After all, most people can only accept what they read.

"Something has to be done about that mess," Jean comments.

"What mess?" I ask.

"Well, we spend over 1/7th of our economy on health care."

"Yes, but is that wrong? Please explain to me why this statistic—and I have no reason to doubt its veracity—indicates a problem. Nobody has yet been able to explain it to me. How much do each of us spend on, say, housing? Is it half? A third? Why is that okay, but 1/7th on health care is considered a national scandal?"

No answer. And so I still don't know why it is considered that we have a crisis in health care in this country. The uninsured? True, some can't get coverage, but others choose to spend their earnings on leisure activities rather than health-care insurance. They then piously claim that they can't afford medical insurance. Is health care a right? If so, why not housing? Why not be able to spend *all* our money on leisure? Evidently, our fabulously wealthy population isn't happy with their lot in life and would like to have even more—everything not only available to them but given to them for free.

---

[1]   Foreign body.

Elaine protests, "You doctors are always opposed to nationalized medicine. You don't want to lose your income."

"Not me," I reply. "I am getting ready to retire. I'm more of an interested—if concerned—observer of this tragic phenomenon that is going on in the country today. And what worries me is not whether we have nationalized medicine or whether doctors will or won't be salaried. What worries me is the bureaucracy. Because in a bureaucracy, it is the individual that gets ground under and swept away. What scares me is that the same nice people that brought us the Veterans Administration and the Post Office are now going to fix up medicine for the rest of the country."

"Well, you have to have administration and regulations" is their response.

"Ah, let me tell you three true stories. I've never worked for the VA. Certainly, some VA hospitals are very fine, especially those affiliated with a university. Perhaps it is only a coincidence that all three of my encounters with non-university-affiliated VAs have been worrisome."

Four years ago, I was in Iowa, and I wanted to send a patient to the nearest VA Hospital. He needed surgery, was a veteran, and wanted to go there. He'd been there before and had surgery there before, so there was no question as to his eligibility. It was his right as a military veteran, after all, wasn't it? I picked up the phone to make the referral. The first person I spoke to was the surgical resident on call, who informed me (before even learning anything about the patient) that he was not empowered to make any sort of decisions with regard to actual admissions to the hospital and that he needed to get the medical officer of the day (MOD) on the phone. And the first thing the MOD wanted to do was get an administrator on the phone, who informed me that the entire telephone conversation was going to be recorded!

"Where is the patient's needs in all this?" I asked them.

All that these people were concerned about were themselves and following this or that regulation, not the patient.

Two years ago, I was in a small hospital in central Minnesota, filling in for another surgeon who was away. I had just finished a breast biopsy. A family practitioner caught my eye.

"Are you the *locum* surgeon?"

"Yup."

"Would you mind looking at these films for me?"

What he showed me were flat and upright abdominal X-ray films showing free air, a sure sign that a catastrophe of monstrous proportions had befallen his patient. Something inside had ruptured. Peritonitis would surely follow. His only hope was urgent surgery.

I responded, "These don't look so good. Somebody has a big problem here. How is the patient?"

"Not very good," he replied. "His white count is over 24,000, and his temperature is 102."

"Want me to take a look at him?"

"Oh no, he is a veteran. As a matter of fact, the VA is already treating him for cancer, and he just suddenly deteriorated last night. I'm going to send him back to the VA, but I just wanted your opinion on the films before I called them."

Later, I saw the family physician. Glum.

"How'd you make out?" I inquired.

"Not too good. They told me that they don't admit patients on Fridays!"

My third story happened many years ago, when I was a medical student. I was on a rotation at a local VA hospital. One day, one of the surgeons was furious. He'd just had his paycheck docked by half an hour's pay. It seemed that he'd been seen leaving the building at 4:30 p.m. instead of 5 p.m.

"But there were no more patients to be seen that day!" he protested.

"Never mind," he was told. "If you leave early, your pay gets docked."

"But last week, I stayed till six with a sick patient. Are you going to give me extra for that?"

"No. If you stay extra time, you are making a *donation* to the VA."

So what did this guy do about it? Well, there was nothing he could do about it, but from then on, no matter how many patients there were or how sick they were, he left precisely at 5:00 p.m. Other similar instances must be the origin of the popular medical "joke" about how dangerous it is to stand in the hallway of a VA hospital at quitting time.

Back to my conversation with Jean and Elaine.

"These three incidents that I have personally experienced are what make me concerned about the future of American medicine. When you have a bureaucrat or a politician in charge, the individual tends to suffer."

"But nationalized medicine would be for the greater good of the population as a whole," protests Elaine.

"Ah, Elaine," I answered. "Let me explain to you how such a system makes decisions 'for the greater good of the population as a whole.' In Great Britain, where they have nationalized medicine, it has been determined by the government that a woman can have only one PAP smear every five years instead of the customary annual exams done elsewhere in the world. As a result, the death rate from cervical cancer in Great Britain is twice the world average. This isn't news to anybody. I am not revealing a great secret. They are perfectly aware of these statistics. You see, it is all an economic decision made for the 'greater good of the population as a whole.' They have determined how much they are willing to spend on health care. Then they have to decide how they will spend that amount. Thus, for economic reasons, they have decided where to spend their resources and are willing to live with twice the death rate from cervical cancer. You don't think that such a thing will ever happen in the good ole US of A? Well, ask me sometime to tell you about mammograms. It will be a decision made for the 'greater good of the population as a whole.' It's the individual who gets run over in the process…

"And you, Elaine, sitting here alive and well, rid of your cancer! Would a national health plan have agreed to fly you to San Antonio once a month for half a year to try out a new experimental treatment? No, you'd have been forced to take the locally available, cheap, conventional treatment that didn't do your next-door neighbor one bit of good! Thus, while many can argue convincingly that nationalized health care is for the greater good of the population as a whole, you, Elaine, would have been one of those sacrificed. That is what I mean when I say that a bureaucracy can sweep away the individual."

Silence.

The next day, as advertised, the weather deteriorated. It drizzled all morning. Betty and I happily hiked the five miles up to the mining town of Kennecott and scrounged through the empty buildings, getting soaked in the process but loving every moment, even as we realized we might not be able to get away. Midway through the afternoon, however, Elaine cast an experienced eye to the cloudy sky and announced that we'd give it a try.

"Fifty-fifty chance of making it," she said.

We had no idea about the weather at the destination (Glenallen) or at any location in between. The concept of instrument flying doesn't even exist out here in the wilderness. Elaine can't do my kind of flying, and I can't do hers. Bush pilots in Alaska all navigate by reference to rock outcrops, dead spruce trees, river bends, etc. I'd be dead within five minutes of taking off. Listening to a pilot describe to others how they made it into this or that location is fascinating. There are no electronic navigational aids, and if you can't see where you are going, you don't go. Some of the pilots become very inventive on getting safely from one place to another.

So it was a take-off and a flight down a river valley in the general direction of Glenallen. As the plane dodged to the left and right of clouds, Elaine and Jean called out landmarks to each other. Alaskan pilots just have to know where the hills are. Novices don't last long. The weather kept improving during the flight, and by 4 p.m., we were safely back in Glenallen. The weather even looked good enough for Elaine and Jean to try the Chickaloon Pass to get back to Anchorage.

After two more days of duty, the Fairbanks *locum* assignment was over. We said our goodbyes and readied our fifth-wheel for the road. Around noon on Wednesday, September first, we were underway for the return trip to Iowa. The first day was a simple ride down a paved highway to Tok—two hundred miles, four hours, no sweat, overnight in a campground, complete with running water, electricity, etc.

Then things became interesting. We drove up the Taylor Highway, through the little town of Chicken (so named because the early miners wanted to name the town Ptarmigan but couldn't spell it), through Boundary, thence via the Top of the World Highway across the Canadian Border to Dawson, in the Yukon. One hundred ninety-three miles for the day, and we were nine and a half hours doing it! The roads were gravel and in various stages of disrepair. We couldn't afford to break anything out here. We were miles and miles from any town, out in the wilderness with few, if any, passersby. We'd noticed that after August first, tourism really slacked off in Alaska. People start heading south, returning Alaska to the natives. There were unmistakable signs of winter. The leaves had all changed and were falling. The Canadian geese had long since departed. So we had the roads, such as they were, to ourselves.

Enroute home, through Canada, from our Fairbanks, Alaska assignment

The day before, pulling into a rest stop, we'd heard a loud explosion.

"Sounds for all the world like we just had a blowout," I said to Betty, but we couldn't find any problem.

I even got a hammer out and struck all the tires to be sure they were inflated. Then when we pulled out of the rest area, we saw the rented camper on the far side of the road with its front tire in shreds. We had heard *his* blow-out. It turned out that he had a jack and spare and was quite able to replace the tire.

Now as we drove along the deserted gravel roads, we heard, from time to time, little sounds or a new smell. It was not unlike flying a single engine plane over the ocean. The engine always seemed to sound a little "rough." Then, suddenly, halfway down a lonely hill, we heard this very loud "Skreeeeeeeeee!." We stopped. What to do? I had Betty let the rig drift forward while I walked around and singled out the left front wheel as the probable troublemaker.

"God, I hope it's not a bearing or something!"

Then I blocked the wheels, jacked the front of the truck up, removed the left front tire, and sure enough, a piece of rock was in there, wedged between the brake disk and the housing! We pried it out, said our little thank-yous and were on our way.

Dawson on the Yukon! Fabulous, fabled Dawson. Dawson that we'd read so much about over the last two years. Other towns had installed new wooden sidewalks to "assume" an air of authenticity. Dawson needed none of that. As near as we could determine, they didn't have one single paved street, and their sidewalks were vintage old boards. Finally, we let our eyes gaze upon the fabled Klondike. We stood right where George Carmack, Skookum Jim, and Tagish Charley found the big strike in August 1896 on a little creek (then known as Rabbit Creek but promptly renamed Bonanza Creek) that empties into the Klondike. This was what started the Great Stampede, the stories of which we have been reading for the past couple of years.

It was the discovery of gold that gave life to Skagway and all the other towns you read about in Jack London's stories. Indeed, Jack London was here. Now rereading his stories, they take on a new significance, as we recognize *places* and not *names*. This was the ultimate destination of some 100,000 sweaty, gold-crazed men from the Lower 48 who were fleeing a depression. From Skagway, they climbed the Chilcoot Trail or White Pass trail to Lake Bennett, and there they built boats to float down the Yukon to Dawson. All they wanted was fabulous wealth that we enjoy—meaning a comfortable life—being in control of their destiny, being able to do what they wanted when they wanted. Ultimately, they were denied these things.

Of the 100,000 who set out, only some 25,000 or so actually reached Dawson. Of these, only 3,000 or 4,000 actually looked for gold, and of those, only the merest handful actually became wealthy. The Klondike did have rich gold fields in terms of the *concentration* of gold; however, their extent was extremely limited, and they soon played out. As it turned out, more money was made selling equipment to the Stampeders than they subsequently found in the Klondike. And so they left Dawson, seeking their dream of wealth elsewhere, in Nome, in Fairbanks. The wealth, the independence, the comfort they sought were the very things that *we common folk* in the here and now have and take for granted.

We enjoyed the history, the museum, the old houses, and yes, simply the sitting along the Yukon. It was so nice to have the freedom to set your own pace in life—to be able to do nothing more than sit if you so desired and to admire a town and the buildings, soaking up the history. A couple of Gray Line buses pulled up and disgorged a few of the season's last tourists, who had just a few hours to assault the souvenir shops and see the sights. I was sure that were I to be in their shoes, the peaceful beauty of that town or its historical significance would have eluded me.

I so much enjoyed this lifestyle! As we sat on the banks of the Yukon, Betty fixed us our lunch. And I said as I munched on a sandwich, as I had said so many, many times to Betty, "Honey, it just doesn't get any better than this!" till she finally laughed and abbreviated it as our own private little joke: IDGAB!

At a nearby bookstore, I had another one of my infamous attacks, and we walked away some $85 poorer. One of the newly purchased treasures was a book written by an early physician in Dawson, Dr. Duncan, who, among other things, related the great amount of "urethritis" (gonorrhea) he treated. It brought to mind the hospital records Elaine and Jean had given us from Kennecott. He went on to relate how he was sometimes called to investigate a suicide. Some of the men with gonorrheal-induced urethral strictures would go into urinary retention and suffer so horridly that they'd either shoot the dogs or turn them loose and then commit suicide. An 18" soft red rubber catheter was all that would have been needed to give them relief.

We take our current lifestyle for granted and forget to be thankful. IDGAB!

Dr. Duncan also related the pathetic story of Dr. Nunn, an even earlier physician at Dawson, whom he'd replaced in 1935 upon Nunn's death. What did Nunn die from? A ruptured appendix. Dr. Nunn knew perfectly well what was wrong with him and what needed to be done. But he was the only physician at Dawson, which at the time was six days by dog sled to the nearest hospital. He died on the way out, and that was just the way things were in 1935 in the Yukon. These days, if somebody dies of appendicitis, there is instant talk of lawsuits. We forget that our fabulous wealth includes the "right" to recover from appendicitis. We take all this for granted and forget to be thankful. IDGAB!

On Saturday, September fourth, we finally tore ourselves away from Dawson and drove south, managing to make only two hundred miles of forward progress, and this despite the good roads. They were still narrow and still had frequent frost heaves, but at least the gravel was gone. Now the problem was me, hopping out of the truck to explore this little road or that field, meadow, brook, bird… Did the early miners appreciate all this beauty, or were they too busy swatting mosquitoes, swearing at the mud, the cold, the damp, all the while desperately searching for gold? In lieu of a campground, we spent a night in a deserted old roadside gravel pit, complete with bonfire. Since the fifth-wheel was completely self-sustaining, we had all the comforts of home—a warm shower, a commode, oven baked casserole, and a warm clean bed.

IDGAB! IDGAB! IDGAB!

CHAPTER 14

The Mayo Health System

While working in a small town in Minnesota, I chanced to give my CV to a Mayo Clinic ophthalmologist who was providing outreach care locally. He took it back to his administrator, and sure enough, when a need arose, they called me to provide coverage for them. This was my introduction to the Mayo Health System. I enjoyed working for Mayo over the years at many of their upper-Midwest facilities. The stories in this and the following chapter come from several assignments at many different hospitals affiliated with Mayo.

Jim Cameron (A Surgical On-Side Kick)

I was asked to see this eighty-eight-year-old man almost as an afterthought. You see, he was admitted to the hospital to die. His troubles had started over a year ago, with an upset stomach, but he went on to bleed. He was diagnosed as having gastritis and was treated for same. But his symptoms progressed. An X-ray of his stomach showed that a severe deformity had developed. It was probably a malignancy. He was sent to the Mayo Clinic in Rochester, and there the experts threaded a flexible fiber-optic gastroscope down his esophagus and examined the area.

It certainly looked like a cancer. True, their biopsies had returned only a "nonspecific gastritis" diagnosis, but gastric biopsies are notoriously unreliable. I have even seen open biopsies taken at surgery come back as negative, only to have the patient die later of widespread cancer. So the fact that a tiny bit of tissue[1] didn't show the expected cancer did not deter the specialists at Mayo. After all, they'd seen the lesion. And so they recommended surgery to see what (if anything) could be done. Jim, however, refused. "Just as well," the experts had noted in their dictation sent back to the referring family physician, for Jim was both elderly and in very frail health—a huge surgical risk. He was sent home to be made comfortable. And to die.

That was some four months before I saw him, and he had progressed exactly as expected. The cancer grew while Jim withered. He was now in his terminal condition. Everything he ate fermented in his obstructed stomach until he regurgitated it. He was then, once more, hungry. Finally, he was too weak to walk. He lived in his bed. Eventually, he became somnolent. His wife called the ambulance, and this extremely emaciated person was transported to the clinic and then admitted to the hospital.

It was, no doubt, with some misgivings that the family physician started the IVs and began to reverse his dehydration. Why prolong the inevitable? Perhaps because Jim's large and devoted family wanted to delay his imminent departure? He was, however, made a no-code status.[2] It was then that I received a consult. The family physician talked to me directly, apologizing for asking me to see this hopeless case. He wondered if I could insert some type of feeding tube so that the family could take him home, where he could complete the dying process without consuming precious medical resources.

And so early December found me up on the floor one evening, poring through the stack of records. There was the large orange DNR[3] sticker on his chart. There were the voluminous Mayo Clinic records. Yes, it was all there, and all was in order. Jim Cameron weighed into the hospital at a mere ninety-three pounds. He looked just like a survivor of Auschwitz. Oh, the horrendous things we do to our friends and relatives!

---

[1]   Gastroscopic biopsies are about only a millimeter in diameter.

[2]   This means that if his heart stopped, no efforts would be made to restart it.

[3]   Do Not Resuscitate.

"Pete, we treat our dogs better than this" was Milt Barrent's[4] lament as he lay dying of pancreatic cancer in 1988.

I spoke at length with Jim and his family. There were several things we could do. For starters, we could remove the IV and let dehydration take its course. Another option could be some type of obscene tube that could be inserted into his intestine, through which liquid nourishment could be pumped, delaying the inevitable. And finally, there could be a long shot—surgery—certainly not with the intention of curing him but simply bypassing the by-now inoperable tumor. That way, he could at least eat in a natural fashion. The food would then pass from his stomach through the artificial opening into his intestine. We would only be delaying the inevitable, but everyone has the right to decide what is to be done with their body. Did Jim want to delay the inevitable or hasten it? Surgery would be extremely hazardous. I went through the calculations.[5] Jim was extremely malnourished. He was only 74 percent of his IBW,[6] and who knew how far off his usual weight he was. One textbook suggested the risk of surgical complication to be 81 percent and the risk of dying after an operation to be nearly 60 percent. Another merely noted cryptically, "As weight loss approaches 30%, the risk of morbidity and mortality approaches 95%." I could imagine now how much Jim must have regretted his rash decision to refuse surgery at Mayo Clinic when he was in much better shape to withstand it. Maybe he could even have been cured. But he wasn't obstructed then. A complete gastric outlet obstruction has a wonderful way of removing a man's ability to deny his illness. His daily vomiting reminded him that something had gone terribly wrong inside.

Jim decided to give it one last great shot. "Go for it, Doc!" But there were some provisos. If I were to find that technically I could not perform a bypass, then I was, under no circumstances, to put in any "damned tubes." Indeed, if that were to be the case, he wanted everything, including IVs, removed to hasten his death. So be it.

---

[4] A beloved senior surgeon I knew, worked for, and cared for in Iowa.

[5] Yes, there are formulae to calculate the degree of malnutrition, and tables to consult listing the percentage chances of death or complication.

[6] Ideal Body Weight.

And so I set about improving his chances of surviving the surgery. A central line[7] was inserted. I went through the calculations of calories, nitrogen balance, etc. His liver function was assessed. The remaining electrolytic abnormalities from his dehydration were corrected. He now weighed in at 108 pounds. True, most of that was water, but we did have the central line in. And so on December fourth, we removed the large orange sticker[8] from his chart and took him to the OR. To the anesthetist's objection that we were undertaking a hugely risky operation, I could only remark that the risk Jim faced without surgery was exactly 100 percent. Acquiescence.

Now here is the wonderful part of this tale. Or is it the pathetic or sad part?

Jim Cameron did not have cancer!

How could the Great Mayo Clinic have been wrong? Well, they weren't. They didn't have a diagnosis, remember? They just had a suspicion, an impression, and Jim had refused that ultimate diagnostic test—the exploratory surgery. No, what Jim had was plain, old-fashioned peptic ulcer disease. It had caused so much scarring that it had obstructed the outlet to his stomach, and he was just starving to death. This new diagnosis did not diminish one iota the huge surgical risk we were facing, but it was with joy that I set about fashioning the bypass between his stomach and his small intestine. No, he was much too weak to have a standard ulcer operation. Just the quickie bypass.

In the post-op period, Jim continued to regain his strength, defying the 80 percent/ 60 percent (morbidity/mortality) odds. At some point in the post-operative period, a well-intentioned nurse glued the orange DNR sticker back on his chart. I promptly ripped it off again.

So what to conclude? It's quite the trend these days to criticize doctors for putting patients through hell as they die, for considering death to be the ultimate enemy rather than a natural process. But

---

[7]   A tiny plastic catheter is threaded through a large vein in his neck, directly into the entrance to his heart. Through this could be pumped a concentrated glucose, protein, and vitamin solution that cannot be given any other way.

[8]   That "Do Not Resuscitate" sticker.

every once in a while, a Jim Cameron comes along and reminds me to never give up. The philosophic question is: If I can add five years of good life to one or two patients, does that justify the suffering that the other ninety-eight people (who really are "hopeless") have to endure? All too often, all the public sees and talks about—and all the newspaper editorials concern themselves with—is the 98 percent, the ones who die after prolonged treatment. They conclude that we doctors don't know "when to stop." Certainly, that is sometimes true, but perhaps, as surgeons, we have to keep on fighting because we, too, are human and don't know what the outcome will be.

Jim Cameron (An Unhappy Follow-Up)

Just when you think you have done well and have beaten the odds, some invisible and malevolent genie named Fate unzips and urinates on your head. Jim did extremely well in the post-op period, and I must admit to a certain degree of smugness on my part. On the evening of his seventh post-operative day, he was sitting up in a chair, smiling and talking to his family. He now weighed 138 pounds. He was enjoying eating food again, without regurgitating. The final pathology report had just come back. He had no cancer, just as my eyes and fingers had told me at surgery. Jim had chronic peptic ulcer disease. Jim's large and devoted family, who had daily rejoiced at his progress, had even begun to allow themselves to look to the future with hope and anticipation.

"Could it really be that we've beaten the incredible odds and will have our dad around for several more years?"

At four thirty in the morning of his eighth post-operative day, my phone rang. It was the second-floor nurse on the line, telling me that Mr. Cameron didn't look too good. He'd suddenly and rapidly deteriorated, and his lungs were "crackling." I quickly got dressed and drove the three blocks into the hospital, letting myself in by the side door with the key they'd thoughtfully provided me. And sure enough, he was barely conscious. His pulse was thin and thready. But he was wheezing, not crackling. Crackles imply excess fluid in the lungs, which leads you down the path to heart failure. Wheezing is akin to an asthma attack. What the nurse had been hearing was air whistling through narrowed bronchial tubes, thrown into an intense spasm by some unknown agent. But Jim had never had an asthma attack in his life. Why now?

There were two possibilities: a noxious agent in the bronchi themselves had thrown them into spasm or some type of reflex spasm. For the first possibility, I wondered whether he had vomited and then aspirated the fluid into his lungs. But why now? He'd just spend the last several months repeatedly vomiting without aspirating. As to the second possibility, well, there was always the dread pulmonary embolus, in which a blood clot silently formed in a hospitalized patient's leg. It could suddenly and unexpectedly break loose in the post-operative period, move quickly through his heart, and be trapped in his lung. The lungs, deprived of blood flow, sometimes go into a kind of spasm.

I moved him back to the ICU and started him on a variety of medications to relieve the bronchospasm and support his failing heart. In case it was a dread pulmonary embolus (that might have happened despite his leg stockings and low-dose heparin), I started him on blood thinners. The lungs responded well enough, but he remained in shock. Worse yet, his kidneys had abruptly ceased to produce urine. It's all like a fragile house of cards. Once one thing fails, the rest comes tumbling down. James Cameron died three hours later. We never learned the precise details of the sequence of events because permission for an autopsy was not granted.

So how does one make sense out of this senseless tale? How does a grieving family deal with these series of events, this rollercoaster of despair and hope? We humans are always trying to "make sense" out of our world. In our longing for comprehension, we have even allowed our priests free rein to make up answers and insist they be true. Something the deceased said or did. Maybe he held an incorrect belief? Or perhaps something the deceased's parents did? Oh, it's all there in their holy books. A huge fraction of the world's population shrugs and concludes it is God's will, Allah's will, or maybe just the Fate that Ernest K. Gann wrote about in his book *Fate Is the Hunter*.

There must be similar answers from all religions, from Neanderthal times to the present. These "answers" are a cover for our ignorance.

The James Cameron tale has happened to me over and over again in medicine. Things happen that I can neither predict nor comprehend. Why did a blood clot form despite our medications to prevent it, if indeed it even was a blood clot? Even more unfathomable is the knowledge that only about a tenth of all blood clots that form in our legs after surgery ever break loose, and of those that do, only a fraction are fatal. There seems to be an element of quirky randomness at work. Quantum physics tells us of things that just happen, popping into or out of existence for no reason at all. Is it because I was a nuclear engineer before I was a physician that I can philosophically take refuge in the concept that there may be no meaning at all to this tale, to the events of the last few hours of Jim's life? If there is a degree of meaninglessness and randomness operating at the human level, I only hope that it isn't universal. Please don't take from me the solace that there must have been a meaning in the eighty-eight years of Jim Cameron's life.

Albert Samuels ('Twas a Dark 'n' Stormy Night)

It was December, and so it was more than "dark 'n' stormy." As I stood late at night, at the end of a darkened runway at the local airport there in Minnesota, it was dark 'n' stormy 'n' *cold*—seventy degrees below zero (wind chill factor) as a matter of fact.

This ain't so bad, I first thought, only to be quickly disabused by the forty-some-mile-per-hour wind as it whipped snow in my face. I went around to the lee side of the ambulance and huddled there while I awaited the arrival of an air ambulance.

It had all started some twelve hours before when Albert decided, for reasons best known only to himself, to go for a drive during the season's first blizzard. Albert was eighty years old and had lived alone since his wife passed away. It had snowed some four to six inches during the night, but it was the northwest wind that crippled almost the entire state of Minnesota on this early December day. I-90 was closed from one end of the state to the other. Travel was definitely not advised. At work in the clinic, I marveled that we could not see the high school building right across the highway. I was also secretly dreading car accidents. Sure enough, at 10 a.m., the first one came. Albert had pulled out in front of a delivery van. The van's driver had quickly applied the brakes but slid on the ice, right into the driver's side of the car, neatly caving in both the car and Albert's left chest. He suffered nine broken ribs, one of whose jagged ends had pierced his lung, creating a hemopneumothorax.[9] The ambulance crew found Albert still sitting in the car, strapped in with a seat belt that did him no good. He couldn't remember the accident. Evidently, he'd also had a concussion. They quickly transported him to the hospital.

The ER doctor expertly placed the requisite chest tube, started IVs, and sent Albert to the X-ray department to find out what else was going on inside this old man. The ER physician happened to be a surgical resident from Mayo Clinic in Rochester, moonlighting in our small hospital. He knew perfectly well what was needed. So I wasn't even made aware of the Albert's existence until sometime after 2 p.m., when all the X-rays and studies were done. It turned out that Albert had, in addition to the injuries described above, a badly bruised liver and spleen, and I learned to my discomfort that he'd also had three previous abdominal operations for a ruptured colon. One of those operations had been complicated by an injury to his left kidney, necessitating its removal. All in all, this was a situation in which it was guaranteed that there would be lots of adhesions that would hamper any attempts for rapid surgical control of intra-abdominal hemorrhage, should that prove to be necessary.

It was the chest injury that made me most uncomfortable. I lived in fear that, on some night in some lonely small hospital, I'd be forced to care for a patient with a gunshot wound to the chest. How long had it been since I'd even assisted another surgeon in the chest?

---

9   The pierced lung develops a leak and collapses into a useless pile of tissue in the chest. The internal bleeding then accumulates around the collapsed lung. The remedy is a chest tube to expand the lung and suck out the blood.

Five years? Ten? And now there I was with a man with a serious but not yet dangerous chest injury. Already he'd lost over 500 cc of blood from his chest. We replaced that, but at any moment, either the liver or the spleen time bombs could go off. Then it would be another one of those high-tension dashes to the OR with an unstable patient in a small country hospital. Usually, you win such a race, but with those adhesions...

These are the cases we send to larger hospitals. Why does this man have to pick this crummy day for his crummy accident? The ambulance crew refused to take him to Mayo. The helicopters couldn't fly. I was stuck with my patient. And so I took him up to the ICU and watched him uncomfortably. He remained stable.

A few hours later, at 6 p.m., I repeated his chest X-ray and found that his opposite lung, the good one, was filling with fluid. Had he vomited and aspirated some gastric contents? He needed somebody to look down his trachea with a bronchoscope and suction out whatever was filling that right upper lobe. We didn't even have that instrument in this hospital. And so 7 p.m. found me on the phone to the State Police. I-90 was still closed. I called Mayo Clinic in Rochester. Could they send their helicopter? No, the weather was still too poor. They told me that they would gladly send their fixed wing aircraft but for the fact that the local airport was closed, as were all the other airports in southern Minnesota. Damn!

I was staring despondently out the ICU window, idly watching a snow plow go by, when a nurse asked me how bad the airport was. Bingo! More phone calls—to the airport manager, to the city police, to the town hall. We could get the runway plowed. We could call the FAA in Oklahoma and notify them the airport was open. (Without that call, we'd be asking Mayo to break the law by flying to an officially closed airport; such are the bureaucratic regulations.) By 9:30 p.m., all was in readiness. Our ambulance, loaded with Albert, was parked on the tarmac at the local airport, the Mayo aircraft on the way, and I was standing anxiously by in case our patient suddenly deteriorated and we had to rush back to our own OR.

The last time I'd been in a similar situation was at a small airstrip in Arizona late one night in December 1990. In that case, my patient had suffered a cardiac arrest in the air ambulance just prior to its taking off. I had managed to get his heart started; he survived the flight to Phoenix and subsequently recovered. (Never give up!) I didn't want to lose Albert at this point.

Mayo Air called in. They were ten miles out. My face now had ceased to be painful. It was getting numb. I turned away from the wind, in the lee of the ambulance. Cupping my gloved hands around my parka hood, I asked the airport manager, who was standing next to me, "How do cows and other livestock manage these conditions? Or deer?" I was thinking of briefly going into the line office when I saw a faint glow above the southern horizon that grew through the snowflakes and transformed itself into a pair of landing lights.

We'd done it! We'd effected an air transport when it was too dangerous to drive! A few days later, I was to receive a phone call from the nice doctors at Mayo Clinic. Upon his arrival in Rochester, the Mayo physicians promptly bronchoscoped Jim, just as I hoped they would. They succeeded in removing vomitus and a blood clot from the upper lobe of his right lung, and he improved immediately. No, his bruised spleen that I was watching did not rupture, and at last report, he was doing just fine.

Trouble in Paradise

I spent most of one summer working in Iowa, happily looking forward to a return to our new home in Florida when, out of the blue, I received a call from the Mayo Clinic. They wanted me to come up to Minnesota and help out in one of their newly acquired satellite clinics. Betty and I talked things over and eventually decided that I would indeed respond to their call, while Betty would visit children and grandchildren and then return to Florida alone.

And so it was that a Sunday in late August found me driving the well-used fifth-wheel RV north instead of south at the completion of my Iowa assignment. The RV was set up in a campground about six miles from town. Not three minutes after I pulled in, and the owner had ascertained who I was, came the unexpected question.

"Say, what's going on at the hospital, anyhow?"

"What do you mean?"

"Why, they just had four doctors quit!"

"Really? Well, I dunno. I just fill in. They don't tell me these things."

So there was trouble in paradise. Hmm. This could prove to be an interesting assignment...

Monday morning was filled with the usual introductions—getting to know people, facilities, names, faces. Nobody made mention of any strife in this medical community. When I was given the cellular phone of one Dr. H., it was discreetly explained to me that he'd "left."

Gradually, I learned more, just little bits and pieces. While the four departed physicians all had their individual, personal reasons for leaving, still it was curious that all were specialists.

Could it be, I wondered, *that the genesis of their unhappiness was rooted in good, old-fashioned dollars and cents?*

Medicine is a big business. Federal funds decreasing or at least more tightly controlled. Health Maintenance Organizations. Affiliations formed. Alliances dissolved. And always the bottom line is dollars and cents. As it turned out, some of the specialists here felt that the generalists were doing too much instead of referring patients. "Turf battles," we call these types of squabbles. One of the attractions of *locum tenens* surgery is that I am largely immune from all this. Of course, nobody ever told me any of this directly. I just managed to gradually get a vague sense that this was part of what was going on. Consider the verbal shot, lobbed my way by their departing surgeon in the doorway of the doctors' locker room? He'd asked what my first case was.

"An incarcerated hernia."

"You are lucky," he said. "The last time a GP tried to fix one, he cut into the bowel and then called me to repair the damage."

Then he was off before I could learn more. Was his concern one of patient care or paychecks? Could be either one...[10]

---

[10] Even if the GPs are doing surgery, the consideration is not whether they are "surgeons" but what their complication rate is. If they have been doing good

On Wednesday, a reporter from the local newspaper visited. Her visit was preceded by a frantic call from the Public Relations Office. They'd heard about the interview and were anxious about what I might tell her.

"What is the interview going to be about?" was the question.

"Oh, all about my folding bike, our fifth-wheel RV, and our travels" was my reply.

And then as I walked downtown to mail a package to Betty, perfect strangers called out to me from across the street.

"How's it goin', Doc?"

"Glad you're here!"

"Saw you in the paper this morning."

Then came the phone call from a woodworker who wanted me to "come over to see" his wood turnings. He was justly proud of their quality. That evening, a knock on the camper door, and it was a machinist who'd driven all the way out from town with a basket of vegetables he'd picked from his garden. He said that he thought, what with being on the road so much, I might not have a garden!

Ah, the people of the Midwest—they are the salt of the earth.

Janice Jackson

It's best not to throw stones. Some bounce back and smite the thrower. Case in point: The departing surgeon, the one who had cast his parting shot at me in the doctor's locker room, complaining about a GP's hernia complication—came to me the very next day, proverbial hat in hand.

This was to have been his last day in town, but he had a problem.

"Can you give me a hand in the OR?"

It seemed that one of his patients had a complication and a pretty bad one at that. He'd done a low-anterior resection of the

---

surgery for years, how can one object to their continuing to do same? Ironically enough, one of the first patients I cared for experienced a major complication from none other than the board-certified surgeon who'd just quit.

colon[11] some eight days previously. All seemed to be going well, and indeed, this was the day she was supposed to be going home. Only now she didn't look very good. She had abdominal pain and looked septic. He'd entertained a diagnosis of acute post-operative cholecystitis;[12] however, the test he'd ordered showed that she had "fluid" in her abdomen. He knew then, no doubt with a sinking feeling, just what was going on. And a gastrograffin enema[13] confirmed his dread suspicion of an anastamotic leak.[14] And so he was not only asking me if I'd help him in surgery but also if I'd take care of her in the anticipated prolonged post-operative recovery after he left town.

We took her to surgery, and all was as advertised in the pre-op X-rays. There was stool and pus everywhere. Peritonitis. Bad peritonitis. There were abscesses above and below the liver and between the various loops of small bowel. He cleaned it all out as best he could and did the necessary diverting colostomy.[15] Now it was up to antibiotics and her own stamina. The next day, he left town for good, and she was all mine.

The family was understandably very anxious that they might lose their mom. Their dad had just died of leukemia at a huge hospital in Minneapolis the year before, and now this. Maybe worst of all, their trusted local surgeon had just quit and left town, leaving their mom in the care of this bearded stranger from Iowa. Or was he from Florida? They were nice and polite, but I sensed their unease

---

[11] A portion of the large bowel, which contained a cancerous tumor, was removed. The "low anterior" part of the operation simply means that the tumor was quite close to the rectum, and the rejoining of the bowel can therefore be technically difficult since it was "low" in her pelvis.

[12] Infection of the gallbladder. He chose this diagnosis because of where her pain was.

[13] Radio-opaque contrast material is injected into the rectum so that the resulting X-rays will outline the bowel and hopefully reveal the cause of the infection.

[14] It means there's a leak in the colon where he'd joined the severed ends together. Stool was now flooding through that opening into the abdominal cavity, creating a putrid mess. Indeed, Janice's life was in great danger.

[15] The end of the colon, just above the leak, is brought to the surface of the abdomen so that the stool will empty into the dread ostomy bag rather than continue to drain via the leak into the abdominal cavity.

and spent as much time trying to reassure them as I did in caring for Janice.

Things progressed for a week or so. Initially, she seemed to be getting better, but then I noticed an ominous slow rise in her white count.[16] I switched antibiotics. Still it rose. She began to look septic once again. And still her white count rose inexorably, seeming to mock the antibiotics we were giving her. The colostomy, which had functioned initially, was now quiet. The bag just lay there, empty, resting on her abdomen, which had become deadly silent. All these things were pointing to the worsening of her peritonitis or perhaps the development of more abscesses. She'd need a repeat CT scan and likely another operation, perhaps more than one. None of this was good news to the family.

One evening, shortly after I got "home" to the trusty fifth-wheel, my phone rang. It was the ICU nurse telling me that the family had decided they wanted their mom transferred to the same large hospital in Minneapolis that had cared for their dad. Now. Now? Well, yes. Now. Even if it was 8 p.m. They were frightened about their mom's continued deterioration and didn't understand that transfers in the middle of the night, while they are done all the time in true emergencies, are not really the most efficient way to do things. For one thing, all you usually get on the receiving end is the resident physician on call, not the particular specialist that your patient might need. For another, if your case is not an outright emergency, you can pretty much bet that not much, if anything, will be done for your patient that night. Things tend to stagnate until morning, when all the various specialists can gather around, go over the case, put their heads together, and decide upon a course of action. In the meantime, the trusty resident physician caring for their mom is likely to be down in the ER, stomping out some true emergency. No, for maximum safety and efficiency, daytime transfers are the way to go.

Thus, while I was not in the slightest bit opposed to Janice going to Minneapolis, it was my firm opinion that we should wait

---

[16]   The white blood cells typically fight infections, and when their numbers rise, you can be sure that somewhere there is an infection lurking...

till the morning. Nothing had changed in her condition, and while it was still serious, it was most definitely not an emergency.

And so in the early evening, I drove back to the hospital to talk to the family and to explain to them why I wanted them to wait till morning. They reluctantly agreed. I drove home again, vaguely uneasy. The easy thing would have been to do just as the family requested, even if it wasn't in her best interest. But now if she deteriorated suddenly in the night, I'd be not only kicking myself but facing a downright angry family.

Wouldn't you know it? At 1 a.m., the phone rang again. Janice was bleeding from her colostomy. No, she wasn't in shock, but clearly she was deteriorating at a more rapid rate than I'd expected. I hauled out of bed, heading back to the hospital for the third time in twenty-four hours.

"Dang!" All my premonitions were coming true. And worst of all, the weather was now foggy, and the wind was driving a misty rain onto my windshield. Now I'd have to transfer her by ambulance instead of helicopter.

Well, as it turned out, she was stable enough for an ambulance transfer. After much phone calling, I at last succeeded in awakening and talking to the colorectal specialist in Minneapolis who would be accepting her in transfer. The ICU nurse then asked if she could call Air Care. I replied that she could, thinking that there wasn't much point in calling because no helicopter could fly in the glop that was still beating against the ICU windows. She was welcome to try. I just knew she'd be greeted with the same loud "horse laugh" from the other end of the line that I'd experienced so often in other hospitals elsewhere in the country. Presently, the ICU nurse hung the phone up calmly and told me that they were on their way. Huh? And, sure enough, within a half an hour, they were there, picking up my patient.

I sought out the pilot down in the ER and asked him how on earth he managed to see well enough to pick his way over to our hospital in such poor weather.

He looked at me strangely and said, "See? We couldn't see a thing. We flew in the clouds."

Oh. Just like the airliners. IFR (all weather) helicopters. They don't do this in Iowa.

And how did Mrs. Jackson do? Well, they repeated her CT scan, but no new abscesses were found. And so they merely continued with the same treatment that I'd been giving her. She gradually recovered. And the family felt better, knowing she was in a bigger hospital where "everything" was being done "right."

CHAPTER 15

More Mayo Stories

Since this assignment took place late in the year, it was a trip from sunny (and warm!) Florida to cold, gray, and dreary Minnesota. It was another weekend of coverage for the surgeons working under a Mayo contract at a small Minnesota town. Imagine! Mayo Clinic flew me halfway across the country and paid me good money to provide a long weekend off for their surgeons—one of the perks of their job.

As I was walking out our front door, I stuffed into my briefcase one more thing to read sometime over the weekend—the September issue of *American Journal of Surgery*. Atlanta was gray with drizzle. During the uneventful flight from ATL to MSP, I paged through my journal. An article on splenic injuries caught my eye. How they do it in Houston… The latest algorithm in the grading and management of blunt injuries to the spleen. Back when I trained, there was no algorithm. No decision. It was simple. We simply removed *all* injured spleens. I was taught that a spleen with even the most minor injury would surely hemorrhage in the post-operative period. So we removed them all. Now we try to salvage them, and there has been considerable research on just how badly a spleen can be injured before you have to remove it. I jotted notes on one of my ever-present 3 × 5 cards.

Minneapolis proved to be gray with no drizzle, but there was a damp chill in the air. I still marveled at the wonders of the internet. Three days ago, I made some keystrokes late at night, and upon my arrival, they had my name, address, phone number, and a compact car waiting for me at the Dollar Rental Car desk!

Later that night, after settling into the hospital's house, I pigged out on Chinese food and enjoyed an uninterrupted night's sleep. Not so for young Daniel Avery.

Daniel Avery (An Injured Spleen)

Even though it was ten at night, Daniel was still busy hauling barrels of dirt out of the basement of his old farmhouse in preparation for pouring a new cement floor. He was using a tractor to pull barrels filled with dirt up the outside cellar steps. He attached the rope from his tractor to the barrel with a bail hook, a large iron hook normally used to haul those big bales of hay around. It slipped off and flew through the air with the greatest of ease, striking Daniel on the left side. Fortunately, the back side of the hook struck him; otherwise, he'd have had a large gash. Still, it hurt a lot, so he and his wife came to the ER. The X-rays were negative, and he was sent home, which was why I slept so peacefully.

The next morning, after my rounds were over, as I was contemplating what sorts of activities I might engage in, my beeper went off. It was the ER, and I was informed that they had a patient with a lacerated spleen. How thoughtful of the Great Surgeon in the Sky to arrange a laboratory session for me to go with the classroom work I'd done just yesterday on the Delta jet!

I examined Daniel and his CT scans. From my recent *American Journal of Surgery* article, I now could casually toss off such lines as "Oh, a Grade II injury. Yeah. Sure. We sit on these." But there was all this blood lying around inside Daniel. It was below his liver, above his liver, and more pooled in his pelvis.

Hmm, I wondered, *does this change the Houston algorithm?*

So recent surgical journal article notwithstanding, I needed some advice. Well now, I happened to be working for Mayo Clinic. Indeed, I knew perhaps half of the surgeons on the staff there because if I was working at any of its affiliated hospitals not too distant from the main clinic, I attended their weekly Surgical Grand Rounds lectures. Indeed, Betty and I were once the weekend guests of one of their surgeons. And so I asked the ER nurse how to go about getting Mayo on the phone.

"Just pick up that phone over there, and push the red button."

And so I did, and presently, the voice on the other end said, "St. Mary's ER."

"This is Dr. Roode. I want to talk to the trauma surgeon."

"I'll page him."

Shortly…a voice on the other end… "This is Dr. Mmmmumble."

"Hi. This is Dr. Roode. I'm a surgeon providing weekend coverage for you guys at one of your affiliated hospitals. I need some advice. I'm sorry, I missed your name."

"Dr. Zafmmmumble" (and with a heavy accent to boot).

"As I was saying, I need some advice. Are you the trauma surgeon?"

Dr. Mumble replied, "I am trauma surgeon."

"Good. I have a patient with an injured spleen. Are you the person that I should be talking to?"

Dr. Mumble, "Are you sending patient?"

"No," I explained, "I just need some advice about handling a specific injury. I can take care of this spleen here. But I want to know the latest algorithm for the non-operative management of splenic injuries and whether the amount of blood in the pelvis upgrades the severity. Are you the person I should be talking to?"

Dr. Mumble, "I do spleen surgery."

I then proceeded to go through the entire history of injury, the patient's present hemodynamic status, the CT scans, and the lab results. At the end of all this—a long pause.

Dr. Mumble, "Maybe you should talk to staff surgeon. I don't know."

I exclaimed, "#$%&*$#%$##@! Why didn't you have the courtesy to stop me and tell me you aren't the trauma surgeon?"

Mumble mumble mumble.

On my next try, I was able to get through to Dr. Farley, a staff surgeon I knew personally. He knew exactly why I was calling and just what the answer was. No, the amount of blood present in the abdomen does not change the grading status. Daniel is still a Grade

II. Yes, the blood will be reabsorbed. Mayo's own specific criteria is to operate if the patient needs more than three units of blood transfusion, and he could tell me exactly what criteria they are using in Minneapolis to boot.

And so Daniel now took up residence in our ICU with our OR crew on standby alert. And I was glad I brought my precious headlight with me on this trip, for their OR did not have one.

Update on Daniel

The next morning dawned gray in Minnesota. (I think that gray is the state color of Minnesota.) Everybody has had a great time laughing at my coat and scarf. It was thirty-five degrees outside, and for me, that was COLD!

"Hey, Doc! Isn't this weather *great!* Heck, it's still T-shirt and shorts weather here in Minnesota!"

On my rounds this morning, the hard-bitten ICU nurse told me she found it necessary to "adjust Daniel's attitude" during the evening. I didn't inquire further, but he *did* have a tattoo on the back of his right hand that said, "DIE BITCH." He had taken to cursing the nurses who wanted him to lie down for an examination. Medically, however, he was doing well. His blood count had stabilized at ten grams of hemoglobin. His abdominal pain was decreased, and he was hungry. I planned to move him out of the ICU later in the day. After a few days, it should be safe to send him home, where he should take it easy for several weeks because the injured spleen would probably be quite fragile. My worry was whether he would listen to my advice to take it easy.

And so splenic lacerations now join an ever-growing list of other sacred cows that have been slaughtered over the past two decades. I keep a list of things that I was assured during my residency training were, for sure, for sure—absolute gospel truths. Things like you must remove a spleen with even the slightest injury or that it is life-threatening to allow a patient's blood count to slip below the sacred number of 10 grams. My list has grown to exceed 50 items.

These honest-to-God, gospel-true, do-it-this-way-or-your-patient-dies truths have been proven to be simply false. The treatment of breast cancer is radically changed. We now know that it is not a rapidly growing cancer. I remember during my training when a staff surgeon rushed a newly diagnosed breast cancer patient to the OR for an emergency mastectomy on Friday afternoon to avoid the chance that it would spread over the weekend. Peptic ulcers are now known to be an infectious illness caused by bacteria, not stress. The list goes on and on and on.

All this tends to breed a degree of skepticism. How much of what we "know" today will be looked upon with amusement tomorrow?

Tracey Coleman

This twelve-year-old boy suffered from ADHD,[1] what we call the "hyperactive kid." Kids with ADHD can drive anybody to distraction and normally are kept quieted down with medication. But even with medication, they live problem-filled lives. Tracey was no exception. He'd been in several altercations in school, where bigger and meaner kids would beat him up. And they so loved to tease him about his bowel habits that he'd taken to holding his normal elimination till the end of the school day, no mean feat in a kid who normally had up to four bowel movements a day. These were all to be ingredients in my diagnosis. But even with these clues, I was unable to make the correct diagnosis before surgery.

I first learned of Tracey when one of the local family physicians called me at 10 p.m. with introductory remarks of something to the effect that he was admitting a kid with abdominal pain, but he didn't think the patient had appendicitis. After he reviewed the physical findings and laboratory data with me, we both came to the same conclusion: I could see Tracey in the morning. I rolled over and went back to sleep.

The next morning, I remembered to look in on Tracey. I found a deceptively normal appearing twelve-year-old who really didn't look

---

[1]   Attention Deficit Hyperactivity Disorder.

very sick. He'd been kept NPO[2] since the evening before, and his mother was quick to warn me that the Ritalin[3] would soon be wearing off and then the nurses would have their hands full. My fingers quickly told me that he could very well have appendicitis despite the reassuring phone call the evening before. Not only did Tracey hurt in his RLQ,[4] but he also had rebound tenderness,[5] as well as tenderness referred to the right lower abdomen when I pressed on the left, something that the average twelve-year-old knows nothing about. So it appeared that he wasn't trying to "con" me in any sort of attention-gathering mode.

However, the lab work quickly offered its cautionary message. Tracey's white blood cell count was normal.[6] Clearly, this case didn't add up. But other patients and problems were calling, so I left Tracey, sans his Ritalin, to the nurses.

Later, in the afternoon, I re-examined Tracey. He was still as tender as before, right over his appendix. And to make things a bit more deliciously complex, he also confided in me that he was hungry.[7] His mother, an RN, was quick to add her contribution to my mental gymnastics. She informed me that Tracey was acting just like she did when *she* had appendicitis. Yes, she also had a normal white count. She also told me that she had colonic diverticulae[8] albeit on the right side that ultimately necessitated a hemi-colectomy.[9]

---

[2]   This is an old Latin leftover from a prior age. It is an abbreviation for *Non Per Oro* or, in plain English, "Nothing by Mouth." He was being nourished solely by the IVs.

[3]   The drug used to control hyperactive children. It can be given only as a pill, but Tracey was NPO.

[4]   Right Lower Quadrant of his abdomen.

[5]   For this test, the examiner slowly presses upon the abdomen and then suddenly removes his hand. If the abdominal pain worsens, the patient is said to have rebound tenderness, indicative of peritonitis.

[6]   Meaning no infection within the abdomen.

[7]   In twenty-four years of seeing surgical patients, I've only known one to have appendicitis and still be hungry.

[8]   Outpouchings of the lining of the colon through its muscular layers. Normally, these are an acquired (by our diet and lifestyle) condition, and normally, they occur on the left side. There is, however, a hereditary form that afflicts the right side of the colon.

[9]   Removal of half her large intestine.

Well, none of this added up to any particular surgical diagnosis. But he was clearly more tender, and so I decided, despite the negative findings (normal white count, his being hungry, etc.), to take him to the OR. My pre-op diagnosis? Somewhat vague: "Acute Abdomen; rule out atypical appendicitis." My incision? Another gamble. His pain was so well localized, I hoped that I could solve whatever his problem was with a little RLQ, appendectomy-type incision. Sure, a midline would be amenable to wider exploration if it proved to be something bizarre, but the little appendectomy incisions heal so much quicker and easier. The only trouble is, you can't easily extend them if you get into an unexpected situation.

Alas, my gamble didn't pay off. I made the small RLQ incision and found a little bloody fluid in the abdomen. Clearly, something was going on, and clearly, it wasn't his appendix. I felt around. Why had he hurt so badly in the RLQ when nothing was there? Then the tip of my index finger felt the mass above, far above, adjacent to his liver, nowhere near where he was hurting on physical exam. I lifted his abdominal wall with a retractor and, with my headlight, could see his omentum.[10] It was almost black. Had it just sealed a ruptured, hereditary, right-sided diverticulum like his mother had? Was it the result of a fight at school? Or was it the result of an infected gallbladder? Clearly, I needed to find out and just as clearly I was stuck down there in his right lower abdomen with a piddly little incision oriented the wrong way for enlarging.

There are times one has to simply change directions no matter how it makes you look.[11] All I could do was close his incision and make a new one in the midline of his upper abdomen. What did I find? No, his omentum wasn't sealing off a perforated colon, nor was it isolating an infected gallbladder. Nor was it the result of a direct blow. The omentum had for completely mysterious reasons simply

---

[10] The omentum is a large apron of fatty tissue that hangs from the transverse colon and drapes itself over the rest of the abdominal contents. It is frequently referred to as the "policeman of the abdomen" because it can seal perforations and wall off abscesses so they don't spread throughout the abdomen.

[11] Oh, for the days of routine CT scans that nowadays avoid this kind of embarrassment!

twisted upon itself, two full turns, and choked off its blood supply. Thus, it was totally gangrenous, but the twists also prevented any toxins from seeping back into the bloodstream, where they would have raised his white count and killed his appetite. How elegant and simple are the explanations *after the fact*. As to why his omentum twisted, I didn't have a clue.

A Heartbreaking Dual Tragedy

It's such a classic accident. You just can't add to it, and it saddens me to tell it. All you can do is silently sit there and stare blankly at the wall. Answers, reasons, and meanings evaporate. When you read the two sentences of the next paragraph of this little tale, you will know the outcome.

An excited young couple bought a used home. The previous owner left an empty old chest-type freezer in the basement. (See? Now you know.)

Their two kids, age four and two, were playing in the basement. "Let's hide in here!" An hour or so later, they were missed. The parents searched high and low. Finally, the father opened the freezer, and four sightless eyes greeted him. Even now, I cannot even begin to imagine the horror he must have experienced. 911 was called. The ambulance transported two lifeless bodies to the ER, but there was nothing that we could do.

And now some minister was going to have to try to make sense out of this purely senseless horror in order to try to give comfort to anguished parents.

Three hours later, the two little bodies were still in the ER. The grief-stricken parents refused to leave. We didn't press the issue. The children were now in the same examining bay, on side-by-side gurneys. It would be touching if it weren't so tragic. A seemingly endless stream of people, relatives, friends came in, trying to console the parents.

Already the guilt started, for I overheard snippets of conversation. Besides the fact that an unused freezer in their basement was a children's death trap, it seemed that their grandmother had invited them over.

"Please, Mommy, can we spend the day with Grammy?"

"No, not this time."

How she must now wish that she'd assented.

Elijah Mathis (A Medical Puzzlement)

"Some Do and Some Don't"—a whimsical quote gleaned from a UFLGR lecture.[12] Or, as I often put it, "Sometimes You Win, and Sometimes You Don't." That's just about all you can conclude about certain events.

Case in point: This lad of fourteen presented with a five-day history of abdominal pain. The diagnosis confounded the family doctor because the pain never localized and his white count remained normal. Indeed, when I first saw him, while I thought he had appendicitis, I also thought it was atypical both in presentation and in progression. Still, I was sure enough of my diagnosis to recommend surgery. And when I took him to the OR, I did so fully intending to use their newly acquired laparoscope, mostly to confirm my diagnosis. And maybe I could remove his appendix with the scope and send him home the next day. Remember, these were the days when laparoscopy was just starting to be widely used; most appendectomies were still done "open," not laparoscopically.

But after he was put asleep, I could now feel the mass in his RLQ.[13] It was now obvious to me that not only did he have appendicitis, but it had no doubt ruptured, maybe a couple of days previously. The "old-fashioned" open operation was clearly in order. Indeed, it was as advertised despite the normal blood count that mocked me. Not only had his appendix ruptured, but a pelvic abscess had formed.

---

[12] University of Florida, Grand Rounds. A weekly teaching conference of the surgery service that I attend when I am home in Gainesville.

[13] Right Lower Quadrant of his abdomen. The reason this mass could not be felt before was that his abdominal muscles tensed (guarded) with the pain and hid it from my probing fingers.

I both drained the abscess and removed a very distorted, abnormal, structure that formerly was his appendix. We then continued him on combination, third-generation[14] antibiotics, all the while smugly congratulating ourselves in how well we handle our surgical problems in this modern era.

Ah, 1995. You just can't beat it.

Only trouble was, Elijah then developed a small bowel obstruction.[15] This was promptly recognized and appropriately treated. The IV was continued. An NGT[16] was placed. He responded well, and five days later, he was home.

Ah, 1995. You just can't beat it.

Only trouble was, Elijah returned to the ER three days later with another bowel obstruction. Now what to do? Operate to divide the pesky adhesion, or try another course of conservative treatment? You can't live the rest of your life with an obstructed bowel, but on the other hand, avoiding surgery has much to commend it. For example, any surgery would quite likely create even more adhesions to trouble him further in the future. Here is where the art of medicine comes into play. It is for these reasons that I have sprouted my crop of gray hair. Ultimately, after not a little mental agony, I once again treated him conservatively, and once again, he responded, and he returned home.

Ah, 1995. You just can't beat it.

For a while. But the obstruction returned for yet a third time, and now it was obvious that he needed reoperation. And so it was done. And so he recovered.

Two operations, tens of thousands of dollars of hospital charges, a month of recuperation, all for a rather simple illness triggered by either bacteria, a bit of hard stool lodged in the appendix, or some thickened lymphoid tissue that the young seem to possess in abundance. I've concluded, philosophically(?), that these things just happen for no particular reason. We struggle for our diagnoses. We oper-

---

[14] High octane.
[15] This was caused by an adhesion at the site of his ruptured appendix.
[16] Nasogastric tube—this puts his intestines to rest while the obstruction hopefully resolves itself.

ate. We watch for the complications and deal with them the best we can as they arise.

What is unique about this case? Well, nothing really.

But during the evolution of these events, my November 1995 issue of *Contemporary Surgery* came in the mail. In it, there chanced to be a small item on Edward VII, born to Queen Victoria in 1841. He had to wait patiently for over sixty years until his mother died before he could assume the British throne. In June 1902, less than two weeks before his scheduled coronation, he developed abdominal pain that localized to his right lower quadrant. And just like my Elijah, he went on to develop a mass there. The Royal Surgeon (one Dr. Treves) was called in. Treves was the acknowledged appendicitis expert in all of England... He'd done the very first appendectomy in that country in 1888. But this was, after all, before the days of antibiotics. Surgery was quite risky. And so Treves temporized. The future king, however, continued to deteriorate. Ultimately, surgery was forced on Treves. What did he do? A simple I+D[17] to drain away the pus. No appendectomy, nothing heroic. Just a small incision to drain the abscess.

How did Edward VII do? Quite well as a matter of fact. No small bowel obstruction. The king recovered and attended his rescheduled coronation and ultimately died of heart failure some eight years later.

How did Dr. Treves do? Also quite well. His grateful patient rewarded him with a baronetcy. He quit doing surgery and devoted the rest of his life to writing travel books, presumably based on his newfound freedom to travel.

So there you have it. I followed the current "scientific" prescription for Elijah. I did more than mere drainage of the abscess. I pursued and removed the source of his disease, the ruptured appendix, all by today's book. My reward was a complication. Treves, living in a simpler time, did a simpler operation, and his patient promptly recovered. What can one make of all this?

Well, before one leaps to a conclusion based on a sample size of two, before one congratulates Dr. Treves, before one begins to

---

[17]   Incision and Drainage.

long for earlier simpler times, consider the rest of the story. When Treves's own eighteen-year-old daughter contracted appendicitis, he knew exactly what to do—wait till a mass forms so that the resulting abscess could be drained. And while he was thus waiting, his daughter's appendix burst. She developed peritonitis and died.

Sometimes You Win, and Sometimes You Don't...

Mary Bernard (Complexities of Bowel Obstructions)

Sunday morning found me on my way into the hospital to make morning rounds and thinking, *Here it is the fourth of September already. I've been here some ten days now, and there's been no memorable patients. Guess I'll just enter a "none" in this column 'cause I'll be heading home again in two days.*

This gypsy life had so gotten into my blood that after only ten days in a very lovely town, I was already getting "itchy" to hit the road again. Upon my arrival at the hospital, the first words out of the shift supervisor's mouth were "Have you seen the bowel obstruction yet?"[18]

Now that startled me. Was I supposed to have seen one? Did I miss a beep, or had somebody failed to call me?

But scarcely had I managed a mumbled "Er, no," she hurried on. "She is eighty-one and came in last evening—middle of the night, really. She'd had the sudden onset of abdominal pain, and the ER obtained X-ray films and thought she might have a bowel obstruction. She's had a really bad night, though."

"How's that?"

"She has had a lot of pain and needed a lot of morphine."

"Well, am I supposed to see her or not?"

"I guess they haven't called you, but they probably will. I just wanted to warn you."

The above words went into my ears pretty much as reproduced above, but there was a peculiar translation somewhere between my

---

[18]   It's funny how we refer to patients by their diagnosis and not their name.

ears and brain. For what the shift supervisor was saying to me, whether she realized it or not, was *gangrene*! You don't have the sudden onset of excruciating abdominal pain with a simple bowel obstruction. The pain from a bowel obstruction usually starts gradually and then comes and goes in waves.

She probably suspected as much, inasmuch as she was an older, experienced nurse. Such individuals often know, in ways they can't express, what is going on before the doctor does. I'd gladly swap a couple of ICU monitor readings for one comment from a grizzled old nurse. "Doc, I don't like the way George looks…"

Then Sunny, the surgical tech, saw me in the hall. "Are you going to 'do'[19] the bowel obstruction?"

It seemed that everybody but me knew all about this obstruction.

Ten o'clock rolled around, and the beeper finally went off. It was the second floor, and the ward clerk put a local family physician on the line who started to tell me about Mary.

"She is a possible bowel obstruction, and I think you ought to see her. Her abdomen is tender and silent. And I think I feel a mass on the left."

Once again, alarm bells. Patients with a bowel obstruction tend to have very noisy abdomens.

"I'll be right up."

And after I talked to Mary and her sister and examined her and looked at her X-rays, my initial suspicion of gangrene was strengthened. The ER X-rays didn't really look like an obstruction to me as much as a so-called "sentinel loop" of bowel. Little old ladies don't have the sudden onset of excruciating abdominal pain out of the blue without a good reason, and when they do, they usually can't safely be observed for twelve hours. And so I found myself writing the words "mesenteric vascular accident vs closed loop bowel obstruction, probable gangrene" on her chart. Immediate surgery was indicated. Indeed, she should have had surgery last night when she came in, but…

---

[19] Meaning: operate upon.

I presented the options, risks, expected benefits of, pros and cons of surgery to Mary (who, by the way, was then barely conscious) but mostly to her husband and family. I was very careful to tell them that I might find that the situation had progressed to the unhappy point that all I could do would be to open and close her. Did they want me to undertake such surgery here, or would they be more comfortable with a transfer to Mayo Clinic, just an hour down the road by ambulance? I was also very careful to explain to them that I was a *locum* surgeon and would be gone in two days, though by then the regular surgeon would have returned and would assume her care. They talked things over and opted for surgery right here at home. And so I went down to the nursing station and asked the supervisor to assemble the OR crew. While I was waiting for everybody to arrive, I reread the chart and pondered how we found ourselves in this pretty pickle.

First, the ER doctor's diagnosis of "possible bowel obstruction" was only one of several diagnostic possibilities and not even the most likely one at that.

Secondly, I noticed that Mary had been admitted to the hospital without ever having been seen by an attending physician. Evidently, the ER here writes the admission orders to save the attending physicians from the dreary chore of actually having to get out of bed at inconvenient times and come into the hospital.

Thirdly, bowel obstruction at this hospital was apparently considered to be a *medical* diagnosis. More properly, it should be a *surgical* diagnosis. Many hospitals routinely admit such patients to the surgical service. I have seen an awful lot more bowel obstructions than has the average GP. Some you can sit on, and some you can't. The penalty of guessing wrong can be gangrenous bowel at best—a dead patient at worst. Despite having operated on hundreds in the past twenty-three years, I am still not always sure which patient is which. Nobody is. As a matter of fact, many surgeons advocate always operating on all bowel obstructions so that you don't miss the ones with dead bowel. "Never let the sun set on a bowel obstruction" is an old adage often taught to surgical residents. A family practitioner who is greatly knowledgeable in many different things might not be expected to know which bowel obstructions can be observed and for how long.

Yet I found myself not angry with either the ER doctor nor the family physician. If I tried to do their jobs, I'd probably miss far more than they do. Just because I know more about bowel obstructions does not mean that they are incompetent or lazy or bad doctors. Nobody can know it all. It is just a crying shame that when we physicians are wrong, other humans can suffer, sometimes even die.

And perhaps worse, way down deep inside myself, where I scarcely want to admit it, was a little secret thankfulness that they dropped the ball because it enabled me to sleep peacefully through the night! "Hey, it's not my fault that they couldn't diagnose dead bowel." But quickly, and not without some guilt, I suppressed that thought. She should have had surgery last night.

My idle ruminations were interrupted by a page to the OR: "We are ready."

We "opened,"[20] and my first view of the bowel was an immense relief to me. It was pink. I now knew that we would have a live patient at the end of this operation. From the nurse's perspective, however, the view was somewhat different. She'd have been happier to find dead bowel, as it would have made this inconvenient Sunday morning chore worthwhile. As I slowly and carefully explore the length of her small intestine, I sight a distended loop and then normal small bowel. Further reassurance for me, for this told me that there was, indeed, an obstruction. We can fix those. Maybe even an obstruction without a gangrenous segment. By now, my personal tension level was way down. The nurses, however, weren't entirely happy until I pulled the black segment of twisted bowel out of Mary's abdomen and commenced to remove it.

In conclusion, our patient had a simple closed loop bowel obstruction that was solved by a segmental resection. And she lived and went home. She even wrote me a thank-you note. Everything was as advertised. A person gets sick, goes to the hospital, has an operation, gets well, and goes home. That is medicine, American

---

[20]   Meaning commenced the operation.

style. And I'm glad for it. But for the *careless assumption* that everything will *always* turn out okay, sometimes bad things happen despite the good intentions of all.

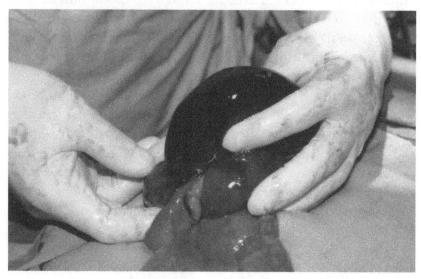

Black Gangrenous Small Bowl

Isaac Hamilton (I Get Superman Envy, Again)

During the week, Isaac was a laborer in a local plastics factory. On weekends, however, he fancied himself being a race car driver. Thus, on this Friday evening, he was tooling around the local race track. Witnesses later told me that he "spun out." Unfortunately, he chose a most inopportune place for this little maneuver—directly in the path of another race car driver. There was a collision, into the side of his car, into the driver's door, into Isaac himself. "T-boned" was how the ambulance drivers described the accident. Both cars were totaled.

My first involvement in this sequence of events was at 10:30 p.m., when the cellular phone rang. It was the ER, telling me she had this race car driver with some "broken ribs."

"Could you come in to tend to them?"

"No problem."

It was quickly evident to me, upon my arrival in the ER, that this was more than a simple case of broken ribs.[21] For one thing, even the initial X-ray showed that the underlying lung was becoming white[22]—and in only half an hour to boot. Usually, it takes much longer for a pulmonary contusion to become evident on X-ray. Evidently, he had sustained a serious injury to his lung. My examination showed the complete absence of breath sounds on the left side of his chest. Ordinarily, that means a pneumothorax.[23] So I rechecked the chest X-ray, but no, no pneumothorax. What was going on, anyhow? Once again, I found myself envying that mythical character Superman, who could simply look inside and see what was going on. The rest of us fumble around. And stew.

If all my instincts, experience, and hunches were right, Isaac would continue to deteriorate, and in a few hours, he'd be on a ventilator. The lab tests showed that already he wasn't getting enough oxygen into his blood. There were, as far as my examination could show, no signs of any other injuries. His abdomen didn't hurt. It was completely soft. In this small hospital, we were not equipped to care for complex pulmonary trauma. It was time to call for Mayo's lifeflight helicopter, Mayo One.

I wonder if the hospital personnel here appreciate how efficient Mayo One is? For one thing, Mayo is quite willing to launch Mayo One often based on a nurse's call alone.[24] For another, after they

---

21   This should *not* be taken to mean that the ER staff had failed to properly assess the extent of his injuries. Emergency Departments are set up to triage their patients. If their evaluation indicates that a specialist is required, further evaluation is then left to said specialist.

22   Ordinarily, a chest X-ray does not reveal much about the lungs themselves. They are full of air. Only if they are to fill with blood or other fluid does their appearance change. On the X-ray, they begin to look whiter and whiter.

23   The lungs are not attached to the chest wall but are merely held there by a slight vacuum. Anything that pierces the lung, such as broken ribs, can cause a leak that destroys the vacuum. The lung simply collapses into a useless pile of tissue in the chest cavity.

24   This was in sharp contrast to a helicopter service, I once encountered in another state. In that case, we literally had to beg them to launch because we

arrive at a hospital, they are the model of quickness and efficiency. In Iowa, it is not unusual for the helicopter to be on the ground up to an hour when they are picking up a patient.[25] And so I am once again an interested, impressed observer when Mayo One touched down.

For starters, the crew bolted out before the rotor blades had even stopped churning.[26] From the time the crew entered the ER till the time the pilot was reigniting his turbines, the total elapsed time was a mere fourteen minutes!

Follow-up: It was with some degree of amazement and consternation that I read a little note taped up on the wall of the ER a few days later. Mayo had called back with a follow-up report on Isaac. Yes, he had broken ribs, and yes, there was a pulmonary contusion. Yes, he was on a ventilator. So far so good.

What had I missed? (There is, after all, a reason this little episode made it into my "memorable patient" files.) For starters, he did have a left-sided pneumothorax, just as my ears were telling me. But our X-ray had said, "No." Did our X-ray lie to us? Or did a small pneumothorax enlarge during the helicopter ride to Mayo? We'll never know. But it must have been obvious to Mayo upon his arrival, for they put in the chest tube that was needed.

And now for the scary part. It was his abdomen, with its perfectly benign exam. If there ever was an abdomen with which I was completely comfortable, this was it. There was no danger of his bleeding to death on the helicopter ride. For whatever reason, they did a CT scan,[27] which was not available to me locally. Guess what

---

hadn't had time to satisfy all the details of the government transfer regulations. That patient, with a leaking abdominal aneurysm, ultimately bled to death due to the forty-five-minute delay even after they agreed to send the helicopter. Governmental regulations do not always guarantee better health care.

[25] They interview the patient. They interview the doctor. They interview the family. They want an IV changed. They want a blood gas repeated. The whole idea of rapid transport is defeated if the helicopter crew dawdles.

[26] Helicopters are powered by gas turbines that must be slowly cooled down if they are to last a reasonable time. This typically takes several minutes, during which time the rotors are turning. I've seen other life flight crews sit inside the helicopter for this entire time, then stroll over to the ER.

[27] Computed Tomography, basically a fancy X-ray test.

Superman would've seen if he was the trauma surgeon on call! A fractured, bleeding spleen, and a severely bruised kidney. Isaac was taken directly to surgery, *then* to the ICU for the ventilator treatment.

And so we live and learn. These events were not as dangerous as they might sound. What I was really doing was lamenting my forced return to "pre-gadget" days (i.e., the days before CT scanners made early and accurate diagnosis easier). Had I been in a location where transfer to Mayo Clinic was not feasible, then I'd have simply carefully observed him. As his spleen continued to bleed, his vital signs would have changed, and so would his physical exam. Then I'd have inserted a small tube into his abdomen, found the blood, and taken him to the OR. But isn't it nice to have all the modern gadgets at hand!

CHAPTER 16

Door County, Wisconsin

Beautiful Door County, Wisconsin, and so far nice and quiet. We were living in our fifth-wheel RV in a parking lot not three blocks from the hospital. Three days previously, when we were setting it up, the local constable stopped by, telling us of a city ordinance prohibiting people living in an RV within city limits.

"Oh. Sorry. We were unaware. Umm. We'll have to look elsewhere. By the way, I am a traveling surgeon covering for Dr. H. for the next two weeks."

Constable, "Have a nice stay here, and do let us know if you need anything."

Friday morning of our third day, at 7 a.m., I step outside and, as usual, wax rhapsodic.

"This has to be the very best assignment we have been on!"

Betty (laughing). "You say that about every assignment." IDGAB!

Just then, my beeper chose to go off. It was the ER telling me about a motor vehicle accident. It seemed that three coast guardsmen were out partying the evening before. All three were drinking, and one was driving when a tree seemed to have inexplicably gotten in their way. The actual accident had happened way out on a lonely country road on Washington Island, off the tip of the Door County peninsula. As best that could be determined, it must have happened around 1:30 a.m. Evidently, none of the three were really seriously hurt. One of them was even able to walk a mile to summon help. They finally were brought to our ER at 4:15 a.m., at which time they were still in stable condition. It was the ER doctor on the phone, who was telling me all this, along with a good deal of normal laboratory and X-ray information. Why was he calling? Well, it seemed that one of them had a rather largish scalp laceration and...

"Would you mind terribly coming in to sew it up, please? I'd feel better if a surgeon were to tackle this one..."

No problem. And I was soon in the ER, inasmuch as my "commute" was a short one. As it turned out, not one but two of the three needed me to sew up largish scalp lacerations. It took me till nearly nine thirty to get the job done, and I admitted one for overnight observation. Yes, they were all basically fine. But, boy, if one had a serious injury, he'd have been dead for sure. You see, the Coast Guard allows the ferry that runs from the mainland out to Washington Island only so many round trips per day. If an emergency arises, phone calls have to be made and permissions obtained for an extra trip. Sort of ironic, eh? The governmental paperwork delayed the evacuation of its very own men. The other irony, of course, was that these three lads spend their days on Search and Rescue boats that rescue stranded vacationers. They board and inspect boats for the proper number of life preservers. And yes, they also make arrests and lecture people on the dangers of drinking and boating...

Sherry Springer (Sherry and the Cow)

This story really starts on a cold winter night in January 1985, when Sherry was delivered by C-section at the local hospital. At the same time, 350 or so miles away, I was just settling into a new surgical practice in Iowa after moving from central Pennsylvania. New town, new challenges, no friends, no reputation. And much bigger Iowa hospitals to provide me with the opportunity to grow beyond what I had been able to achieve in rural central Pennsylvania.

Snap ahead to June 1994, I now find myself secure and happy in an entirely different world, that of *locum tenens* surgery. I have been able to adapt to and succeed in everything from a four-hundred-bed medical center to small rural desert hospitals. Now our days include plenty of free time to share. On this afternoon, for example, Betty and I rode our folding bikes through Potowatomie State Park and discovered a picnic table near an abandoned ski lift. There we sat, looking over a peaceful and beautiful valley.

Unbeknownst to either of the two players in this little drama, events were transpiring that would lead my path and Sherry's to cross. As Betty and I sat at the picnic table, soaking up the beauty, some twelve miles south, in a barn, Sherry was investigating whether their new cow had calved yet. It had, and it became alarmed. As it struggled to rise, Sherry got kicked in the head. She fell to the stall floor, and the cow ultimately stepped on her abdomen. Shortly thereafter, my beeper went off, and we met in the ER. Her exam was remarkable for the hoofprint on the left upper quadrant of her abdomen. Although her vital signs were stable, her abdomen was exquisitely tender and silent. If we didn't have CT scanners, the decision would be easy—operate. But we have all these diagnostic "toys," and they were meant to be used, especially on kids. Perhaps the injury is one that can be observed. Avoid an operation. Trouble is, the tests take time. Can we afford it? That was judgment call number 1. Although the typical radiologist says it only takes ten to fifteen minutes to do a CT scan, I have found that it really takes more like an hour, when you add in the transport time, the interminable IVs, Foleys, etc.

Lessee now… Vital signs are stable. If I set up the OR, and if she deteriorates, I can always rush her over there. Besides, we won't have blood available for another half an hour anyhow. This isn't the big city, you know. So let's go for it. Do the CT scan!

It is a calculated risk. Kids will be stable up till the time they lose 40 percent of their blood volume. Then they just suddenly crash. And there is simply no way to know how far along that path they are at any one time. They will be stable one minute and crash the next. And there you are, sucking wind into your lungs and wishing you'd done something else instead.

Now to make things really dicey, I learn that the local orthopedic surgeon wants to tie up the OR with a wrist fracture. He says it will only take ten minutes. Where have I heard that line before? Judgment call number 2.

Lessee now. He'll take half an hour for sure, but so will the CT scan. If I have them set up the second OR, then I still have an out. So, okay, give him permission to get started with the wrist, but tell him to be damn fast.

He was, but I wondered if he appreciated that I took a chance simply for his convenience so that he could go home while I later operated on Sherry. Why do I always try to be the "nice guy" anyway? Someday I'm going to get burned…

Things proceed along at their usual frustrating snail's pace. Why do X-rays always seem to take so damned long? Sherry still has stable vital signs, just a little tachycardia, but that is all kids will show as they are bleeding to death. I wonder how far along she is toward the dread 40 percent cliff edge? No way to tell.

"What is the delay?" I ask of two X-ray techs after they have snapped the chest X-ray and are just sitting there.

"Waiting for Dr. W. to check the chest X-ray."

Does anybody share my anxiety, my sense of urgency with this little one? I urge them on…

"Forget Dr. W. Get her into the CT scanner!"

Well, maybe those weren't exactly my words, but then I tend to get excitable around broken kids.

Finally, the CT images came up on the screen, one at a time.

"Hmm. Blood in the left upper quadrant, so it's undoubtedly the spleen. Can't see any other injuries, but this definitely isn't something that I feel comfortable observing. Time to go to the OR."

It is now nearly 8 p.m. It has been something like three hours since the cow stepped on Sherry. Three hours! What would that sound like in court if Sherry doesn't make it? "What took you so long, Doc?" But it all adds up little by little.

Sherry's mother had to wash off the cow manure so she'd be presentable in the ER. Then she drove her to the hospital. The ambulance crew then had to "rescue" her in the parking lot, taking the time to strap her onto a board and apply an unnecessary cervical collar. Then the initial nurses' evaluation, the ER doctor's exam, the call to me, my exam, the decisions about CT scan, the IVs, the drawing of blood for lab tests, the trip to the X-ray department, the trip to the

CT scanner, the trip to the OR. Nobody was wasting time, but look at it! Three hours have dribbled by!

It never ceases to amaze me how long things take. I know this kid is bleeding inside, and I just want to put a stop to it before she falls over the 40 percent cliff, and I have to sit and fidget while all this other stuff takes place. And it is always the same—big hospital or little.

Well, it was her spleen. When I opened Sherry's abdomen, some blood and a piece of her spleen floated out. We try to salvage kids' spleens so they don't get serious infections later in life. But you can't save all spleens, just the ones cracked near the edge. And I had never succeeded in saving even one. This one didn't look too promising, with a huge crack going right into its center. But it isn't bleeding too badly.

I think to myself, *So why not give it a try?*

I set about mobilizing the spleen, moving it up to the midline so that I can work on it. All went well—too well.

God, I'm getting good at this, I think to myself as the spleen moved quickly up to the midline. And still it isn't bleeding much. Why haven't they been this easy in the past? Pretty soon, I have the spleen in my hands, and you know what? *I don't recall putting any ties on the splenic artery*, I think to myself.

Slowly it dawns on me what has happened, and (as usual) all things are crystal clear—after the fact. Sherry's spleen had been avulsed by the cow, literally ripped off its stump, and was hanging there only by a few shreds of peritoneum. That was why I was so "good" at mobilizing it. And that is also why it didn't bleed very much. Any self-respecting nine-year-old child's artery knows exactly what to do when it is torn in half. Even big 1/8-inch splenic arteries know what to do—go into spasm. I look back into Sherry's splenic bed, and sure enough, there it is, like a pulsating earthworm. I slip a clip over it and crush it. Probably not necessary, but I want to be sure. The artery has done a bang-up job of sealing itself. I just don't want it to get tired later on in the night and start bleeding in the post-op period.

"How much have we lost?" I ask the circulating nurse.

She checks the suction bottles. "280 cc." So add in another 20 cc to make it a nice round figure, then multiply by 100 and divide the product of 23 times 80 into that. And what do you get? The nurse anesthetist had a small calculator. "Sixteen," she announces.

Sixteen! Sherry had lost only sixteen percent of her blood volume.

"Well, shit!" is all I can say.

We could have screwed around all night in the CT scanner, and Sherry wouldn't have bled to death. No wonder her vital signs remained stable. She'd stopped bleeding all on her own, thank you. Of course she still needed the surgery to remove the dead spleen. In the 1800s, she'd have died of sepsis five or six days after the injury, and we'd have read her name on a grave marker and never know the elegant details of her death...

"What are all those numbers, Doc?" asks the nurse anesthetist.

"Nuttin'. I was just realizing how unimportant we sometimes are. Mother Nature was way ahead of us on this one." (Later, I explained the calculations to them.)

Other, smarter, surgeons could have told you in advance that given the choice between a cracked spleen and one literally ripped out of its socket, with the splenic artery torn in half, the latter injury was the lesser. Of course, it is... The artery will go into spasm. But I had to have a cow and a nine-year-old girl remind me how remarkable the human body is.

17

Surgical Catechisms

In 1996, I provided coverage to two hospitals in northern Minnesota. Things went well for five assignments spread over many months. Then I was asked to participate in a frankly unsafe medical practice, one quite against the standards set by a national organization. I refused, and as a result, I was "let go." Well, let's be blunt: I was fired. One must do what one considers moral. I left with a clear conscience. Did I suffer for taking a stand on principle? Hardly! The phone continued to ring, and I had the usual choice of deciding on my next assignment.

Here then are several stories of memorable patients from these two Minnesota towns, which shall remain unnamed.

Raymond Harding (Trauma Code!)

This assignment involved a clinic associated with a Catholic hospital—a *very* Catholic hospital. Every morning, at 8:00 a.m. sharp, somebody would read a prayer over the loudspeaker system. Shortly after my arrival, I was given a packet of information regarding what types of surgery were allowable. They were deathly afraid of the ecclesiastical consequences of doing any operation that might render a person infertile. And so they had a printed policy that announced that tubal ligations were to be decided in an *ethical* manner. And quite naturally, they had an Ethics Committee to help a physician make Ethical Decisions in these ethical matters. And of course, none of the forbidden were permitted to be done in their hospital. But here was the curious thing: in a facility administratively separated from but still physically a part of the hospital, tubal ligations and vasectomies were done left and right, on demand. The church hierarchy found it convenient to look the other way and was thus able to technically satisfy its obedience to whatever divine ordinance its members perceived to exist—and make money in the process. I found it amusing that they seemed to be worshiping a god that could be fooled so easily.

There were other amusing euphemisms lurking around.

One day, I heard the following over the PA system: "There is green grass growing in the basement."

Nice. Wonder what that means, I thought.

When I asked a passing nurse what was going on, she replied, "Fire in the basement."

"Why do they call a fire 'green grass'?" I asked.

She shrugged and said, "Well, we mustn't alarm anybody, must we?"

And so, to get into the spirit of these things, I will tell Raymond's story, sad though it is, in a suitably religious narrative mode.

Shortly before ten o'clock on a morning about a week after my arrival, the Devil Himself appeared to Raymond and said, "*Pssst!* Why don't you get into your grandfather's vintage '76 Corvette and take it for a spin? Never mind that you don't have your driver's license yet. Sure, you can do it. Anybody can drive one of those things!" It just *had* to be the Devil, didn't it? No sixteen-year-old boy would dream of going on a joy ride alone in his grandfather's vintage 'vette would he? Nah. It had to be the Devil.

Well, by and by, through circumstances that we'll never know, Raymond rolled the Corvette over while traveling at a high rate of speed. Since he wasn't wearing the seat belt (for all I know, perhaps cars didn't come with seat belts back then), he was ejected and flew some fifty feet through the air. When he landed, the impact converted the left side of his brain into mush and broke his neck. A passerby called 911, and shortly after that, my beeper went off.

"Trauma coming in... Trauma code in the ER!"

My first view of Raymond was at 10:40 a.m. and was not particularly reassuring. He was not only unconscious but was breathing deeply and rapidly.[1] Worse than that, both his arms were extending themselves in that peculiar configuration known as decerebrate posturing.[2] When I pried his eyelids open, I found his eyes to be staring steadily to the left and one pupil was larger than the other, the so-called "blown pupil."[3] Clearly, we needed to stabilize him and then get him to a major medical center pronto for the services of a neurosurgeon. IVs were started. Lab tests were drawn. An X-ray of his chest showed it was clear, but the X-ray of his neck revealed it was fractured and appeared unstable. The cervical collar was therefore left in place. Sandbags were placed and secured on each side of his head. A call was made to the nearest major medical center, and their helicopter was launched.

In effecting a transfer of the critically injured, we referring physicians have to be certain that our patient is stable enough to endure the transfer. Have a patient bleed to death during the transfer and all Hell breaks loose. (See? I'm still in the religious narrative mode.) The accursed lawyers will proclaim that their client would have survived and lived a long and productive life if we hadn't so hastily put him in the ambulance or helicopter. I had to *know* that Raymond wasn't bleeding internally. If he was, and at a sufficiently brisk rate, then I'd be forced to take him to the OR—broken neck, mush brain, and all. And so I did a DPL[4] to detect any internal organ injuries. Yes, it is old-fashioned but quick and easy to do. Thankfully, my own silent prayers were answered. The tap was negative. Raymond would no doubt survive the ride to the tertiary medical care facility.

---

[1]   A sign of irritation to his brain stem, from blood in his spinal canal.

[2]   The arms extend parallel to the body and twist so the palms face outward. It is a grave sign that the brain has become unwired at a very basic and deep level.

[3]   It usually means bleeding within or adjacent to the brain, and later, the CT scan obtained in the medical center to which we transferred Raymond confirmed this physical sign.

[4]   Diagnostic Peritoneal Lavage. In this test, a small plastic catheter is inserted and sterile saline used to rinse out the abdominal cavity to test for the presence of blood.

It was eleven thirty when the helicopter touched down on the grass outside the hospital. I was outside as it landed and hit the button on my stopwatch. Precisely eleven minutes later, Raymond was being loaded onto their gurney, and sixteen minutes after touching down, the pilot was hitting the igniters of his turbines. Now *that* is the way trauma is supposed to be handled. What a contrast with the nameless town in Virginia where we had a patient bleed to death because of their pokey helicopter service!

Yes, Raymond survived the transfer, but heaven only knows how he did at the center since we never received any further reports on his condition.

Haley Jones (The "Straight and Narrow")

Herein lies yet another episode in my never-ending guessing game, otherwise known as physical diagnosis. The public, the government, and the accursed lawyers all think physical diagnosis is a simple matter. Just ask a standard set of questions, request a standard set of lab tests, and presto! You have your diagnosis. Pure and simple. Why, you could even have a computer do it. Once you have a diagnosis, then treatment immediately and logically follows. Even that could be handled with a suitable computer algorithm. Only trouble is, it's not quite that easy, hence my gray hairs.

It was midmorning when I received a phone call from a local family practitioner (Dr. J) of the neighboring clinic that was in competition to the one that had hired me. The details of past politics in this small town in west-central Minnesota concerned me not a whit. Thankfully, I get paid to provide medical care irrespective of clinic allegiances or a patient's ability to pay. Dr. J's regular surgeon was out of town. Indeed, I was the only surgeon in town.

"Are you covering for Dr. A?" was her question. Her unspoken question, of course, was "Would you, despite the fact that you are working for a different clinic, would you…be willing to see one of my patients? Please?"

"Beats me" was my response. "Nobody told me if I was supposed to be covering for your clinic. But what's the problem? I'm available."

So she proceeded to describe a fourteen-year-old girl with abdominal pain, coupled with a slightly elevated blood cell count, nausea, and vomiting. She wasn't too sure what was going on. It could be early appendicitis, or it could just be a flu bug. Ordinarily, she'd have her own surgeon get involved for a second opinion, but since he was out of town, she decided to settle for a telephone consult to review the case with me. And she was profusely thankful that I'd even be willing to see her patient. My allegiance is to patients, not some clinic. After she described all the details of her physical exam, I tended to agree with her. It could be early appendicitis, but it was too early to diagnose with assurance. The patient could safely go home and return if the symptoms worsened; in any case, she must return to their clinic in the morning for a repeat blood test.

Early that evening, my beeper went off. It was the same family physician who had called me earlier. She was seeing Haley back in her office. The pain was much worse. Haley now had rebound tenderness.[5] The WBC was higher but not a whole lot. She had decided to admit Haley to the hospital and would appreciate it if I'd come in and see the patient yet this evening. She thought it probably was appendicitis. I readily agreed to see her patient in the hospital. After supper I told Betty not to wait up for me. I'd probably be doing an appendectomy and wouldn't be home till after 11 p.m.

And so 8 p.m. found me examining Haley. I can't simply take another physician's word for a diagnosis if I am going to be doing the surgery and taking responsibility for the outcome, including any

---

[5] A physical examination technique that is widely taught in medical schools. In this test, the examining physician applies pressure to the patient's abdomen, then suddenly releases it. If the patient then experiences increased pain, it is called rebound tenderness. It used to be thought that this was indicative of peritonitis. However, recent studies have shown that rebound tenderness is present in only about 50 percent of patients with proven peritonitis, and since it is definitely uncomfortable to the patient, its routine use has been questioned.

complications along the way. To do this, I try to wipe all previous information from my mind, hopefully to give me a fresh approach to the problem at hand. But is this right? An experienced family physician's opinion doesn't count for nothing. So even though I start from the beginning with each new patient, I must admit that my mind is often colored. It certainly was in this case. I had it in the back of my mind that we'll surely be doing an appendectomy in a half an hour or so.

"When did your pain start?" is one of my standard questions, which often has to be further clarified by "When was the last time you felt *perfectly* well?"

But even that needs to be validated with additional questions. I'll go back to before the pain started and ask how they slept or how they ate or how their appetite was or how their bowels moved. I am looking for clues as to when and how the illness really started and how it progressed. It is an incredibly complex and deliciously difficult problem to ferret out the details of an illness. The fact that some patients are forgetful while others will deliberately lie[6] to you doesn't make things any easier. It has taken me *years* to get good at this game, and still it seems that all, too often, patients have me floundering around.

Haley told me the pain started sometime between 9:30 and 9:45 p.m. the night before. Now this is a tad unusual, and it caught my attention. Most people with appendicitis are not this specific as to just when the pain started. It piqued my curiosity. I decided to pursue that lead. Could a computer algorithm be fashioned to pick up on information that is *too* accurate?

"What were you doing when the pain started?"

"Taking a shower."

"And it came on suddenly?"

---

[6] Now who would conceivably lie to their physician with surgery hanging in the balance? Easy. A pregnant, unmarried teenager whose strict mother is sitting with her in the room—that's who! Sometimes we have to throw the mother out of the room to get accurate information. Once, I even had such a patient lie to me as she lost consciousness while bleeding to death from a ruptured ectopic pregnancy.

"Yes. It threw me down!"

"Down?"

"Yes, it threw me down in the bathtub."

Well, that is *not* how appendicitis starts, and as my interview continued with Haley, I quietly shelved any plans to do emergency surgery that night. Those four little words—"It threw me down"—kept nagging at me during my interview and examination of this girl. Yes, she certainly had a *very* tender abdomen, right over her appendix, so it could well be appendicitis. But in the end, I thought it was simply those four fateful words that impelled me to change my plans for surgery to a plan of watching and waiting. Happily, as the days progressed, Haley slowly got better. She was discharged two days later, still with some pain, but it certainly wasn't appendicitis. I had, after all, made the right choice.

Well then, what was causing her pain? What was her diagnosis? As time permitted over the two days before she was discharged, I returned to examine Haley's abdomen repeatedly. I asked her more questions.

One afternoon, I asked her, "Are you sure nobody bumped or hit you on the abdomen?"

"No." Then, "Oh, wait… Jeff *did* punch me there two days ago."

So there it was! Her story had changed. You'd think that there would be only one story for any given illness, but I tell you, it's not that unusual for two physicians to obtain two markedly different histories from the same patient. It is partly in how we relate to our patients, partly the questions that we ask, and partly the reliability of the patient's memory. In this case, after thirty-six hours, we finally stumbled upon the explanation of Haley's pain, a bruised rectus abdominis muscle that suddenly goes into a cramp—an abdominal charley horse as it were.

Well, what's so special about this tale? I chose not to operate, mostly because of a teenager's choice of overly dramatic words ("It threw me down"), and as it turned out, she didn't have appendicitis. I was lucky; not every physician would have reached the same decision. There were plenty of factors that did point to appendicitis.

Suppose she hadn't used those four fateful words? I wonder if we could turn the clock back and "play it again, Sam," a hundred times with different surgeons. Perhaps she'd experience an "unnecessary" appendectomy on thirty or forty of those occasions? Remember, at the time, I rejected surgery as an option we still had no diagnosis. Yes, she could easily have been explored that evening.

Now suppose, just suppose, that I had operated. But then let's further suppose that she'd had a surgical complication. The family could have been upset or even angry that the daughter had a complication as a result of an "unnecessary operation," especially by some kind of vagabond surgeon from Florida. It would have been obvious to all concerned, after the fact, that she didn't need the operation.

It is even possible that I could have been the subject of a lawsuit, in which the attorney could have stated his case (using the after-the-fact information) as follows: "Ladies and gentlemen of the jury! Here, we have a case in which a young girl is playfully punched in the abdomen by her boyfriend, then developed a painful cramp in the underlying muscle. Despite 'normal' laboratory tests, this traveling surgeon from Florida carelessly and negligently chose to rush in and operate rather than prudently observe his patient. As a result of this unnecessary operation, my client has suffered such and such a complication, and her life is *blah, blah, blah...*"

Does the above sound far-fetched? Am I becoming paranoid? Perhaps, but precisely just such a scenario did happen to me two years previously, one night in Arkansas.

A thirty-eight-year-old man presented to his family physician with a four-day history of severe abdominal pain. He had a markedly elevated blood count. The family physician assured me that the electrocardiogram was normal (we now know it wasn't). Moreover, a lab test that I'd requested to test for heart attack was not reported to me as being abnormal. And so, fearing to neglect some abdominal catastrophe, I took him to surgery and didn't find a thing. Then additional tests showed he was, after all, having a heart attack.

The internist that I then consulted to help care for this patient managed to obtain a different history than either I or the family physician had obtained. This was surprising to neither of us, but the man's attorney assumed I'd neglected to ask the proper questions. He then used all the after-the-fact information as well as the changed history to make it appear that we were just being careless. He alleged that, as a result of my "obviously unnecessary operation," his poor client had been made into a cardiac cripple and will be on disability for the rest of his life, unable to hold down a respectable job or enjoy a vigorous life. I neither gave this man his bad heart nor forced him to smoke (which he did) nor to eat greasy hamburgers (which he did). Nor did my surgery make his preexisting heart attack any worse; but upon the advice of my malpractice insurance company, the case was quietly settled out of court for a nominal amount. It was done as a matter of expediency, the cheapest way to settle the matter.

And while we are playing these mind games, suppose that my "hunch" about Haley was in error, that she really did have appendicitis. Further suppose that I opted to observe it. What if I found a ruptured appendix the next day? Once again, the accursed lawyer would have smugly known the answer: "This traveling surgeon from Florida didn't want to trouble himself to work at night when my client obviously had an appendix that was about to *burst!*"

In this crazy business, if you get a perfect result, it is just taken for granted by the public. That's the way it's supposed to be, isn't it? We surgeons have to bat 1,000 all the time. And after a while, it gets mighty tiresome to be held to a higher standard than are the accursed lawyers. And when it comes time to retire, I'll not be sad...

A pox on all lawyers!

Programming a Waitress

In summer weather, we generally lived in our fifth-wheel RV when on assignment. Winter in Minnesota is an entirely different matter. Motel living is much more appropriate. The ice on a nearby lake becomes so thick that tents, huts, and shacks are dragged out on its surface so the locals can ice-fish in comfort. Come springtime, bets are made as to when the ice will melt sufficiently plunge any remaining debris to the lake bottom.

In such times, my life was divided between a sterile motel room and the hospital. One of my idle amusements was programming a waitress in a restaurant I patronized. Naturally, I ate alone, often with a book propped up in front of me. When I was done, I preferred to get up, pay the bill, and leave. Sometimes this meant trying to catch the waitress's eye to ask for the bill. If she were to lay it on the table halfway through my meal, it would expedite my exit. And so one day, I set about seeing if I could silently program this behavior into one of the waitresses. On a day that I had to hunt her down to get the bill, she received no tip. If, on the other hand, the waitress had quietly placed the bill on my table midway through the meal, she received a handsome tip. Within just a few days, the bill always showed up halfway through the meal. Amazing. Evolution in action!

Owen Jones (Constipation Can Kill You)

I was called to see this sixty-one-year-old resort owner who was a mere eleven days out from coronary artery bypass grafting done at the nearest large medical center. In this operation, a vein is taken from the patient's leg and used to bypass an obstructed coronary artery and thereby, hopefully, avoid a more serious problem, as in a heart attack.

All was going well in the postoperative period until Owen became constipated. Ordinarily, we tend to think of constipation as more of an inconvenience, an annoyance, not a life-threatening health condition.[7] Old-timers know better, as do their surgeons.

It was on a Saturday morning that the family doctor manning the ER in the nearby town I was also covering called me. He had to mention only one single number to me, sort of an insider's code word, for me to realize that I'd promptly be driving the twenty miles or so to see this patient. The number he mentioned was sixteen,

---

[7]   The particular form of constipation I'm describing here is known as Ogilvie's Syndrome. It is a peculiar condition affecting older people after major surgery or trauma and is best described as a form of colonic paralysis. There is no actual mechanical bowel obstruction.

though anything over twelve would have done the trick. Dr. H. was referring to a measurement he'd made on Owen's X-ray, with an ordinary ruler. And that measurement was the diameter of his cecum in centimeters. The cecum, residing at the beginning of a person's colon, is that portion of the large bowel to which the appendix is attached. It is also the thinnest part of our colon, and if the colon is over distended to the point of danger of bursting, (one of the dangers of constipation), the cecum is where the action is going to be, for that is where the colon will burst.

I was impressed with the ER doctor because I'd seen any number of specialists (read: radiologists) describe in detail the gas pattern they saw on a set of X-rays and inexplicably fail to reach for their handy dandy ruler to make that one measurement that would tell us clinicians whether we had to do anything about the gas pattern. Here, we happily had a family practitioner who had correctly assessed the danger to Owen and called me, asking if I could "decompress" his colon.

Owen was as advertised—distended and uncomfortable, with a cecum that did indeed measure sixteen centimeters on his X-ray. Last year, I had heard a surgeon at Mayo Clinic's surgical grand rounds weekly conference characterize the number sixteen as being "truly frightening." Thus, there was no time to lose. I noted with some concern that our patient had lost hepatic dullness to percussion.[8] And so I had them obtain an upright chest X-ray, looking for free air under the diaphragm.[9] Two tiny bubbles.

---

[8]   Ever have a physician go "thumping" around your body with one middle finger on another? It's called percussion, and it is amazing what you can learn. For example, your abdomen normally sounds "hollow," but if your physician were to "thump" over your liver, he expects the sound to be dull and flat, as befits a solid organ. Owen, however, sounded hollow even over his liver. Could the cecum already have ruptured? You see, when a gas-filled organ within the abdomen ruptures, the gas is free to wander willy-nilly around the abdominal cavity. It goes to the high point and collects between the liver and the abdominal wall.

[9]   This is a fancy way to double-check on your fingers. If there is free air (meaning the cecum has "blown"), the colon gas will rise and form a layer under the diaphragm, where it is easily seen on a chest X-ray.

Hmm, I wondered. *Could that be free air or not?*

In free-air situations, we are used to seeing an entire layer on the X-ray. But the longest journey starts with the first few steps and, presumably, a layer of free air starts with just a bubble or two…

Well, I thought. *We can at least try to save Owen from the need for major surgery.*

A colonoscope[10] was readied. We gently introduced it into his rectum, advanced it through the colon, and suctioned out a great deal of the gas that was causing his distention. He felt better. I didn't. Those two little bubbles, less than a quarter of an inch in diameter, on his X-ray… And so I arranged for a second set of X-rays to be done in three hours.

I spent the intervening time doing chores around the trusty fifth-wheel: cleaning, filling the water tanks, and cooking. I looked at my watch. Quarter to four. Time for me to drive back to recheck Owen. A glance at his chest X-ray left no doubt where he'd be spending his evening—in the large medical center where he'd just had his coronary artery bypass surgery done. There was now, clearly evident, a definite layer of free air under his diaphragm. My colonoscopic decompression had failed to help him. He had probably ruptured even before I'd seen him earlier in the day. Neither those two tiny bubbles, nor my fingers, were lying to me this day.

Owen went to the medical center not because we couldn't have dealt with the surgical problem locally but because that was where he'd just had his heart surgery, and that is where he wanted to go. He felt better being in "The Mecca." Years ago, I'd probably have felt bad, but I have long since grown beyond the need to prove anything, either to myself or anybody else. There was, after all, much to be said for a quiet evening at home. And it was nice to hear from Owen's surgeon a few days later. He'd tolerated surgery well. The perforation was, as expected, in the cecum. And he did well after his emergency surgery.

---

10 This device, looking like some relic of medieval torture chambers, is a black rubber tube about a yard long. But it is jam-packed full of fiber optics, irrigation, and suction channels, as well as wires to enable us to move the end, to guide us through the human colon, and to allow us actually see, without surgery, what is going on in there.

Fred and Lillian (Orthodoxy versus Heresy)

This is the story of two hospitalized patients. Both had the same condition, perforated sigmoid diverticulitis,[11] and both needed surgery, although two separate surgeons were involved. Their stories differ in significant ways. Remembering that I was now working in a *very* Catholic hospital, I shall once again revert to the religious mode in telling this tale.

In the Sunday school days of our medical education, we are introduced to catechisms, which must be memorized exactly. The "surgical catechism" tells us how to treat various conditions. These catechisms must be repeated verbatim to various examiners, else we are sure to be thrown into "outer darkness where there is weeping and gnashing of teeth" (read: you failed your board exam; now go find another career). But then, at a later date, we learn that heretics have arisen. They usually inhabit secure havens otherwise known as universities. Dare I say it out loud? Some of our faithfully memorized catechisms are thought to be—ah, er, how can I say it—false! Let me illustrate this with these two patients.

Fred happened to come under the wings of Dr. A (of the "other" clinic), who immediately obtained a state-of-the-art CT scan,[12] and based on the results of this test, Fred was taken to surgery where the diagnosis of his diseased, perforated sigmoid colon was confirmed.

Now for some background material. The catechism that we all memorized in training mandates that the only way to safely deal with a diseased and perforated colon is to remove that portion of colon, clean up as much of the mess as you can, and temporarily divert

---

[11]   In this condition, an opening forms, more or less spontaneously, in the patient's left colon. The explanation is the prior formation of weak points in the colon. Known as diverticuli, they are thin outpouchings of the lining membrane of the colon, between bundles of the muscular wall. Their formation is attributed to a combination of our diet lacking in bulk-forming fiber, and, possibly, the high-tension state our society induces in certain of its members.

[12]   Computed Tomography, basically a fancy X-ray test.

what is euphemistically known as the "fecal stream"[13] by means of the dread colostomy. But various heretics have successfully rejoined the severed ends of the colon after the diseased portion has been removed. They gleefully report in the surgical literature that the catechism is wrong.[14] One can only trust in their honesty, hoping that they haven't found one excuse or another for failing to mention those patients whose colons failed to heal. And yes, over the years, I have violated the sacred catechism on occasion. Once, I recall, was with a profoundly retarded inmate of a mental institution, and pardon me for being judgmental, but I glibly concluded, "What do I have to lose here?" A second was a Roman Catholic priest, where I concluded, "How can I possibly go wrong with a holy man?" Both healed uneventfully, and the dread colostomy was avoided.

As for Lillian, she came in to see me also with probable diverticulitis. The infection seemed mild, and there was no evidence of perforation. Complicating the situation, however, was the fact that she was on steroids, which not only suppress the inflammatory response but also make it more difficult to diagnose the perforation if and when it develops. Being reassured by her benign examination, yours truly advised the attending physician to start antibiotics. Not until four days had passed, when she developed a small bowel obstruction, did I wake up to the awful fact that there was more to Lillian than I had suspected. I found myself belatedly obtaining the requisite CT scan. It showed that Lillian's diverticulitis had indeed perforated, with formation of at least one but more likely two abscesses. Dang! How *dumb* I sometimes feel, when, after the fact, the true nature of things become clear to me. Surgery was obviously in order.

Dr. A, who had operated on his patient Fred for the same condition two days previously, was standing nearby on the second floor. He noticed that the activity and asked, "Whatcha got, Pete?" There can be a brotherhood to surgeons, even though they may be working

---

[13]   Isn't this an amazing euphemism? Is it supposed to give one a vision of a sparkling mountain brook when in fact what we are dealing with is a smelly, semi-solid, brown substance.

[14]   One even titled his report in an otherwise staid medical journal "A Stake Through the Heart of Colostomies."

for different clinics. And so I told him about Lillian and the revelations of her CT scan. He remarked that he'd just "done" a patient with identical conditions. And so I inquired as to how his patient had presented, how he'd made the diagnosis, what he found at surgery, etc. I am always looking for ways to improve, to avoid being caught with my proverbial pants down. Dr. A then regaled me with his immediate CT scan and what he'd found. He remarked, as polite advice to me no doubt, that he *always* gets an *immediate* CT scan on cases of suspected diverticulitis. Good advice. (When I'd inquired as to what operation he'd done, I was really asking him which camp he pledged allegiance to—orthodoxy or heresy.) He made it clear that he'd done as he usually did—removed the diseased portion of the colon and immediately rejoined the severed ends.

So, I thought, *he is heretic, and his patients avoid the dread colostomy. Good for him. Maybe I shall be as lucky with* my *patient.*

Back to Lillian. Upon opening her abdomen, I found that, having perforated a number of days before (while I was counseling antibiotics alone), the only thing I felt I could safely accomplish was the dread orthodox colostomy. Such was the inflammation obscuring her anatomy that I did not even feel it was safe to remove the inflamed, diseased portion of her colon. That would have to wait till later. The next day Dr. A asked me what I'd found and what I'd done.

When I told him, he clucked, "Well, she is headed for more trouble someday down the road—that's for sure." Possibly, but I certainly hoped not.

Five days went by. I happened to be in the X-ray department, checking on X-rays of an unrelated patient. The technician pulled freshly developed films from the processor and flipped them up onto the view box. The films had nothing to do with those I was studying; she was merely checking the quality of these newly developed films. I, however, could not help glancing at them, more with the view of diagnosis, not film quality.

Hmm. Free air. Somebody is in trouble. I looked at the name. It was none other than Dr. A's patient Fred!

Dr. A's heretical surgery had obviously gone awry. Fred would need further surgery. He would, this time, undoubtedly be getting the orthodox colostomy. Meanwhile, my Lillian was having meatloaf for lunch, possibly wondering in the back of her mind if the dread colostomy that the itinerant surgeon from Florida did was really necessary, and if so, how long she'd have to endure the smelly plastic bag now glued to her side.

Well, what's the point of all this? It's not that the Old Masters, authors of the catechism, were any more correct than modern-day university heretics. It's not that Dr. A is a dolt. And it's certainly not that Dr. Roode is a genius, knowing when to cling to orthodoxy and when to forsake it for heresy. You can't draw any conclusion from a single population of but two instances with opposite outcomes. It's just a true story. I just happened to luck out with my patient, and I only know that now, after the fact, because Lillian is munching on meatloaf.

And for those of you who think that medicine is all science, not art, or that it is a simple matter for us physicians to choose what to do, well, think again.

Medical Use for a Quarter

A few days later, I was giving serious thought to sending Lillian home. Fred was still in the ICU, slowly recovering from his second operation.[15] Neither one was aware of the other's existence, and that was just as well. It avoids their playing the what-if game. I was making rounds. First, I looked at Lillian's chart to see how things were going, and I noted (but was not terribly surprised) that the nurses had not been taking Lillian's temperature regularly. I'd noticed this two days before and had written on her chart "VS QID," which, in medicalese, means "Take the blood pressure and measure the temperature four times a day."

Nurses are, after all, human. They get busy and take shortcuts. It is not uncommon to find such blank spaces in any hospital anywhere in the country. Just a week or so ago, with another patient,

---

[15] And yes, the second time around he did get the orthodox colostomy.

I found I had to make repeated requests to have all the little blank spaces filled in on the I+O[16] record. Things improved, but then I saw a sign posted in the nursing station wall by a well-meaning nurse.

It said, "ACCURATE I+Os ON ALL OF DR. ROODE'S PATIENTS!"

I protested to the shift supervisor that they should treat my patients no differently than any other physician's. Accurate I+Os ought to be the order of the day for *all* patients.

Back to the problem at hand. More blank spaces. No temperatures on Lillian. I needed that information to make an intelligent decision about sending her home. But the problem was more than missing temperatures. It's the general problem of getting people to do a good job. Various doctors have attempted at various times to solve this problem in various ways: yelling, screaming, or intimidation are techniques that have all been tried. Indeed, I had tried all these in the past, but the results (if any) were temporary and just made you look bad. Realizing that there are few (if any) truly bad people or nurses, I had more recently been trying an educational approach.

"Say, what was Lillian's temperature this morning?"

Nurse, showing surprise. "Isn't it on the chart?"

"I'm sure it is. Somewhere. I just can't find it."

She looked, saw the blank space. "Oh, June hasn't charted this morning's temperature yet." She hunted down June, and sure enough, there was a number there in her pocket, written on a scrap of paper.

"What about yesterday's temperatures?" (There were three more blanks there.)

"I wasn't working yesterday."

"Yes, I know, but I need the numbers."

She checked and confirmed the blank spaces. All she could do was mumble that she wasn't working. My problem, of course, was what they were going to do the rest of today and tomorrow. The lost data was lost. There was no sense making a scene about it.

---

[16]   Intake and Output record. We use measurements of the volume of IVs infused and urine output to gauge a patient's hydration status. The numbers that a nurse records on a patient's chart are used to make adjustments in the IV infusion rate.

She checked the orders. VS QID. "You are absolutely right," she concluded. "If you wrote VS QID, then it must be done. We have no excuse. We should have done it."

I knew that this wasn't going to solve the problem because we went through all this with the I+Os and with the temperatures just two days before. The problem was that they didn't understand *why* the temperatures were so important.

"No," I said. "The problem is that you all don't realize how badly I need these numbers. Let me try to explain."

And so we gathered together all the nurses and aides who might have occasion to see or care for Lillian. I started out by explaining to them.

"You see, we surgeons aren't all that smart, though to listen to many of us, you'd never know that. The problem we face is that we don't always know what to do. Take Lillian, for example. She is just recovering from surgery for perforated diverticulitis. She has been on antibiotics. The question at hand has to do with when it is safe to stop them. If we stop too soon, the infection will return. But we can't leave her on antibiotics the rest of her life. Some authorities say seven days, some say ten, and some say wait till the WBC is normal. I hate to say it, but absolutely nobody really knows *for sure* which is the right answer. We just don't know. It's sort of like religion, where you have a lot of strongly held opinions but precious little objective knowledge. So what to do? In cases like this, I have a medical decision-making device."

Here, I reached into my pocket and fished out a quarter. They all laughed. Politely. They didn't understand. The use of probability, of a random outcome, has a long history in decision-making. In olden times, it was supposed that, since humans don't control the outcome of a coin toss, then God must. So a nifty way to decide what to do was to cast lots. That was how, for example, they decided who got Jesus's clothing. That was how the first king of Israel was chosen. (See how well I am staying in the religious mode as I tell this story!)

I tossed the coin and announced, "Heads. Seven days. So I stopped the antibiotics two days ago. And by the way, her WBC was also normal. So I'm probably okay with seven days, but I am not *per-*

fectly sure. I don't mean to cast doubts on the utility of my little 'decision-making machine.'"—I point to the quarter—"but it is always wise to double-check, especially when a human life is involved. That's where you come in. You are my eyes and ears. You can tell me if my decision-making machine was right or wrong. If we stopped the antibiotics too soon, the patient will spike a temperature. How will I know I have gone astray if you aren't taking temperatures?"

They all agreed that the temperatures should be recorded, and hopefully, they would be (for a while). Maybe it was helpful for them to know that they weren't just filling in the blanks on a form that some dolt in the nursing office dreamed up. It was not make-work at all.

I saw that they were amused by my use of a quarter as a decision-making machine. And they were a nice audience. They seemed interested, if unconvinced. And things were slow this morning. I decided to give them another example.

So I continued, "I know you think I was just kidding about the quarter, that you don't believe me deep down inside. But I really wasn't. Let me tell you about rebound tenderness.[17] We have all been taught to do this test as part of our physical diagnosis. It is supposed to tell us if a patient has peritonitis." They all nodded knowingly.

"I am not kidding you, but we don't know what to make of rebound tenderness. Sure, the books all tell you to test for it, but today's books are merely repeating what yesterday's books said, and they in turn repeated still earlier editions. It all goes back to a famous and hoary figure of the past—perhaps Osler?—who first said it. The point is that everybody just took the other guy's word for it, and nobody bothered to put the cold-hearted, unblinking eye of statistics to the matter. Statistics don't give a fig who Osler was. And when statistics were applied, we found to our astonishment that testing for rebound tenderness is only 50 percent accurate! I hope you find this as amazing as I do. You get equally accurate information out of

---

[17] In this test, a physician presses his hand on a patient's tender abdomen and then suddenly releases the pressure. If the pain gets worse, it is called rebound tenderness.

another little decision-making machine"—I dig a dime out of my pocket and toss it—"as one does with our test for rebound tenderness! So why not use the dime? It is a whole lot more comfortable to our patients and equally accurate."

Had I changed things? Probably not. But perhaps at least a few of the nurses would know that I was not just being a bastard about insisting that all the blanks got filled in on my patients. I did use the information.

Lillian remained afebrile and was discharged from the hospital the next day. On that same day, Fred moved from the ICU back to his old room. I wish that I could say that was the end of his problems, but it wasn't. Fred went on to develop additional abscesses and was sent to the big medical center for further surgery. It brought to mind the surgeon I most admired during my training.

Dr. Carl Konvolinka once said to me when we had problems with an elderly patient, a Mr. O'Shinski, "Pete, you gotta get it right the first time. You can't keep operating and operating on these older people indefinitely."

Oh, and how did Lilian do in the long run? Well, after waiting several months for all inflammation to quiet down, I was able to perform the second operation, in which I removed the diseased colon that I had to leave behind and, in the same operation, restore her intestinal continuity, meaning her dread colostomy was removed.

Fired!

At the conclusion of my fifth (and last!) assignment at this small hospital, I was informed that I would not be invited back. They'd found somebody else, somebody to replace me, somebody who would "play ball" with them. There were two points of contention:

1. I was unable (unwilling in their view) to provide them with the *continuous* coverage they needed to replace their beloved former surgeon.

2. The second point of disagreement revolved around an unsafe medical practice situation in the nearby town that I was also covering. They had decided to resume providing obstetrical services, and so they needed C-section backup coverage. I was perfectly agreeable to this request until I visited that hospital and was astonished to learn that they had no regular, in-house anesthesia services available. I had never done any surgery there. Anesthesia was to be provided by CRNAs,[18] who would drive over from a homebase over seventy miles away.

I remember thinking, *This simply cannot be. There must be a mistake. When a baby gets in trouble, it has to be rescued immediately.*

And so I gently remarked that surely they must routinely call anesthesia in whenever a woman went into labor. To my further astonishment, I was informed that, no, they would wait until an emergency arose, and *then* they would call anesthesia! It appeared that this was a purely an economic decision. Why pay a CRNA perfectly good money to sit idly by for the unlikely event that his or her services would be needed for a C-section? But this also meant that whenever a baby got into trouble, the infant could not be rescued via C-section for well over an hour. This is an unconscionably long time, far exceeding the standards set by the American College of Obstetricians and Gynecologists, which mandate the ability to start a C-section within thirty minutes of the time one is deemed necessary. Fetal brain damage can start in a matter of minutes, not hours. Yes, it is difficult for small hospitals to meet this standard, but it can be done. In a previous assignment in South Dakota, we were able to assemble the OR crew and start a C-section in just about twenty minutes. At the other extreme, I was once involved in (but ultimately dismissed from) a lawsuit in which the hospital took fully fifty-four minutes to prepare for an emergency C-section. The hospital lost that malpractice suit on that one point alone.

---

[18] Certified Registered Nurse Anesthetists.

But even worse, from my point of view was the fact that there were qualified CRNAs available and within twenty miles. "Wrong clinic," I was told. They were the competition. We were not permitted to use their services. So here we had healthcare decisions being made strictly on economic grounds. The fetus was an innocent pawn in the whole process. And so I refused to do C-sections there.

They were likely annoyed because I phrased it something to the effect that "You guys are nuts! You have no business doing OB if you can't do a C-section faster than that. This is a multimillion-dollar malpractice suit just waiting to happen."

They took offense, retorting that they never had a problem before when they were providing obstetrics to their community.

"Good!" I said. "You can keep right on doing what you want, but don't involve me."

(Ah yes, it reminded me of the apocryphal tale of the man who fell off a tall skyscraper, and as he plunged past the third story, he was heard to remark that it wasn't so bad, that nothing had happened to him yet.)

And so I was fired. Obviously, I was not "working out," as they put it. I wished them well and felt no regrets whatsoever with my decision. There comes a time when one must draw a line in the dirt and refuse to step over into an area that is both unsafe and morally wrong.

This was the only instance in my 244 assignments where I was "let go." In the good old days, one had to suffer when one took an unpopular position on moral grounds. Alas, I didn't even get the chance to endure any privation, for not a week later, I received a phone call asking me to work elsewhere.

18

Locum Tenens at Home

The collapse of my multispecialty medical group in Iowa was what prompted me to first try and then embrace the *locum* lifestyle. Though Betty and I still lived in Iowa, it merely served as the base for our *locum* travels. Then one of the two remaining hometown surgeons relocated. Suddenly, the other multispecialty clinic in town, the one that had previously given me a "We have no need for you, Dr. Roode" response when I had inquired about working for them, now asked me to join them. Well, no, thank you. So they then asked if I could provide *locum* coverage for them until such time as they could recruit a replacement for their former surgeon. Now *that* I could do.

My first assignment at home lasted only eight weeks, for the clinic was then lucky enough to hire not one but two general surgeons, a husband-and-wife team to boot! And so I was once again unemployed, but that is the usual fate of a *locum* surgeon. Additional needs arose from time to time. All told, I was employed right in our hometown on no less than seventeen separate occasions!

Here then is a smattering of my memorable patients from the twelve years during which I was asked to provide temporary coverage in our hometown.

Sam (Motorcycle vs River Barge)

Sam was driving his motorcycle home late one Saturday night. He was heading west on a highway that traverses several Iowa cornfields. Suddenly, to his amazement, he saw a huge Mississippi river barge lying squarely across the highway! Yes, he had been drinking. Yes, he knew he should not be driving in his condition. And he also knew that there was no way on earth that a Mississippi river barge could be way out there in the country, lying across a highway in an Iowa cornfield. He sensed that it must have something to do with the booze. Yup, that barge just surely had to be a beer-induced hallucination. No doubt about it. So he proceeded to nonchalantly drive right through it.

The next thing he knew, he was lying in a brightly lit room with me peering down at him. While examining him, I was able to inform him that:

a. No, he had not been on his motorcycle.
b. Instead, he had been in a motorboat on the river, and
c. Yes, there really was a Mississippi river barge in front of him.

He had seven fractured ribs, a right-sided hemopneumothorax,[1] and several nasty abrasions, with tissue loss. After inserting a chest tube, I had to take him to the OR to debride, wash, cleanse, and close the lacerations as best I could. He made an uneventful, if slow, recovery.

Flossie

I had performed a mastectomy on Flossie many years previously, long before we adopted the *locum* lifestyle. She appeared one Tuesday afternoon at the clinic I was working at, with a small sebaceous cyst just in front of her left ear. She was just as I remembered her, a rather unkempt old woman. She'd heard I was back in town and had hired a cab to drive her the twenty-five or so miles to town. All she could think of for a reason to see me was the cyst, which I

---

[1] Collapsed lung with accumulation of blood and air in the pleural space.

excised in the office. While I was doing that, she regaled me with tales of her adventures with another doctor at another office. She had been thrown out of his office for being disorderly and loud. This was followed by tales of the problems she was having with her husband, etc., etc., etc. I sympathized with her, gave her my card, and went on to the next patient.

But my relationship with Flossie was just beginning. I received a phone call the next day; she wanted more of my cards for her friends. I reminded her that I was here only on a temporary basis and would soon be leaving. No matter, she still wanted the cards.

The next event in our relationship was the large "Thank You" notice that appeared in the local newspaper. This was followed by several phone calls, in which she updated me on her marital woes, including the information that she had bought a completely black outfit to wear to her divorce hearing in the courthouse. (She'd been a virgin when she was married in white, and so she thought it only proper to divorce in black.)

About a week after that, she reappeared in the office, calling my attention to a small seborrheic keratosis on her face. I reassured her about this, whereupon she produced this huge bag of goodies she'd made for me. Such a collection of unappealing things! They ranged from "homemade" brownies jumbled together on a paper plate to a handful of "party mix," three ears of partially shucked corn, a few dirty potatoes, etc. At this point, she asked me if I was married, and when I replied in the affirmative, she said, "Oh well, keep this stuff anyhow!" Since her cooking ability (not to mention her personal hygiene) was of dubious quality, I passed along the corn and potatoes but threw the rest out.

Marilyn Berry (Bestirring Oneself at Midnight)

Not all of my "remembrances" are flattering to everybody, myself included. Here is an instance where I could have done much better.

It was nearly midnight one evening when the clinic physician called me about a patient he was seeing in the ER. Marilyn Berry was a sixty-three-year-old woman with a two-day history of abdominal pain. Her white count was elevated (24,000), and he thought he felt a mass in the left lower quadrant of her abdomen. He was admitting her with the diagnosis of acute diverticulitis.[2]

"You don't have to come in and see her tonight, Pete," he added. "I'm starting her on antibiotics." He was just letting me know about her in case she deteriorated during the night.

Well, what to do? Sometimes acute diverticulitis is a surgical emergency. Would Don (a family physician) recognize such an emergency? That white count was awfully high for a simple case of diverticulitis. What if it was perforated? But it was nearly midnight, and we all get tired. And the tiredness influences our judgment and our decisions, even though we only admit it in private, and then only rarely. If I went in, and it were perforated, I'd probably need to annoy the radiologist by requesting emergency X-rays or CT scans. And then if we had to go to the OR, it would be more like 2 a.m. till we even started surgery. I'd be up all night.

He didn't ask me to come in.

Probably he is right about the diagnosis.

He's an experienced GP.

It should be safe for me to go back to sleep.

But that invisible "Little Green Man" that my mentor (Dr. Carl Konvolinka) had placed on my shoulder way back in my surgical residency kept nagging me: *That white count is awfully high.*

I chose to ignore him.

The next morning, on rounds, I tried to look Marilyn up. But she was downstairs, getting a CT scan. And so with one interruption after another, I didn't get around to examining poor Mrs. Berry until early afternoon. I was horrified to find that she was, after all, a genuine surgical emergency.

---

[2]   Inflammation of the sigmoid colon usually caused by infection in a small outpouching of the colon's lining.

"Do you feel worse now than you did last night?" I asked her, hoping that she really wasn't this bad last night.

"No, not really."

Damn, I thought to myself as I wrote on the chart that, she'd "apparently" deteriorated since her admission the evening before. Who gets "fooled" by these notes anyhow? Hopefully, the accursed lawyers!

And so it was that we explored Mrs. Berry that afternoon, finding that a large portion of her small bowel was gangrenous. Small bowel, not diverticulitis. But from what? We'll probably never know. Nor will we ever know if it was gangrenous when she came to the ER the evening before, or if the gangrene had developed during the night when I was sleeping peacefully with the "knowledge" that her family doctor had made the right diagnosis. While operating, I found these thoughts flitting through my mind:

She had the pain for two days before admission; therefore, it must have been gangrenous when she came to the ER.

Maybe the gangrene just happened during the night.

We had to get her volume restored and give her antibiotics.

I hope we didn't do her any harm by waiting.

We probably didn't hurt her any by waiting a lousy twelve hours or so, did we?

If this all sounds like whistling in the dark, then you have heard that sound before.

And Mrs. Berry? Well, she did fine after I removed the gangrenous small bowel. Neither she nor anybody else ever suspected how much I'd kicked myself over her care.

Amateur Night in the ER

Friday night, about 8 p.m. I received a STAT call to come to the ICU. One of the internists thought he had a tension pneumothorax[3] on his hands. And so, quite naturally, I hustled right on in and found a bluish man in the ICU with a chest tube already in place! A chest tube is used to *treat* a tension pneumothorax. How could a tension pneumothorax develop in a patient who already had a chest tube in place? What the heck was going on?

When a chest tube is inserted, it is connected to a pleur-evac, which allows the abnormal pressure in the pleural space to be vented away. But there were no bubbles going through the pleur-evac connected to his chest tube. So the chest tube could be plugged.

My first action, therefore, was to irrigate the chest tube with sterile saline. It flushed nice and easily, so it wasn't plugged. But I did find that a small amount of dark blood came out at the end of my irrigation.

Hmm. That's peculiar. What's going on?

The saline went in and came out so easily. The tube just couldn't be clogged, could it? But something continued to act like an obstruction. Well, sort of. The chest tube wouldn't bubble, drain, or even fluctuate unless the suction was off, and then it drained nicely. Put the suction on, and it stopped. Could something be on the inside, sucked up against the tube and blocking it when the vacuum was applied?

But, no, I thought, *there must be eight or ten side holes in that tube. What could suck up against all ten of them simultaneously and block them?*

Maybe I was just imagining that there was a blockage. Still, Carl didn't look good at all. What the hell was going on anyhow? My next step was to get a chest X-ray. When we looked at it a short while later, it was evident that there was no tension pneumothorax. True, he did have a residual 10 percent pneumothorax, but that seemed, if

---

[3]   The lungs are not physically attached to the chest wall. Instead there is this slight vacuum that holds the lungs expanded and allows them to move as we breathe. If this vacuum is broken, the lungs collapse and it is called a pneumothorax. If there is some sort of leak involved, pressure can build up in their pleural space, forcibly compressing the lung and even pushing the chest contents to the other side, interfering with the heart and the other lung. This is called a tension pneumothorax and is a true emergency.

anything, improved over the chest X-ray that had been done in the ER. And the chest tube seemed to be in perfect position.

"It's *not* a tension pneumothorax," I reassured the internist, but I still didn't understand why this patient looked so bad nor why his pleur-evac neither bubbled nor fluctuated.

Looking at his chart, I discovered that he had widespread lung cancer. He had apparently been a big-time smoker (naturally, that's how he got lung cancer in the first place) along with severe COPD,[4] asthmatic bronchitis, etc., etc., etc. He was a patient both at this hospital and at the University of Iowa, and he'd had previous pneumothoraces and previous chest tubes. Finally, a chemical pleurodesis[5] had been done at Iowa City to prevent further pneumothoraces. Evidently, however, it wasn't a perfect job, inasmuch as he seemed to have gone on to develop yet another pneumothorax. And then there was the matter of a chronic broncho-pleural fistula[6] on his other side, the side with the inoperable lung cancer. To solve that problem, Iowa City had created a permanently open window in the back of his right chest, isolating the fistula away from the rest of the lung so it couldn't collapse. This created the unusual situation of a man with a hole in the back of his chest that communicated with his bronchus, and ultimately with his mouth. I was told that Carl could talk out of the back of his chest!

So much for his past history. What had happened earlier in the day was that Carl had been found unresponsive at home. A quick 911 call had summoned the ambulance. He then had the dubious honor of being the first "field intubation"[7] done by one of the EMTs. Carl was then rapidly transported to the ER, where the pneumotho-

---

4   Chronic Obstructive Pulmonary Disease

5   Placement of an irritating substance, usually talcum powder, into the pleural space, to so irritate the lung and the inner chest wall that adhesions form. When this happens a pneumothorax cannot form. The lung is held to the chest wall.

6   An abnormal opening between a bronchus and the pleural space. This also leads to a pneumothorax.

7   In which a plastic tube is inserted into a non-breathing patient's trachea so that we can breathe for him or her.

rax was discovered and treated. And as it turned out, it was the ER doctor who had inserted Carl's chest tube. While all this was taking place, earlier in the afternoon, I had been happily making rounds elsewhere in the hospital, blithely unaware of Carl's problems. As a matter of fact, I had been on my way out the back door when I ran into John, an EMT, who ecstatically shared his joy with me.

"Doc! I did it! My first field intubation. It was great! Boy, am I wired!" And off he rushed, down the hall, to share his joy and excitement with others, barely hearing my "Congratulations!"

Then I left the hospital and went home to Betty, only to be shortly called back by the internist.

I wandered downstairs to talk to the ER doctor. I was disturbed about the blood I had found in the chest tube when I irrigated it. A small amount of watery blood would have been okay, but this was so thick and dark, not diluted by pleural fluid like you sometimes see after a chest tube is inserted. It looked like pure blood to me—not a large amount, not life-threatening, but just curious and disturbing. My talk with the ER doctor was both informative and unrewarding. No, it wasn't a difficult chest tube insertion, and when I told him about the blood, he stressed the fact that he had been careful to go over the rib.[8]

"What about your finger?" I asked.

"Huh?"

"Did you put your finger into his chest to feel for adhesions?"

Well, it seemed that he hadn't. As a matter of fact, he'd also used the trocar. *Arghhh!* What do they teach in ATLS[9] about trocars? (They teach amateurs *not* to use them.) You are supposed to make an incision and gently insert just the naked tube. The trocar is a sharp metal rod that can safely (if you do it properly) be used to quickly insert the tube. But amateurs can easily spear things.

I went upstairs again, to the ICU. Carl wasn't doing well, and his chest tube still didn't seem "right" to me. But I couldn't put my finger on the problem. For lack of anything better to do, I irrigated it

---

[8] Chest tubes are always place over a rib, because blood vessels (that could be injured) lie under them.

[9] Advance Trauma Life Support

again. No, it still wasn't plugged. It still irrigated freely but this time I felt a peculiar "thunk" at the end of the irrigation. I'd never encountered such a sensation before. What was going on? Should I remove and replace the chest tube? But why? The X-ray showed there was only a piddly 10 percent pneumothorax. And the chest tube was in perfect position to boot. Therefore, repositioning it wouldn't improve him clinically. Listening to his lungs revealed that they were awfully tight—lots of broncho-spasm. That alone could easily account for his respiratory distress. The blood? Well, he'd had the pleurodesis, and probably the ER doctor had torn an adhesion putting the tube in. There wasn't enough blood to be concerned about. Still, I wasn't satisfied that I really understood what was going on. I needed to think this puzzling one through.

I've often said that there is a simple, clear answer to every problem. The only trouble is, we often don't learn the answer while we are dealing with the problem at hand. Only later, after we get additional data—the result of a test, an operation, or worse, an autopsy—do things finally make sense.

Carl didn't give us time to think of any more elegant explanations as to what was going on. He abruptly deteriorated and stopped breathing. A cardiac arrest code was called. Decision time. No more thinking. Another one of these "firing line" decisions, open to second-guessing by everybody after the fact. Should I try to replace the tube while they are conducting a code, applying CPR compressions to his chest? Could I have misread the chest X-rays? Could there indeed be a tension pneumothorax after all? Was the X-ray lying to me? To test this last possibility, I took a long 14 ga needle and inserted it several places into his chest while the code was underway. No rush of air. No tension pneumothorax. Stick to your guns. The chest tube will not be changed.

Carl Mackay died. An autopsy was done. The next day, I sought out the pathologist, with my usual curious mixture of anticipation and dread. What had I missed? What killed him? The pathologist told me that he'd found the chest tube residing *inside* Carl's lung! Not in the pleural space between the lung and the chest wall where it was supposed to be. Now in a rush of understanding, it was all too clear to me. It was that damned trocar. I had never tried to irrigate a chest tube that was completely *inside* somebody's lung, so I wasn't familiar with the sensation that one would encounter. As a matter of fact, I'd never even seen a chest tube placed inside a lung. Should I have (or could I even have?) been able to imagine, to deduce, to predict how it would irrigate and then conclude what was going on?

A smarter doctor would have done so immediately. For me, it took the autopsy to reveal that, even though his lung was completely surrounding the chest tube, somehow it accepted a large volume of irrigating fluid freely into a closed space. Then when we aspirated, it would collapse all around the tube, returning the fluid to me before occluding all the suction holes at once with that peculiar "thunk." I tried to take comfort from the fact that the autopsy also revealed that it was probably his cancer and his rotten lungs that really killed him. Had I removed and changed the chest tube, it would not have helped him. Still, we didn't really do him any good that night.

The hospital in this town in Iowa was one of the few that, at the time this story took place, didn't require its ER doctors to take the ATLS course. At universities even medical students are required to take that course before they are allowed to serve on a learning rotation in the ER. ATLS advocates insertion of the finger first to feel for just the type of adhesions that Carl had and to gently insert only the tube so that the sharp trocar doesn't push the tube into something valuable, like the heart or the lung. As Carl's bad luck would have it, the site chosen by the ER doctor for the chest tube just happened to be one with a dense adhesion between the lung and the chest wall. When he inserted the trocar'd chest tube, it went straight into the lung. He probably felt a slightly increased resistance as the trocar pushed the tube into the lung, but not having done very many chest tube insertions, he didn't appreciate that the resistance he encountered was too high or out of line. The trocar strikes again...

And one other thing: The ultimate irony is that Carl didn't need the chest tube in the first place. His pleurodesis operation done at the university hospital was working just fine. He only had a 10 percent pneumothorax because that was all he was capable of having. The incorrectly placed chest tube neither helped nor probably greatly hurt him for that matter. It was his cancer and horrid lung disease that did him in. For me, this whole episode was an interesting mental exercise. For the ER doctor, hopefully, it was a learning experience that served to make him a sadder and wiser physician. If so, Carl's death will undoubtedly help somebody in the future.

James Miller (An Old Dog Learns a New Trick)

It was not till 5 p.m. on a Monday afternoon that a local family doctor called me over to his office in the clinic to discuss one of his patients, who had abdominal pain and a slightly elevated white count.

When I examined the patient, I found that in addition to his pain, he also had a mass in the right upper quadrant of his abdomen. It could be an infected gallbladder or maybe a perforated colon cancer. The white count was only 12,800, but it was my fingers that told me we needed to operate that night.

In preparation for his admission to the hospital, a careful H+P[10] was done. I happen to use a three-page checklist that patients fill out. Then I go over it with them, gathering further details about the responses. It both saves time and ensures that we don't miss any vital information.

Jim, it turned out, was a veteran—a VA patient, no less—who had not taken very good care of himself. There was a long history of alcohol abuse, though he hadn't indulged for the past three years or so. And despite his emphysema, COPD, and asthmatic bronchitis, he persisted with the cigarette habit. I noticed the nicotine stains on the fingers of his left hand.

He must be putting away a couple of packs a day, I thought, *and smoking them right down to the butt to boot.*

The rest of the history proceeded smoothly enough. We discovered that he also had hypertension and a severe walking disability

---

[10]   History and Physical Examination.

about which he was vague. The VA had told him there was nothing that could be done about it, but he didn't know what the problem was. A check of his record, however, revealed that he had been diagnosed as having an ataxia of cerebral origin, probably secondary to his alcohol abuse. In plain English, the booze had rotted that part of his brain that controlled his balance. We also obtained the complete list of medications that the various doctors had prescribed for him. Now it was time to send Jim to the hospital for the additional tests that would be necessary prior to surgery.

Later that evening, we explored him, and it turned out to be a gangrenous gallbladder. I set about its removal, which proceeded smoothly enough despite the cirrhosis in his liver. About three quarters of the way through the operation, however, his lungs decided to fizzle out. Anesthesia was able to get him through the surgery, but when we were done, he was neither interested in nor capable of breathing on his own. He was wheezing, and it was obvious that he was going to be spending the rest of the night in the ICU, on a ventilator. What was going on with this man?

Of all the information I had gathered on Jim that evening, only two items were the result of physical examination. One was the tender mass in his abdomen, and the other was a laboratory determination of elevated white count. They told me that I needed to operate. But all the other information I had obtained from Jim himself or from his records. It is in the history that we get most of our information. "Listen to your patients," goes one old adage, "for they are trying to tell you their disease." How true it is, and how often I need to relearn that simple lesson.

The checklist that I used helped, but the events of the evening were to prove that it was still far from perfect. True, I knew of his bad lungs, but then I was lulled by the normal physical exam. His lungs sounded plenty clear to me. What had I missed? It was only after the surgery, when I talked to his wife, that I obtained that one little bit of vital information that he'd neglected to tell me and I had neglected to specifically ask for, and that explained to us why his lungs crapped out.

When I told his wife that it was "only" a gangrenous gallbladder (not the dread "C" word), her comment was: "So it wasn't the pills, eh?"

"What?"

"Well, Doc, he thought that it was his Theodur[11] that was upsetting his stomach and giving him the pain, so he quit taking them about three or four days ago."

Of course! How simple and elegant the explanation! And, as per usual, obvious only after the fact. Now it all made sense. Sure, I had gotten the entire list of medications that were prescribed for him, those he had at home in bottles in the bathroom. We even had his family bring them in, to be sure we hadn't missed any. But nobody (myself included) had asked him if he was *actually taking them*! It's funny how one can discover such a simple lesson after playing this game for twenty-three years.

And Jim? Well, he did fine. Once we knew what the problem was, we loaded him up with Theophylline[12] again. He spent the night on the respirator in ICU. As a matter of fact, that, to him, was the single most unpleasant part of his entire adventure. I had filled his abdominal incision with a dilute solution of Marcaine,[13] so he had no pain from the surgery itself. But there is absolutely nothing that you can do to make an endotracheal tube pleasant. That is one of the prices that people eventually pay for their tobacco habit.

But for the Grace of God (A Surgical Horror Story)

I watched another surgeon remove a couple of inches of the common bile duct last week. For the uninitiated, the common bile duct is the one and only channel that the liver uses to discharge its waste products. If it were to be blocked, you would become deeply jaundiced and die. So you'd think that such surgical carelessness would horrify all onlookers, but I tell you, not one person in the operating room that day realized what had happened. True, I'd had

---

[11]   Medication for his chronic pulmonary disease.
[12]   A medication for asthmatic pulmonary disease.
[13]   Local anesthetic.

a vague feeling that something wasn't perfectly "right," but like the audience in front of a master magician, I couldn't put my finger on it. Things seemed to go so smoothly.

It wasn't till the operation was nearly half over that I became uneasy and suspicious. I hesitantly questioned the surgeon. But no, that can't be. One does not remove the common bile duct so easily. I must be wrong. And how could I question a more experienced surgeon? So after he reassured me that he'd done nothing wrong, that everything was fine, I was quiet again.

I asked him the next day how the patient was, and he replied, "Fine… I sent her home."

So I must have been wrong. I must have been imagining things. Dang! A week went by, and the surgeon called me. He said he had a problem.

"Do you remember Mrs. Hastings?"

"Sure do."

"Well, I may have put a clip[14] on her common duct."

"Oh no!"

"I'll need your help with her tomorrow."

"I'll be there."

It seemed that Mrs. Hastings had developed jaundice—bad jaundice as a matter of fact. When I looked at the chart, I saw that her bilirubin was highly elevated.[15] He had consulted a local gastro-enterologist, who had performed an ERCP.[16] I wandered down to radiology to look at the X-rays that had been taken. They showed an abrupt blockage of the dye that the gastroenterologist had injected into the lower end of the common bile duct.

---

[14] Metal clips are used to close blood vessels before dividing them. In the removal of a gallbladder they are also placed on the small cystic duct that needs to be divided before the gallbladder itself is removed.

[15] When a red blood cell's life is over, it disintegrates, and the content (hemoglobin) is degraded into bilirubin, a yellow substance that the liver excretes via the common bile duct. If the bile duct is obstructed, the bilirubin backs up into the bloodstream, and the patient begins to look yellow (jaundiced).

[16] A fiber-optic scope is inserted through a patient's stomach so that a thin plastic tube can be inserted into the common bile duct from below and an X-ray obtained.

"Could be a clip," I mused, "or worse."

I remembered the operation… I'd been scheduled to assist the local surgeon with this lap chole.[17] Being an assistant chiefly involves the holding of a couple of retractors. In many hospitals where I have worked, this function is fulfilled by a nurse or a surgical tech, but this surgeon preferred to have another surgeon help him. In any case, I'd never seen Mrs. Hastings until the day of her surgery and then only after she was already in the OR, on the table, and asleep. To me, she wasn't even a person. She was a name stamped on a bit of sticky label paper that I stuffed into my pocket later that evening to enter into my computer.

Initially, things didn't go smoothly. An equipment salesman was present, trying to get the local surgeon interested in using a new trocar,[18] one having a cute little spring-operated knife built into the tip. By using a miniature camera chip, you could actually watch the progress of the trocar through the abdominal wall. However, this required the prior creation of a pneumo-peritoneum[19] with a thin needle. This surgeon, however, wouldn't even insert such a needle into the abdomen for fear of injuring the bowel. He was a super cautious, super careful, methodical-to-the-point-of-plodding-along type of surgeon. Instead of using either a needle or a trocar, he always created the initial abdominal wall opening surgically, under direct vision, so that he was positive that the bowel had not been injured. The equipment salesman therefore suggested we just try the spring-loaded knife-trocar without a pneumo-peritoneum. It didn't work, and finally, our surgeon became frustrated and excused the equipment salesman from the OR. He then reverted to his comfortable, safe, tried-and-true technique.

---

[17] Medical slang for gallbladder removal, using the new-fangled minimally invasive laparoscopic equipment.

[18] A sharp, spear-like instrument that is thrust into the abdomen to make a passageway for the various laparoscopic instruments that are used to perform minimally invasive surgery.

[19] Filling the abdominal cavity with air to distend it so that one can safely insert and manipulate instruments and thereby perform a "minimally invasive" operation.

Mrs. Hastings's gallbladder proved to be chronically inflamed. Worse, the inflammation had created scar tissue that obscured the normal anatomy. The surgeon began gingerly dissecting, looking for the cystic duct,[20] but initially without success. Nothing looked like the cystic duct. At this point, a remarkable interchange took place. Darla, a mere aide, had been asked to scrub into this case for the sole purpose of holding the camera. She had done it many times when the OR staff was short-handed. We were astonished when this ordinarily reticent aide watching the operation and holding the camera had the temerity to open her mouth and ask the surgeon if he planned to open.[21]

"No, just give me a little more time. I might have to open but not yet" was his polite reply to this unexpected query from the aide.

He continued to search for the cystic duct. I continued to watch. Finally, he dissected around the lower end of the gallbladder, leaving the crucial anatomy encased in inflammatory tissue well below and out of harm's way.

He explained to us all, "I want to be safe, so I'll divide here, up higher, on the lower end of the gallbladder itself rather than hunt for the cystic duct. That way, I'm sure to be well above the common duct so that I do not injure it." A little while later, he said, "There! Do you all agree that's the end of the gallbladder?"

"Uh...I guess so. Sure looks thick, as it is supposed to. I dunno. Yeah, I guess so" was my reply.

He'd done more of these laparoscopic operations than I had. If it were me, I'd open, but then I was not in charge of this case. I was the assistant, and he already indicated to the lowly aide that he wasn't ready to open. Why ask him again since he had already proposed to continue in a way that appeared safe to him?

So clips were put on the wide neck of the lower gallbladder, and it was divided. He then proceeded to remove the gallbladder in

---

[20]   The duct between the gallbladder and the common bile duct.

[21]   That is to convert the operation to the "old-fashioned" tried-and-true method in which an incision is made and difficult dissections can be done by hand with more room and better visualization.

the usual fashion, from below up. But halfway up, he encountered a peculiar wide band of tissue coming out from the liver.

"What is that?" I wondered out loud.

But without answering me, he proceeded to put clips on it and then divide it.

Must be fascia... I thought to myself somewhat uncomfortably. Then a gallstone suddenly appeared. *That's unusual.*

"Where did that come from?" I asked.

"Oh, right out of here," he said, indicating the lower end of the gallbladder.

But how can that be? I wondered. *He'd just put a clip on the lower end of the gallbladder. How can a stone come out through the clip?*

"Are you sure?" I asked.

"Yes."

He went on with the dissection, and I interrupted him yet another time, somewhat to his annoyance.

"I don't like the look of that 'thing' coming out of the liver" was the best that I could do.

I wasn't sure just what was going on, if anything. He'd safely divided the gallbladder high so as not to injure the common bile duct. What was I worried about? A bit of tissue? But it seemed to have swollen and was it darker in color than it was a few moments before? Was it distending with bile? Or was I just imagining things?

All I could say was "Is this thing okay?"

"Yes, it's all right, Peter," was his firm reply.

Okay. I had caused enough trouble, and he had, after all, done far more laparoscopic operations than I had. It was best to keep quiet. He must be right. He couldn't have made any mistakes. I'd just watch from now on.

And the rest of the case went fine. Mrs. Hastings went home the next day.

I pondered over this conversation as I walked down the hall to the pathology lab, wondering if they still had the specimen or if they'd chopped it all up. I sought out the pathologist.

"Say, can you pull out Mrs. Hastings's tissue from last week?"

After fumbling with a stained logbook, a number was looked up, and a smelly plastic container was retrieved from an equally smelly cabinet. I peered inside, and *mirabile visu*, Mrs. Hastings's gallbladder was virtually intact. The pathologist must have been in a hurry that day. Was it the end of the day? Or was he just careless? He sees hundreds of gallbladders, and his attention is focused on being sure to document the presence or absence of stones or disease, not to check for the presence or absence of a common bile duct hanging out the bottom. Nobody removes common bile ducts, so why should he bother to look for one? All he'd done in this case was to remove a small bit of tissue from the top of the gallbladder for his microscopic exam. The rest of the gallbladder was floating there in the formalin.[22]

"Here, let me look at this more closely," I said as I pulled on a pair of gloves.

"What's wrong?"

"Nuttin'. Well, maybe. Dr. T has a problem with this patient. She has an obstructive jaundice. We have to operate tomorrow, but I want to examine the specimen. It might help us determine what's going on, what we need to do."

"Sure, go ahead."

"What do you make of this?" I asked him, pointing at the lower end of the specimen.

"It's the cystic duct."

"Is it? Look more closely" was my reply.

And with the aid of a couple of probes, there it was, all too clearly evident. There was a good two inches of Mrs. Hastings's common bile duct attached to the lower end of her gallbladder. And with a rush of understanding (my, aren't things always so clear *after the fact*), I realized just what had happened. He had divided not the lower end of the gallbladder, like he had thought, but the common duct itself. The inflammation had obscured the anatomy so that it wasn't evident what he was doing. Then that peculiar upper "band of tissue," the band that I was worried about, the one that swelled and got darker, why, it was the other end of the common bile duct. Of

---

[22] Preservative, essentially an embalming fluid.

course, it swelled after the clip had been applied—because now it was obstructed. And the stone that had unexpectedly appeared evidently had been in the common bile duct. It popped out when he divided it. It was all too clear now *after the fact*.

And do you know what the pathologist said to me?

"Gee, do you think I should change my dictation?"

We surgeons deal in flesh and blood, in humans and tragedies, while pathologists deal with dead tissue and paper.

And so we reoperated on Mrs. Hastings and swung a loop of small bowel up and attached it to the end of her severed bile duct. As I wrote these words, she was doing fine. Still, I expected this to result in a lawsuit, one that would be quietly settled out of court. Lawyers will make it look like a couple of surgeons were just slap-happy, whacking away without a care in the world, being careless and hurting poor Mrs. Hastings. Well, that's simply not the way things were, but these things are still settled out of court, inasmuch as a surgeon isn't supposed to remove portions of someone's common bile duct, and if you do, there really isn't any defense.[23]

A week went by. I was now engaged in a lap chole of my own. This one, like Mrs. Hastings, also was inflamed, but I had no trouble in locating the cystic duct. I put three clips on it[24] and asked for the scissors. I inserted them, opened the jaws, encircled the "cystic duct," and was about to squeeze the handle when this little voice inside my head, for no good reason at all, said, *Are you really sure it's the cystic duct? Ain't it kinda wide?* Maybe, maybe not. And so to the amazement of the nurses present, I removed the scissors.

"What are you doing?" was their question.

"We're going to do an operative cholangiogram"[25] was my reply.

---

[23] In an interesting follow-up, there was no lawsuit. Such was the surgeon's excellent rapport with his patient that she accepted his explanation that the unfortunate complication was the result of her disease and the inflammation it had caused. She trusted him and knew he had done his best.

[24] Two below and one above my intended point of dividing the cystic duct.

[25] X-ray the common bile duct to be sure it is open and my clips are nowhere near it.

If I could have lived that first operation over again, this was just what I'd have suggested to the other surgeon. But by the time I became suspicious, it would have been too late. Well, at least it wasn't too late for my patient. And guess what. No filling of the hepatic radicals.[26] We tried again. Still no filling.

"We're opening."

And sure enough, my clips were on my patient's common bile duct, and I had been about to divide it! My god!

It is a common misconception that we doctors are always in collusion with one another, protecting the incompetent. What seems to the layman to be an obvious careless malpractice—the removal of a person's common bile duct—in reality simply didn't happen that way. Nobody is carelessly cutting things out. A great deal of attention is taken to doing things safely, and still mishaps occur. I do not refrain from criticizing the other surgeon out of any misguided sense of protecting him but because I have this inner dread that I can just as easily stand in his shoes. Indeed, but for the grace of God, I nearly was…

Russ Churchill (A Slice of Life at 3 AM)

The same event can trigger remarkably different emotional responses in different observers, making for fascinating observations of human nature. Take this evening, for example. Russ, thirty-seven years old, and having a marital dispute (we'll never know all the details) decided to "end it all."

My first involvement in this particular tragedy was at 3 a.m. on a Saturday morning when the beeper went off. Upon dialing the indicated number (it was the ER), I heard the ER doctor telling me that an ambulance was bringing in a gunshot victim, who was deteriorating rapidly, and so he'd appreciate if I could come in as soon as

---

[26] These are the bile duct branches that come from inside the liver. If the common bile duct were open, the dye would have gone up into them. And so the X-ray was telling me that the common bile duct was obstructed by my clips.

possible. At this point, no additional details were available. Was it a barroom brawl? A family dispute? An accident? Was alcohol involved?

The twin emotions recorded at this point were relief on the part of the ER doctor and anxiety on my part—relief for the ER doctor, as he'd have help in caring for this shooting victim, and anxiety on my part because if the victim was rapidly deteriorating, it meant a major vessel injury. Sure enough, I could hear an ambulance siren wailing in the background.

As I dressed, my mind started its usual litany: *Dang! It's probably a handgun, and the low-velocity bullet will have torn the liver, aorta, vena cava, or God knows what. How am I going to be able to fix that? With my luck, the patient will be stable enough to make it to the OR. What if I manage to get a cross clamp on the aorta? Then what? That will be like holding the proverbial tiger by the tail. It has been over twenty years since I've even helped with an aortic graft. I don't even have hospital privileges to do that sort of operation. But they have no vascular surgeon in this town. He'll bleed to death. Damn. Why me?*

I pulled into the ER shortly after the ambulance had made its arrival. The nurses quickly ushered me to the trauma bay, one of them even holding out a gown and gloves for me.

"Pretty messy" was her comment.

And sure enough, there was blood all over the place. Since the advent of HIV, we have all come to view blood as poison that should not be touched. But our victim, with a gaping hole in his abdomen (he had used a shotgun), had no blood pressure and soon lost all heart rhythm. He was essentially DOA.

"This is useless," muttered the ER doctor as he told everybody to quit the resuscitative efforts. As near as I could determine, once we reached this stage, he simply lost all interest in his former patient.

I hung around the ER for a while, now merely a bystander, an interested observer in the parade of emotions.

Upon learning that this was a suicide, I wondered if the victim's last emotions might have been smugness. "There! Guess I showed her a thing or two!"

Soon, the new widow was brought to the ER. Her emotions were of horror and shocked disbelief. She kept wailing "OH GOD! OH NO! How could he!" as relatives and nurses tried to comfort her.

One of the OR nurses, called into the hospital in the hopes that we'd be able to operate, reacted with outright anger to the interruption of her night's sleep. "This was stupid," she berated the ER doctor. "You shouldn't call me in until you have at least examined the patient to see if I'd be needed."

And what were my own personal emotions? Hard as it might be for outsiders to understand, my own reaction, which I carefully concealed from even the medical bystanders, to this man's violent death in the small hours of Saturday morning in a small town in Iowa was one of relief and even gratitude! Worse than that, I found that I had actually been hoping that he'd die quickly in the ER! Can you imagine a seemingly more inappropriate response to this tragedy? How can this be? Have I become an uncaring monster over the years? Any number of surgeons, however, would understand. Later, when I related this story to Betty, she understood immediately.

I was thankful, for selfish reasons, that he died quickly, because it spared me the mad life-and-death rush to the OR. It spared me from assuming the horrendous responsibility for this man's survival. As things now stood, his death was his fault and his alone. This crazy litigious society has succeeded in transferring responsibility of anybody's actions to another. Sometimes it seems to me that nobody is responsible for his or her own actions any more. Take him to the OR and have him bleed to death on the OR table, and everybody—from the widow, to the bystanders, to the accursed lawyers—could blame me rather than the victim. And curiously enough, this transfer of responsibility even rubs off on some of us surgeons.

I, too, would probably blame myself if I had been unable to save him, especially if it were a close one: "If I'd been a little faster with my clamp or a little more skillful with the sewing or a little more bold with a resection…" No, thank you. I was purely relieved to be let off the hook so easily.

By and by, the police showed up at the ER. The grizzled old veteran, who over the years has probably seen far too much human violence and tragedy, summed up his emotions in one sentence: "Doc, there ain't no woman worth a man shooting hisself over."

Russ Duncan (Another Motorcycle Accident)

It was nearly 5 p.m. on a Friday afternoon when my so far month-long sedate pace on this assignment was shattered in the form of a call from the ER. I was up on the hospital's fourth floor, about to see a patient with abdominal pain.

Before I could even answer the pager's beep, the ward clerk dashed into the room to give me the message. "They need you right away in the ER."

So down I went and found the usual crowd of personnel and activity that characterizes an ER in the midst of a trauma case. I poked my head in the first trauma bay, only to see the on-call ER doctor engaged in CPR on a large black man. A peek at the monitor revealed that his heart had stopped and seemed to be resisting all efforts on restarting it. One of the EMTs informed me that he'd been unconscious since being found at the scene of a motorcycle/automobile accident.

Must be a massive injury, I thought, *probably nothing a general surgeon can do about.*

But there was a second victim in the adjacent trauma bay. Upon looking in there, it was evident that I did indeed have something to do, for there was no physician present. The patient had just been unloaded from a second ambulance. Apparently, he was the passenger on the motorcycle. And so I donned the requisite gloves and went to work.

My man proved to be conscious, complaining of abdominal pain, and had reasonably stable vital signs. We could proceed in an orderly fashion: starting an IV and asking X-ray to obtain films. All went well for about ten minutes until we noticed that his blood pressure was falling. Abdomen still tender. Time for a DPL[27] and a call

---

[27]   Diagnostic Peritoneal Lavage. In this small hospital, it was the quickest way to determine intra-abdominal injuries. Were I to have been elsewhere, in a larger medical center, it would have been a CT scan that I'd order.

to the OR to hold a room open at all costs. As it turned out, this latter action greatly angered the local orthopedic surgeon, who had been planning to set a teenager's broken arm. In fact, he was so angry with having to wait to do his nonemergency case that he childishly refused to even see my patient despite the fact he had fractures of both arms and one leg. Even though he was the only orthopedic surgeon available in town and even though he was on call, he sneered. "I refuse to become involved." With that he stalked off in a huff.

"Fine, I'll do it myself" was my disgusted response, feeling somewhat like being in the children's story in which *The Little Red Hen* had to make bread all by herself.

The DPL yielded pure blood and lots of it. No time for further X-rays. Russ was rapidly bleeding to death. We took him to the OR as quickly as possible, where I found the motorcycle accident had shattered his spleen, torn his liver in several places, blown out the wall of his duodenum, bruised his right kidney, and torn his cecum.

I am not even conscious of the passage of time in these situations when I am madly repairing things in the order of their severity, addressing the most life-threatening injuries first. For example, bleeding takes priority over a bowel injury. And so I was somewhat surprised at the end of the case to find that only an hour and a half had elapsed, even though I had managed to remove the spleen, staunch the bleeding, and repair the bowel injuries. It was now time to get this man to a larger hospital, where they could manage the broken bones that our "noble" orthopedic surgeon "refused to become involved with." Arrangements were made, a helicopter landed, and Russ was whisked off to the University Hospital.

As I walked back to the ER, I chanced to see my old friend Mallinger,[28] who fished a plastic baggie out of his uniform pocket.

"Hey, Doc! Lookit what I found in the pockets of the guy who didn't make it!" he chortled.

It was a white substance. Funny. After all these years of taking care of patients, of reading about cocaine in the newspapers, I'd never actually seen the stuff. He also informed me that the motorcyclist

---

[28]   City policeman.

was one of the town's biggest drug dealers. I asked him about the accident. It seemed that an elderly lady had pulled out in front of the speeding motorcycle. Had she failed to look? Did she look and not see? Did she see but misjudge the distance and speed? If the motorcycle driver hadn't been on cocaine, could he have stopped?

And as for Russ, how did he do? Apparently well, though the university never called me.[29] However, word did filter back to the ER via a friend—something to the effect that the doctors at the university commented that whoever the surgeon was who took him to the OR in such a small town, he did a "helluva job."

It's the little things like that that keep me in this crazy business.

Mary Hughes (Some of Us Get to Die Twice)

I did not actually participate in the care of this patient. My only involvement was listening to another surgeon in the locker room on Monday morning tell me about his "nuisance patient" over the weekend. Mary's problem was neither new nor unusual. But I listened to his tale with an eerie sense of déjà vu.

Mary had been transferred in from a nearby nursing home that offered hospice care. A few months previously, she'd undergone surgery at another hospital and was found to have an inoperable rectal cancer. The tumor had invaded the walls of her pelvis, was large and bulky, and had spread widely within her abdomen. All that could be done was a diverting colostomy. Now this did not cure her, it merely altered the manner of her forthcoming death, hopefully sparing her a great deal of suffering. Following this surgery, the situation was explained to Mary and her family. They declined chemotherapy (it had little chance of helping), and arrangements were made for her to enter the hospice. They planned no heroic measures. One would presume that everything was explained to the patient and her family,

---

[29] It is always nice to learn how patients do after being transferred to larger medical centers. Many are very conscientious about informing the referring physician regarding the status of referred patients. Others much less so.

that they had the support of their minister, family, friends, hospice staff, etc.

On Friday evening, Mary commenced to bleed from her tumor. This was just another form that her impending death could take. It is not a painful process, just a bit messy. The pulse rises, then the patient slips into a coma and quietly sleeps. All was proceeding as expected, but here is where the tale goes awry.

Phone calls were made from the hospice to inform the local physician of Mary's bleeding. He was not available. An attempt was made to contact Mary's surgeon in the other city, but they couldn't get through to him. And so yet another physician was contacted. Unfamiliar with her story, he suggested to the distressed nurses at the hospice that Mary be expeditiously transferred to "the nearest hospital." By the time she arrived in the ER, she was peacefully comatose. The family was anxious. The ER staff was anxious. And so my fellow surgeon, the one telling me about his "nuisance patient," was called to care for her. He had never seen her before.

In this country, it seems that it is perfectly okay to die of pneumonia, cardiac arrest, liver failure, uremia, or any number of other conditions, but it is manifestly not okay to bleed to death. I have often pondered this strange phenomenon. Is this because it is so alarming to bystanders to see bright red fluid pouring out of the hopelessly ill? Is this because we (supposedly) are able to do something about bleeding? Still, it's not logical. Just because something (transfusions) can be done to delay the inevitable doesn't mean that it should be done. We often withhold antibiotics, IVs, or other treatments in the hopelessly ill but sometimes don't seem to be able to withhold blood transfusions.

My first exposure to this curious phenomenon was during my internship too many years ago. We were caring for a man with throat cancer. He'd undergone radical surgery. His tongue, voice box, and half his jaw had been removed. He breathed through an opening in his neck. Still, the tumor had returned. It ate a huge open hole in the side of his neck. He was given radiation treatments. That worked for a while, but then the tumor returned and continued to enlarge. The hospital Tumor Board carefully considered his case and determined that nothing more should be done. And so there he lay in the hospital with a huge obscene open sore on the left side of his neck. One evening, when I was on call, I got a STAT page to his room. He was hemorrhaging. Massively. The tumor had eroded into his carotid artery. What to do? Knowing this man's history, I simply wedged a pillow and several sheets against his neck and sat there, holding his hand, while he bled to death. Yes, it was messy. No, he didn't suffer.

But later, the attending surgeon took this young intern aside and quietly suggested that he'd made a poor decision.

"What should I have done?" I asked.

"You could have put a clamp on his carotid artery and called me."

"Then what?"

"I'd have come in, and we'd have taken him to surgery."

"But the Tumor Board had already determined that he wasn't a surgical candidate," I protested.

"Yes, but now he was bleeding. The situation was different" was his reply

"What would you have done in surgery?" was my next question.

"Some kind of a bypass graft."

"Would that have cured him?"

"No."

"Wouldn't he have had a stroke and been paralyzed from the clamp I was supposed to have placed on his carotid artery?"

"Very probably."

"And so we'd then have had a man with an inoperable, recurrent cancer and now paralyzed on one side of his body to boot?"

"Well, it would be unfortunate" was his response.

Suffice it to say that we never did agree on how I should have responded to this emergency one evening long ago in Pennsylvania. It was almost like discussing religion. Each saw the other's point of view, and neither could agree which was correct. I remained convinced I had done the humane thing, and the attending surgeon was convinced I'd erred. But it was me who was on the firing line late at night, who had to make a decision on the spot, open to later criticism, while he, the attending surgeon, was comfortably home in bed.

Back to the present. Back to Mary. It was the same story all over again but now with a different outcome. My fellow surgeon ultimately deferred to the family's wishes and ordered the transfusions. She was brought back to consciousness, back to this world.

What do you tell such a patient? I wondered.

"Hi! You're still here! We brought you back so you could die a *second* time!"

CHAPTER 19

A Hangman's Fracture in Alaska

Back to Alaska again, this time to answer a call from its capital, Juneau. It was a long and tiresome trip, made longer by a loud bunch of Californians on the final Seattle to Juneau flight. They were coming to Juneau to drink and fish and, not being able to fish on the airplane, decided to get a head start on the other half of their agenda.

Juneau is savagely beautiful. It is nestled on a narrow strip of land between the Gastineau Channel and a three-thousand-or-so foot mountain. Ordinarily, you might even be tempted to use the word "cliff" when describing that mountain. Here, however, it is clothed in pine trees and other greenery, occasionally interrupted by a rock slide that reveals the true nature of the mountain. A long stream flows two thousand vertical feet down the rock slide. It would be a beautiful waterfall if the rock face was just a little steeper.

The air is full of sea planes busily attending to their business. It is like a roadway some five hundred feet or so in the sky. Traffic keeps to the right (as on land), and the arriving Alaska Air 737s, like aerial buses, use the middle of the channel, the little fellas staying carefully out of the way. If the pilot of one of the float planes wants to cross the channel, he looks left and right, then scoots across, not unlike a pedestrian crossing a highway.

At ordinary airports such as we have in Gainesville, Florida, the ILS (Instrument Landing System) aligns you with the end of the runway. Fly the numbers on the instrument panel, and you are guaranteed perfect safety as you break out of the clouds only 250 feet above the ground with the runway right in front of you. Here, that will not work. The runway is on a spit of land aligned at an acute angle with the channel and pointing in the general direction of nearby mountains. There is no way the ILS can be flown to the end of the runway unless you have developed a way to fly through solid rock. So they have imaginatively aligned the instrument approach path with the Gastineau Channel. Fly the numbers well at Juneau, and you will not see a runway ahead of you when you break out of the clouds. Instead you will be in the middle of a mile-wide channel with mountains on both sides of you, rising up and disappearing into the clouds above you.

Here, you damn well better have flown the numbers flawlessly. Follow the channel two miles north, miss the float planes, make a skidding left turn at three hundred feet altitude, and there at last is the runway. Being a curious instrument-rated pilot, I had once perused the approach procedure. Now, as a passenger, I *followed* the approach. It works, but it is uniquely Alaska.

(Update from 2021: The above approach description was written more than twenty years ago before GPS approaches were widespread. Perhaps there are different, less "interesting" approaches in use today.)

Why can't I get a surgery assignment like this for more than a week? Here, the mountains are magnificent. Betty and I were put up in a first-class B&B, complete with living room, dining room, kitchen, and bedroom.

Sights and Sounds of Juneau

The start of my first full day in Juneau was characterized by my failure to convince my body that it was not time to get up. The clock said it was 3 a.m. My body said it was 7 a.m. and definitely time to get up. After brewing a pot of coffee, I sat down at "Ye Olde Computer" and watched a gloomy morning dawn. A few mouse clicks, and I was in touch with my friends around the country. A few more, and I was reading the *London Times*! How different from my first trip to Alaska eleven years ago!

The living room picture window of our superb living accommodations faced the Gastineau Channel. The mountains that line this channel have their heads in the clouds all day long. Just under the cloud layer is the continual air traffic, mostly float planes and helicopters, but with an occasional arriving Alaska Air 737 breaking through the overcast, right in the middle of the channel, then proceeding north toward the airport. The airliners arrive with wheels hanging out and all lights on, no doubt with their pilots diligently looking for any fools in the middle of the channel. But the local traffic stays either to the sides of the channel or very low. One can recognize the tourist helicopters by their peculiar flight manner; they fly sideways so that the tourists in the back have a good view of the scenery!

Juneau is the only continental state capital that you cannot drive to. Access is either by air or sea. With a population of 35,000 or so, it is Alaska's third largest city (after Anchorage and Fairbanks). Though there are the usual government office buildings, the main downtown section is devoted to the fine art of separating tourists from their dollars.

The small hospital where I was working was caring for an amazing number of seriously ill patients. I made rounds with the local surgeon before his departure and was now responsible for five patients, two of whom were recovering from burst colons. One was an eighty-four-year-old man desperately ill and on the ventilator. He was definitely university material, but one must remember that transfers to larger hospitals are difficult. Anchorage is 570 miles north, while Seattle is nearly 890 miles south. A transfer would be like sending a patient from Gainesville, Florida, to Chicago. And so Alaskan physicians have to be incredibly well rounded and resourceful. They routinely care for conditions that similar physicians in the Lower 48 would refer to specialists in larger hospitals. I once thought that the general population would be more understanding when things go awry as compared to those in the Lower 48. Not so! The malpractice rate here is higher than most places in the States, and so I carry with me thirty-some-odd medical textbooks (on CD-ROMs that my laptop computer can read) and found myself referring to them constantly. It was a challenging week.

Dodging a Bullet

There are surgeons who enjoy the challenge of trauma, with its rush of excitement. And judging from the ever-popular ER shows on TV, one would think it is all grand and glorious. I know otherwise. The problem is that the patients never have the courtesy to come in with a clear list of problems and injuries that are hidden deep inside. The penalty for guessing wrong, being careless, being rushed, or neglecting a symptom can be disastrous.

Today was a blissful day in which all my patients had been seen by noon. Betty and I then walked happily hand in hand along the piers. There were three huge cruise ships at the docks, not even looking like ships as much as skyscrapers lying on their sides, two of them looking shapely—one an ugly box, obviously designed to hold the maximum number of tourists. They travel by night; during the day, they are tied up at their various stopping points: Ketchikan, Sitka, Skagway, Juneau. The ritual is always the same. The tourists rush ashore and make a frontal assault on the souvenir shops. (The shops always won.) The locals disdainfully separate tourists into two categories: the newlyweds and the nearly deads. Here, you could buy three six-ounce cans of smoked salmon for a "mere" $54.95 (but this included FedEx shipping to anywhere in the US!). In another store, I saw watches for sale—a bargain at $3,600 each.

The sun was shining for a change. Juneau enjoys roughly 219 rainy days a year. After picking up a fistful of brochures from a travel agent, we wandered back to the bed and breakfast to plan how we would spend our planned three "play days" at the end of my assignment.

This idyllic scene was shattered by the beeper at 4 p.m. The ER nurse told me there had been a motor vehicle accident—three critical victims, one bleeding "from every orifice."

"I'll be right in."

It seemed that three teenagers were driving on the one good paved road about twenty miles north of town. The driver, the only one using the seatbelt, was horrified to see an oncoming car veer into his lane. Was that oncoming driver distracted by something? The teenager swerved violently to miss the car, lost control, and rolled his car several times. The two unbelted passengers were ejected. One was lying motionless in the middle of the road, the other in the ditch.

The first to arrive in our ER was the road victim, an eighteen-year-old boy who was unconscious. His vital signs were stable. My physical exam, coupled with CT scans, disclosed that he was suffering from a severe head injury. This hospital was not equipped to care for such an injury, so he would need to be air evacuated out. And no, he was not bleeding "from every orifice."

The second victim was a seventeen-year-old somewhat hysterical girl who had been ejected into the ditch. She had multiple complaints, was slightly abusive, and loudly demanded that the protective cervical collar tightly wrapped around her neck be removed. It hurt her. The cervical collar had been placed by the EMTs at the scene of the accident to stabilize her neck in case it was fractured. We, of course, refused to remove it until the precautionary X-rays were done. She had lacerations on her forehead, elbow, leg, but no broken bones. Other than that, her examination was entirely normal. She could move all extremities, could feel me touching her, had a soft and nontender abdomen, and clear lungs.

The cervical spine X-rays were read as normal by the radiologist, who was still in the hospital but intending to head home at any minute. "It's cleared," said his handwritten message, meaning that it was safe to remove the neck collar.

It is often the practice to simply have the nurse remove it. This is not the best practice in the world but is done often enough around the country. Normally, I choose to remove it myself. The first thing I did was gently touch each bone on the back of her neck. She cried in pain. Was she just an immature wimp? Then as I moved my fingers higher, I felt a soft squishy spot where I could indent the back of her neck. It hurt her. I couldn't say that I had ever felt such a sensation there.

Hmm... Maybe it's nothing. Maybe it's normal to feel a little soft there. I touched the back of my own neck. *Maybe. Maybe not.*

Was this all nothing more than a whiplash? Remember, I had a set of "negative" X-rays on the wall. The radiologist himself even said so. And my neurological examination was normal as well. She had normal sensation, movement, deep tendon reflexes, etc. It should be safe to remove that neck collar, eh? Well, for a reason that I was still not too sure of, I put the collar back on Ashley, over her loud and pro-fane protests. She said the collar was what was making her neck hurt.

"Let's get a CT scan."

"Okay," said the nurse.

The radiologist, however, opined it was not necessary. I asked him to just humor an old man. "Suit yourself."

Later, in the CT control room...

The radiologist exclaimed, "Well, I'll be damned!"

Even I could see the broken bones—several of 'em. The pattern was that of the classic hangman's fracture, the same injury executed criminals suffer. It is caused by a violent snap of the head. And while I don't know what Christopher Reeve's injury was, I suspect the same sort of pattern.

I went back to the ER and asked Ashley to move her arms and legs. She could still do it. I pinched her toes, and that made her mad, but I had demonstrated her sensory nerves were intact. I then taped her head to the bed board, put sandbags on either side of her neck collar, and I called Harbor View Trauma Center in Seattle. Tonight Ashley will have her own private jet ride 893 miles south to the near-est neurosurgeon.

I felt like I was the luckiest person in Juneau. Had I succumbed to the temptation to just take the collar off a wimpy teenager with a whiplash and "normal" X-rays, she might well have wound up spend-ing the rest of her life in a wheelchair—or worse. I had no idea what made me request the "unnecessary" CT scan or stick to my guns over the objections of the radiologist.

Oh, by the way, Ashley's response to all this?

"Take this g*d**nd f**ing thing off my neck, it's hurting me."

"No, dear. Your neck is broken."

"You're lying to me."

This story has a happy ending. She made it to Seattle without becoming paralyzed. She had the requisite surgery, and after recovery, she was able to walk normally. And perhaps most unusual of all, I actually received a thank-you note from Ashley in the mail.

CHAPTER 20

Adventures in Wisconsin

Caleb Yoder (Choosing Your Surgeon)

The ER called me in one May afternoon when I was covering for a hospital in a small town in central Wisconsin. They were seeing an Amishman's son with possible appendicitis. Our fifth-wheel RV was parked in the slot normally used when the mobile CT scanner was not in town. It was but a short stroll over to the ER, where I examined a freshly scrubbed fourteen-year-old boy. My examination confirmed the ER physician's impression, and so I told the anxious parents that their son needed surgery. As is widely known, the Amish don't have insurance. But they always pay their bills. So they had twin anxieties—the welfare of their son and the hospital bill.

Unfortunately, I used the word "probably" when I described Caleb's illness, as in "It's probably appendicitis..." They picked up on that real fast. I could see their mixed anxiety for Caleb, for the upcoming hospital bill, and now here was a stranger to the community, a wandering, vagabond surgeon who only "thought" it was appendicitis. They wanted a surgeon who *knew* what he was doing, who was positive that it was appendicitis for sure, for sure.

Ultimately, they agreed to surgery. I found that my diagnosis was correct and was able to remove his appendix through a miniature incision using the special instruments and headlight that I carry in the RV. No, this small hospital did not have any laparoscopic instruments. Many surgeons routinely used four- or five-inch incisions for an appendectomy. Since my incision was just over an inch long, Caleb was able to go home the very next day. Everybody was happy.

But it wasn't any fast talking on my part that convinced the anxious parents that the surgery on their son was what they should agree to. Nor was it the fact that this local hospital had "credentialed" me. No, what convinced the Amish family to let me operate on Caleb was the fact that during our conversations in the ER, they learned that I'd just served on a *locum* assignment in south central Iowa. Mr. Yoder had once lived there. In fact, Caleb's brother had had appendicitis, and it was removed in that very hospital I had recently served. Since that hospital had hired me, ergo I must be a good surgeon. Not only is it a small world, but people chose their doctor or reach conclusions on his capability based on the most amazing, coincidental, and sometimes extraneous information.

Warm and Dead

I was invited back to this same Wisconsin hospital for a second, longer (three-week) assignment, this time in the dead of winter. One day, I happened to be in the hospital, making rounds, when a nurse from the ER asked me to be sure that I'd stay nearby. The ambulance was bringing in a man who had been cutting down a tree, only to have the tree fall upon him. I was told that CPR was in progress in the ambulance. So I went down to the ER and saw to it that all was in readiness. Chest tubes were laid out in case his chest was crushed. IVs were hung and ready to go. The portable X-ray machine was standing close by. Soon, the ambulance roared up with its siren screaming and lights flashing. It was sucked *into* the hospital. (You know you are in the frozen north country when the ambulances pull *into* the hospital and a door closes behind them because it is too cold to unload patients outside.) Yes, indeed, there was a young blue man on the litter, and yes, they were pumping up and down on his chest.

I followed them into the ER, asking one of the ambulance attendants, "Just where did the tree land on him?"

She gave me a puzzled look and said he was just found out in the woods, lying *beside* a tree.

So, far from being a trauma case, it turned out to be a heart attack case, and he was only thirty-six. But then his daddy had died at a young age of a heart attack, as had a brother. We hooked up the cardiac monitor and looked for a heart rhythm. There was none. His heart was stone—cold, dead, stopped. We gave him epinephrine and atropine. Nothing. We intubated him, gave him oxygen, and continued to pump up and down on his chest. Nothing. In between all this, I asked the ambulance attendants when this had all happened. Well, his collapse in the woods had not been witnessed. So nobody knew how long he'd been lying out there.

Hmm...

"What's his temperature, anyhow?" I asked.

The nurse took it, and it was 96°. That meant he might have been lying out there a fairly long time. Somebody suggested that we could call it quits. However, there is an old adage in the ER business: "A man isn't dead until he is warm and dead." That is, you don't give up on CPR until the victim is fully warmed up because hypothermia can look just like death.

A few years ago, an ER doctor in New York State had stopped CPR before the patient was fully warmed up, and the ER nurse reported him, not to the Board of Medical Examiners, but to the District attorney. He was investigated for possible murder! Such is medicine in different parts of the country.

So I said, "We'd better warm him up," to which everybody agreed. Now I hadn't had a lot of experience in this matter, only what I'd read. I do most of my work in the operating room, not the emergency room. I was eager to learn. Everybody must be used to doing this here in Wisconsin, eh? Somebody was sent up to the OR and got the Bair Hugger, a device that blows warm air on a person in the recovery room who might be shivering after surgery, and we hooked that up. Ten minutes later, I asked what his temperature was. 95°

Hmm... Progress the wrong way.

But there are other tricks I'd read about. If the person is real cold (temp less than 83°), you are supposed to run in warm IV fluids to speed the warming process.

Let's see how that works.

We sent for two bags of warm IV fluids and ran that into his veins. His temp rose to 94°. We put a nasogastric tube down into his stomach and pumped warm water into him. His temp came up to 93°. We put warm water in his bladder via a Foley catheter. His temp increased to 92°. I was down the hall when another doctor gave permission for them to stop the CPR, to everybody's immense relief. I had no idea how hard it is to warm up a cold, dead body.

The next day, we received the coroner's report of the autopsy. Yup, it was indeed a massive heart attack, and he was dead before the ambulance picked him up. But I continue to marvel at how hard it is to warm up a cold, dead body.

A Man Named Florence

I had no sooner gotten the fifth-wheel safely parked behind the hospital in this little Wisconsin town not too far from Madison when I was beeped to the med/surg floor. There I found not one but two surgical consults. The first was for a man who'd fallen and broken several ribs. All he needed was a chest tube, and then he did well during my remaining time on this assignment.

The other consult was for an eighty-year-old man named Florence. He had been transferred from a nursing home the night before. There was very little information available except that he had abdominal pain of four days' duration. His X-ray films were suggestive of a bowel obstruction. Upon seeing him, however, I became discouraged, for he proved to be a very elderly man with a history of several strokes in the past, lying there in bed, unable to speak, his mouth a great big O. Even if I made the correct diagnosis, intervened, and corrected whatever was going on inside his abdomen, what would we have at the end? A frail old man lying in bed, unable to speak.

Enough of this gloomy thinking. I cannot be judgmental.

An examination of his abdomen yielded conflicting information. Yes, it was soft, but it was also quiet. Abdomens with bowel obstructions are often noisy, sometimes even with diagnostic sounds. When I pressed on his abdomen, old Florence screwed up his face in obvious pain. But as to how bad it hurt, when it started, or how it had progressed, well, for that, I had no information at all. The general public does not realize how much we physicians depend on the history of an illness related to us by the patient to tell us what is going on. More often than not, we make our diagnoses based on the history and not X-rays or lab tests.

So what should I do? Watch a bit more to see how his symptoms progress?

At this point, all I had was just a single picture, one snapshot in time. Or maybe I should take him to the OR... But what were the risks in operating on a very sick old man? What if he died? I was a stranger in a strange hospital, and I sensed the usual distrust that greets me when I step in to fill the shoes of a beloved town doctor.

Florence's family was clearly suspicious of a bearded, itinerant surgeon. Where did he come from? And above all else, *why* does he travel? What is he running from? A troubled past? Substance abuse?

The long and short of it was that I did take Florence to the OR and found both a ruptured appendix and a bowel obstruction. It appeared that his appendix had burst a number of days previously, but there was surprisingly little peritonitis.[1] His bowels had efficiently walled the burst appendix off and, in the process, suffered an obstruction. The appendix was removed, the area drained, and the bowel obstruction relieved.

And now came the amazing part.

On my routine rounds two days later, when I walked into his room, Florence was sitting up in a chair. He eagerly motioned me over, and he spoke to me in a nearly normal voice, thanking me profusely! What a transformation! What we had here was an old man with such poor cerebral circulation that even a little toxicity drove

---

[1]   Infection spread through the abdominal cavity.

him over the edge into aphasia.[2] My initial impression was woefully wrong. He was not a hopeless stroke victim, one for whom one could question the wisdom of even thinking of surgery. True, he couldn't trip the light fantastic, but his family had their dad back again…

Marley Benson (Contemplating the Senseless)

I never knew Marley either as a human or a patient. I only saw his twenty-five-year-old body, freshly dead, in the ER late one Friday afternoon. It was a stupid farm accident that killed Marley.

I happened to be entering the hospital via the ER when the charge nurse said to me, "Oh, don't go away, Dr. Roode. There has been an accident nearby. We are expecting the ambulance in ten or fifteen minutes."

"What's up?" I asked.

"All we know is that a man is pinned between a Bobcat [a front-end loader] and a concrete wall. There has been a lot of bleeding."

"Call me."

And I went upstairs to see another patient. I was, however, back in the ER well before the ambulance brought in our young victim. He was essentially DOA. The ambulance crew had wrapped his head with bandages. Pulling them aside, I saw that most of the left side of his brain was visible, mixed with grass bits and dirt. A large portion of his skull, including his left eye, was simply missing, no doubt lying out there somewhere in the barnyard. The rest of young Marley was perfectly intact. Whatever it was that hit him nearly missed. Had his head been a mere three or four inches to the right, it would have been one of those "close calls" that leave your heart pounding but which you forget about in a few days. I was sure he lost consciousness immediately, though it took his heart another twenty minutes or so to die.

---

[2] The inability to speak.

Once I realized the hopelessness of this unfortunate situation, I simply turned and walked out of the ER. Could it be (I later thought) that I had peered into the most sacred space of another human being (his brain) with virtually no emotion? Had I seen too much death over the years? Was I becoming callous? What a contrast to the emotions that must have engulfed his wife (if he had one)! Later, I learned further details of this horrible accident. Not only did Marley have a wife, but she, as well as his three-year-old daughter, had witnessed this gruesome accident. He had apparently stuck his head outside the Bobcat he was operating, no doubt to get a better view of where the front-end loader scoop was, when it unexpectedly lowered onto his head. Desperately, his wife tried to operate the unfamiliar controls to raise the scoop. I could imagine her crying, screaming, praying, all to no avail.

This afternoon's tragedy is one that only a few of us have to endure as our daily fare. The average inhabitant of this planet encounters these senselessness events perhaps only a few times then beats a hasty retreat to his/her minister for an explanation. But it cannot be explained, not by your minister, not by anybody. It's too unreal. It's too horrible. A common initial reaction is that it did not really happen.

Perhaps when they told Marley's mother, her reaction might have been "Oh no! That cannot be! No! Tell me it's not true. It must be a sick joke."

And even if Marley were back here, his reaction would have been the same. "No! It didn't. That can't have happened to me! The morning was so sunny and bright. The sky was so blue. Surely this must not have happened."

But the still-warm corpse on the litter, behind the drawn curtains in the ER, silently said that it really did. Not only had it happened, but it was both senseless and beyond comprehension.

Many try to take comfort in the fantasy that it didn't really happen. Even though we have the evidence of our eyes and fingers, we deny that it happened: "He's not really dead. He is somewhere else." But when the skeptic asks where, the answers are vague. Isn't this, then, the origin of religion? Senseless accidents, death, pointless suffering have been with us since Neanderthal times. I dunno.

Early in my training, I helped care for a nine-year-old girl who suffered almost the same injury in a car accident. A happy laughing little girl had her head hanging out the window when her mother allowed the car to get too close to another car traveling in the opposite lane. In an instant, half her head, like Marley's, was horribly torn open, parts of it falling on the street. Still, her heart continued to beat. So an IV was started in a small local hospital, and she was transferred to us. It was hopeless, of course. Back then, I was unable to simply turn and walk away with seeming indifference. Then my emotion was pure anger that such a horrible accident could happen to such a pretty girl.

But life goes on, and the same senseless accidents happen over and over again. When I was younger, I wasted much time pondering the why of such events. My good friend, the Rev. Dr. Battles, once commented to me "I dunno either" before observing that even Jesus is reported to have turned aside "why" questions with but one word—no—before abruptly changing the subject.[3]

Perhaps a reasonable conclusion is that tragedies such as these simply have no meaning. They result from nothing more than the misfortune of a person simply being in the wrong place at the wrong time—the "time and chance which happens to us all" mentioned by that ancient seer Qoheleth nearly 2,500 years ago. At least, such a philosophy serves to protect those of us who regularly deal with these tragedies by psychologically distancing us from their horror.

---

[3] Luke 13.

CHAPTER 21

La Crosse, Wisconsin

Having worked for the Mayo Health System in several of their upper Midwest locations, it was natural that when a need arose at their affiliated Franciscan-Skemp Clinic in La Crosse, I received a call asking me to provide coverage for a shortfall occasioned by an illness. The associated hospital of about 250 beds was accustomed to handling major cases. Betty and I both fell in love with La Crosse—the clinic, the hospital, and the people.

Wally Dixon (A Swing and a Miss)

As per usual, the "new kid on the block" was welcomed both warmly and with a degree of curiosity that sometimes bordered on faint suspicion. They were glad for the help, but could this guy really "cut the mustard"? My first two major cases (a hernia and a bowel resection) went well. Then I met Wally. Could it be that the Great Surgeon in the Sky was amusing himself at my expense again? "Let's see how Roode handles *this* one. Heh, heh, heh…"

Wally, a twenty-three-year-old laborer, had presented to the walk-in clinic the day before, complaining of nausea, vomiting, and vague stomach pains. The exam was unremarkable and that, coupled with a normal blood count, was enough for him to be sent home. The diagnosis? Flu.

The pain persisted, and so the next morning, he returned, this time the ER. The pain was now in the right lower quadrant of his abdomen, right over his appendix. His white count was elevated at 13,800. Thus, everybody agreed that the new diagnosis was (for sure, for sure) appendicitis. Since I was on call, he was referred to me. After examining him, I agreed with the diagnosis and called the OR to schedule him for an appendectomy. Thinking that I'd show them how I could get an appendix out of a mere one-inch incision, I made my incision over the most tender spot, which is usually just over the appendix. That should make it easy to fish the offending organ out despite the small incision.

Alas! There was no appendix there. I was puzzled and embarrassed. Feeling around through that small incision, I could not feel anything firm that would be indicative of inflammation. Dang! Where was that pesky appendix? Eventually, I found it a good two inches below my incision, and with much fumbling around, I managed to fish it out. There was a polite silence among the OR crew when they saw an obviously normal appendix. What to do? Since I had no other diagnosis, I removed it and closed my little incision. My hope was that it was just a very early appendicitis and that the pathologist would find at least a few signs of inflammation on microscopic examination.

Alas, it was not to be. When Wally woke up, he was no better. He still had his abdominal pain.

Grrrr! What have I missed?

The next morning, it was brought home clearly to me that I must have missed something, for his white cell blood count was still elevated. Later that day, a completely normal pathology report on the appendix was placed in his chart.

What is going on?

I needed a more complete workup. Because of his youth and lack of any chest symptoms, I had omitted a routine chest X-ray from his initial work-up. Omission of "unnecessary tests and X-rays" was all the rage in those days. Now, searching for disease and despite his lack of cough, fever, or other signs of pneumonia, I ordered a chest X-ray. Very rarely pneumonia can present as lower abdominal pain, and nobody knows why. I had never seen such a case, only read about it. But the X-ray showed the telltale basilar infiltrates.[1] And so

---

[1]   X-ray sign of pneumonia.

I put him on antibiotics, and he recovered. Nobody was upset with me (except me), but even if I'd gotten a chest X-ray, I wondered if I would have had the guts to not operate in such a classic case of appendicitis because of an abnormal chest X-ray.

Herbalist with Breast Cancer

To her horror, Ms. Patel felt a lump in her breast about two weeks before I appeared on the scene in La Crosse. She called for an appointment with a surgeon, and because my schedule had oodles of free spaces in it, she wound up in one of my examining rooms.

I found her to be a very nice and very frightened sixty-one-year-old herbalist. This lady placed a great deal of faith in home remedies, in the use of "natural" and "organic" products, and in the herbs she grew herself. For her, hospitals were a last resort. But a lump in your breast is a frightening prospect, so she immediately applied a poultice to her breast and then made an appointment to be seen in the clinic.

My examination confirmed her worst fears. The lump, whatever it was, had attached itself to Cooper's ligaments, which then revealed its presence by dimpling the skin. Breast cancers often do that. When they do, you can diagnose them by sight alone. Of course, we always confirm our impression with a biopsy. So I knew her diagnosis from the moment I saw her breast, and as a result, I could not really be very reassuring.

At this early stage of our relationship, I found myself saying, "Yes, we have a problem that we will have to work through together." I gave her no hokey assurances that the lump was inconsequential.

In the course of our initial interaction, she told me she'd taken the leaves of African violets, crushed them, and applied them to her breast. She also had made Essiac tea out of slippery elm, burdock, and yellow dock. She was a walking encyclopedia of various natural and herbal remedies, all of which she recited at the least provocation. (Well, remember that aspirin and digoxin both initially came from plants.)

Let modern medicine discover something new, like T-cells in AIDS, and alternative medicine immediately discovers an herbal remedy that "boosts T-cells."

Incidentally, her husband thought the matter of the violet poultices was all wrong. He was convinced she should have used oil of mustard! The dilemma this woman and her husband faced was not that unusual, but it illustrates the unfairness that can result when the government sticks its grubby fingers into modern medicine. And so the tale is worth the telling. Bear with me.

It turned out that Ms. Patel was of the Baha'i faith. She'd traveled to and even lived in India for several years, being a teacher in one of the Baha'i schools there. It was there that she met and married Surendra, another schoolteacher. They were both back in the States now; he was unemployed, she was working as a coffee attendant in a local convenience store. They were good people, had devoted themselves to others, had no insurance, and shared the same fears and medical needs as the rest of us. They had never earned much money, but they had been frugal and set aside a little money against their eventual retirement. They feared this modest retirement would now be taken from them.

Modern medicine in this country is very expensive. But it is worse than that. When a hospital cares for an elderly patient, the bill is sent to Medicare. However, Medicare makes its own assessment of how much any given service is worth. Even then it doesn't pay the reduced amount that it thinks is reasonable. Medicare pays 80 percent of it. The patient is responsible for the other 20 percent of the reduced payment. No doubt Washington politicians pat themselves on their backs and think smug thoughts of how frugal they are with taxpayer money.

But this leaves the hospital with a huge shortfall. Their submitted charges have been sharply reduced. What are they to do? How do they make up their lost charges? They have no choice but to charge private paying patients more than the usual costs for their services. So what the government has really done is sneakily pass a hidden tax upon all Americans who are not on Medicare.

Back to our patient. Because she had neither Medicare nor other health insurance, they would have to pay for her care out of their pocket and at the inflated rate to boot. They worried about what that hideous lump in her breast was, worried about how they would pay for her care, and worried about the loss of their meager retirement savings. Were they eligible for Medicaid? Who knew? An application would require them to reveal all their assets, and they were afraid to do that.

On with my story. I biopsied her breast mass, and to nobody's surprise, it proved to be a cancer. To save money, I did it as an outpatient. But I did more than a mere biopsy. I also added a wide excision (lumpectomy) and a simultaneous sampling of her armpit lymph nodes. I did all this as an outpatient to save them hospital charges.

She needed chemotherapy. She needed radiation. I had no idea whether she would agree to this, now that the lump was gone. She had agreed to at least talk to the specialists. She undoubtedly continued with her violet compresses. She couldn't help but be suspicious of a medical care system that was both outrageously expensive and made her pay more than her fair share.

"How do I know they aren't recommending radiation just to pay off their fancy machine?" she asked me.

Oh, one last little tidbit. In the medical field, we have lots of jargon. With respect to breast cancers, there are a variety of types, but the most common one is the infiltrating ductal type, which pathologists nickname the "garden variety" breast cancer. I manfully refrained from telling Ms. Patel, the herbalist, that she had a "garden variety" breast cancer.

The Hmong People ("Who-uda Thunk?")

Who would have thought that a thirty-five-year-old SE Asian conflict (read: Vietnam War) would reach forward through time and across half the globe to touch me personally in Wisconsin?

My involvement with the Hmong people began late on a Saturday night when my beeper went off. It was the family practice resident in the ER informing me that she was admitting one Panhia Khaab, sixty-eight years old, to the medical service, with a "hot" gallbladder. She asked me to see her patient.

"Sure, no problem," I replied.

"But I must warn you," she continued, "Panhia is one of the Hmong people."

"Huh?"

Knowing that I was a stranger in La Crosse, she explained, "They are Laotian. You see, they sided with the Americans, and when South Vietnam fell to the north, they were viciously persecuted."

"Oh."

"So our government relocated thousands of them to our country, many of them to La Crosse."

"I see. Why La Crosse, Wisconsin?"

"I don't know. Somebody in the government must have just made a decision." She continued, "I have spent the past forty minutes convincing her family that she needs to be in the hospital. You will likely have problems convincing them that she needs surgery. But at least I have laid down the groundwork."

"Well, er...thanks."

She added, "They still believe in spiritual healing..."

Odd, I thought, *coming from an employee of this very Catholic hospital. Where have I last seen black-garbed men and women publicly offering up prayers to the Deity, beseeching Him to set aside His own natural laws, to intervene and miraculously cure this or that patient?*

Well, at least I now understood why there were so many Asian food stores in La Crosse.

A short while later, I introduced myself to Panhia and a large assembly of her relatives. No, she didn't speak English, but a daughter who did was present. I had reviewed the chart, the lab results, the X-rays. Yes, Panhia would need surgery and soon. Her gallbladder was badly infected; indeed, it was a life-threatening situation. And so I proposed the only logical solution—I should operate and remove her gallbladder. Being prepared by the resident, I was not surprised at their initial refusal. Indeed, the chart revealed that, a full two years previously when her gallstones had been first diagnosed, surgery was recommended. They had refused. Back then, the gallstones were merely annoying. Now, with her gallbladder full of pus, the situation was life threatening. Nevertheless, they still wanted to avoid surgery.

As I talked to them via the only one who spoke English, it gradually dawned on me that it was not the surgery that they were opposed to but the anesthesia! Indeed, they wanted me to remove their mom's gallbladder with a local anesthetic. Now why was that? It seemed that the Hmong People, observing that general anesthesia induces a state that is seemingly close to death (you feel no pain, you are unconscious, you are unable to breathe or move, etc.), have concluded that the human soul can leave the body when a patient is anesthetized just like it does at a person's death. Who is to guarantee that her soul will find its way back to the recovery room and re-inhabit her body when she is waking up?

Well, er… I dunno.

How would you, gentle reader, give these people the assurance that general anesthesia, which is routinely given thousands of times a day all over this country, always returns to us the same person they were before?

The upshot of all this was that, faced with the grim alternative, they finally agreed to surgery. But not before they could hold their own shaman religious ceremony in her hospital room. Colored yarn was wrapped around her wrist and those of her family members to keep them "united" during the stressful period when she was asleep and her soul was (presumably) wandering around in downtown La Crosse. Then they brought a chicken's egg into the hospital and took it through the floors and up to the operating rooms, transferring various evil spirits into the egg.

"Dr. Roode, what are you allowing them to do?" exclaimed a somewhat amused OR staff.

"Trust me, I'm trying to save the life of a Hmong refugee."

(I could only presume that they later disposed of that egg in an environmentally proper manner—too bad for the evil spirits that were trapped inside.)

And so, on Sunday afternoon, I took Panhia to the OR and removed a very badly infected gallbladder. I had done this oh so many times before; it was familiar territory to me. The results were predictable. She would get better.

Pre-operatively, they had insisted that afterward I should bring the surgical specimen, the gallbladder, to the waiting room. And so I did. To my astonishment, they grabbed the specimen, in its container, out of my hand. They wanted to take it home. They explained that they must have it so it could be buried with her someday. Burial of incomplete bodies was not proper, they said.

"But you can't take it," I protested. "These things must be examined by the Pathology Department—state law, you know." Then an inspiration came to me. "Would a picture of her gallbladder serve as an adequate surrogate so that she will be 'complete' when buried?" After conferring among themselves, they made an exception no doubt to humor me. I also threw in the gallstones, which we were allowed to give to patients.

What a huge gulf that exists between our cultures!

On Monday evening, Panhia was doing just fine, just as our modern, orthodox, scientific, medicine predicted she would. I couldn't restrain a "See? I told you so" remark to her visitors. They were unimpressed, attributing her recovery to the colored yarn and egg.

Each culture sincerely (indeed fiercely) believes in its own heritage. The Hmong People must look disbelievingly at this Catholic hospital—with its little figurines in every room, each neatly pinned to crossed wooden sticks. Our "shamans" wear black clothes with the reversed collars, carried the little vials of water and black books and muttered incantations to unseen spirits. To the Hmong, we must be lost souls, and we look upon them the same way.

What to make of all this? When I related this tale to Betty, she had perhaps the best answer of all: "Everybody needs a shaman from time to time," she said. "Next time you are called in to take care of one of the Hmong people, bring a little colored yarn and an egg with you."

Roger Winston

And now, in the for-what-it's-worth department, it seems that the fates were not through pitching me curve balls. Do they snicker when I swing and miss?

Roger, a twenty-year-old college student, who was out "boozing" the night before, came into the ER with abdominal pain of about four hours' duration. His white count was normal. He didn't look all that sick. The ER doctor thought it could be appendicitis, but I was dubious. It didn't sound like appendicitis to me. Although the literature says that fully 10 percent of appendicitis patients have a normal blood count, every time I have operated on a person with a "for sure, for sure" appendicitis by physical exam and history and who had a normal blood count, the appendix turned out to be normal.

ER doctors' diagnoses are cheap. It isn't their name that goes on the chart. They don't decide whom to take to the OR and then lamely explain to everybody why they were mistaken and the appendix was normal. They are only interested in moving patients. Get 'em in, get 'em diagnosed, and get 'em out. If they call it appendicitis, then it falls into my court. And they are off to their next patient.

I'd already taken out one normal appendix during my short stay here in La Crosse. No, I was not going to operate on a dubious case. Instead I admitted him and examined him several times during the day.

His white count remained normal. I ordered an ultrasound examination of his abdomen. It was entirely normal, including appendix and gallbladder. Still he hurt in the right lower quadrant of his abdomen, right over his appendix. The pain refused to go away.

Finally, a full day later, I decided to look inside with the laparoscope, the then new-fangled instrument that we now routinely used to remove gallbladders. Sure enough, he had appendicitis that mocked all of modern scientific medicine. After the appendectomy, his pain went away, and we are all living happily ever after.

Herbalist with Breast Cancer (A Follow-Up)

Well, as luck would have it, Ms. Patel's pathology came report came back with mixed news. Yes, I did get all the cancer out, and no, it had not spread to her lymph nodes. But there was a second condition present in her breast, DCIS,[2] and I had not removed all of it. You can't see, feel, or detect DCIS except under the microscope. But it went right to the edge of the large specimen I had removed. Undoubtedly, it was widespread in her breast. The safest treatment now was a mastectomy. I presented this recommendation to her, and she went home to think. She then came back with a most startling request, one that took me completely off guard. She agreed to the surgery but asked me to remove her other breast at the same time!

"But there is nothing wrong with your right breast!" I protested.

"How do you know?" was her response, though she phrased it in suitably herbalist terms. She had observed the same weeds growing in various places in her herb garden. Plus, there was the added expense she would have to face if one day in the future, she would need surgery on the other breast if it developed cancer. She'd concluded that it would be far cheaper to take care of a potential future problem right now and be done with it.

Well, she had a point. I had done prophylactic mastectomies twice in the past. Once it worked, and once the person died of cancer despite the prophylaxis. Of all things, a new cancer had developed in a microscopic remnant of breast tissue that is invariably left behind! So I promised to think it over.

Hmm... Lessee now. I am a locum surgeon in a Catholic hospital. What will they think if I remove a perfectly normal breast? What will the members of the Tissue Committee say? Will they conclude that I am engaging in unnecessary surgery? Lessee now... This is a Catholic hospital. I bet they have an ethics committee that would just love to render an opinion. Better run this one by it for my own protection if nothing else.

And so I did, with the most surprising of results. As soon as the committee realized that the problem did not involve the uterus, tubes, ovaries, a vasectomy, or an abortion, its members lost all interest. I was dismissed almost in midsentence with the observation that "This is not an ethical problem. Do whatever you want. We don't care."

---

[2]   Ductal Carcinoma In Situ. It is a sort of precancer that, if left to its own devices, will inevitably turn into real cancer.

22
CHAPTER

A Newborn

Today I was the awed admirer of a newborn—a newborn rock. The new arrival made its appearance at 2:30 p.m. (local time). The proud parents (Mauna Loa and Pele) took the event in stride; it was the visitors who oohed and aahed. The birth took place from the Pu'u O'o vent in the side of Mauna Loa on Hawaii's Big Island. But I fear I am getting ahead of my story.

I had been covering for a hospital in Hawaii for almost a week and finally had a day off.

Yippee! I will get to explore the Big Island.

Saturday morning dawned anything but auspiciously. Two hours before I was to be off duty, the ER doctor called and told me he was seeing an unrestrained victim from an MVA (motor vehicle accident).

Uh-oh! This could spoil my entire day off...because putting Humpty-Dumpty back together again often takes the major portion of a day. There goes my planned adventure.

There was nothing to do but hide my disappointment and head into the ER.

There I found Stan, forty-one years old, snoozing peacefully with a huge eight-inch laceration in his forehead. The windshield had nearly scalped him. Fixing that would be the easy part. What about the snoozing? I could rouse him, albeit with difficulty, and when awake, he seemed reasonably coherent. But his eyes had this disconcerting behavior of going off independently of each other in different directions. Now if he'd been drinking, I'd have happily admitted him to sleep it off. But his blood alcohol was zero. Ditto for drugs. He was the passenger in a car without a driver (This meant that the driver found reasons to be elsewhere as soon as the accident was over. Well, that was now a police problem.) So we didn't know when it happened or where they'd been or what they'd been doing. The ER doctor had gotten CT scans of everything, and all were normal. Still, Stan snoozed. No, it was not anywhere near a coma, but still I wondered. And worried.

So as I began to stitch up the humongous forehead laceration, I asked the nurses, "Say, do you have a neurosurgeon available at this hospital?"

"No."

"How about a neurologist?"

"Yes, but he's not on call."

"Uh. Er… Well, I think I'd like to talk to him."

Eventually, he was located, and he agreed to come in. His assessment: "I think we have a brain stem contusion here. This chap needs to be in a closed head injury unit somewhere else." That instantly translated into two things in my mind—a life-flight for Stan to Honolulu, and I'd get to go see the Kilauea volcano after all!

By and by, all transfer arrangements were made. After the transfer took place, I headed back to the condo to change into shorts and T-shirt. Before I left the ER, I asked one of the nurses about seeing the lava flow. After she had given me the directions, she added the helpful suggestion that I wear old shoes, as the cooled lava would cut shoes to shreds (if they didn't melt).

Lava flow in Hawaii

Uh-oh. I only had my super-comfy operating room shoes with me, and I paid way too much for them to melt. But on the way back to the condo, I saw a Goodwill Industries sign.

Screech! The car swerved into the parking lot. There I found a dandy pair of decrepit loafers. "Seventy-eight cents." The clerk smiled, and I handed her a dollar, telling she could keep the change.

And that was how I came to be at the end of the Chain of Craters Road at two thirty in the afternoon. The lava changed course every few days or so. Sometimes it flowed down over old lava fields; sometimes it was diverted to a new pathway. Today the lava was flowing through a wooded area where it hadn't been before.

As I approached the area, my nose was greeted with a strange odor, a mixture of wood smoke (sweet to me) and a sulfurous stench. At the end of the road, there was a barricade. The sign that read, "Do not go beyond this point," somehow translated itself in my brain as "Something very interesting lies down this road." And so I parked on the berm, and after looking around to be sure there were no officials in sight, I proceeded to hike down the road. I was eventually greeted by another stench but this time of burning asphalt. Today the lava was gently and slowly flowing across the paved road, setting it on fire. I could walk up to within five feet or so before the heat drove me back.

A black tongue of shimmering lava is seemingly "set," but then it will start to glow dull red. Soon more lava, about the consistency of thick toothpaste, begins to ooze out from the side. You can throw a rock on the red lava, and it will dent the lava before it bounces off. This lava was cool enough that it was setting as fast as it flowed. It would well up out of the flow, move a while, set, only to be followed by still more lava oozing out. Fascinating! I'd just seen the ripples of Pahoehoe lava form! About a hundred feet away, red lava was dripping into the ocean, which greeted its arrival with great clouds of steam.

Back at the top of the Kilauea Crater Rim sits Volcano House, which Mark Twain visited in the mid-1800s. Tongue in cheek, he wrote that he found the "smell of sulfur is strong, but not unpleasant to a sinner." When he visited Maui, he climbed to the top of

Haleakala, where he found himself in a location few in his time ever got to see, but which we all now take for granted—that of being above the clouds.

He wrote these words: "Vagrant white clouds came drifting along, high over the sea and the valley; then they came in couples and groups; then in imposing squadrons; gradually joining their forces they banked themselves solidly together, a thousand feet under us, and totally shut out the land and ocean—clear to the horizon, league on league, the snowy floor stretched without a break—not level, but in rounded folds, with shallow creases between, and with here and there stately piles of vapory architecture lifting themselves aloft out of the common plain. It was the sublimest spectacle I ever witnessed, and I think the memory of it will remain with me always."

Wouldn't a time machine be nice if you could go back and offer Mark Twain an airplane ride!

On surgery call during one of my numerous trips to Hawai'I

23
CHAPTER

Lied To!

These surgical adventures took place in Iowa, where I was covering a pair of hospitals located about twenty miles apart. Over the years, I was called to cover for their surgeon on thirteen separate occasions. Sometimes Betty and I brought our fifth-wheel RV to live in, and at other times (especially if it was in the winter), we would fly commercially and stay in either a bed-and-breakfast or a motel.

Carolyn Clavier

On my very first day covering this small rural hospital, I was asked to see a very pleasant eighty-six-year-old lady. She had been admitted by her family doctor with excruciating abdominal pain. The abdominal X-ray showed free air within her abdominal cavity. Her story was quite consistent with an obstructing process (likely cancer) in her colon, which had then ruptured and was now spilling feces all over the place. Without surgery, this is a lethal condition. That much was obvious, but the really interesting, tough question was "Where should the surgery take place?" At this point, I had no idea of the capabilities of this little hospital.

After I'd seen Carolyn, I called her attending family physician to convey my diagnosis. The necessity of surgery was obvious to both of us. There we were, like two old junkyard dogs suspiciously sniffing each other. He asked me if I was comfortable doing such surgery. I replied that I was. Then I countered with a question as to the capability of his hospital in rendering care in the post-operative recovery period. I mentioned that she'd need to be closely monitored, could go into heart failure, and might very well need a ventilator. He assured me that they had all necessary equipment and that he felt comfortable in managing the medical aspects of her case. I took him at his word. And so it was agreed. We'd undertake to do the surgery locally if that was what the patient and family desired.

The local family physician immediately became effusive, remarking, "Good! I'm glad you are not like those other *locums* we've had before. All they want to do is transfer patients away to bigger hospitals. I'm glad you're willing to work!"

I guess, at this point, I should have been suspicious; sometimes I am too trusting.

Surgery was proposed to Carolyn and her family, and so it was agreed upon. When we had her in the operating room with her abdomen open, it was all as expected. She did indeed have a colon cancer, with a half-inch hole in the side, leaking feces out into Carolyn's abdominal cavity. After three hours of work, the offending tumor was lying in a basin at the foot of the OR table, her peritoneal cavity had been rinsed and washed with copious amounts of saline and antibiotic solution, and the operation was over. She came through it fine and was breathing on her own, albeit a little weakly.

As I was preparing to leave the hospital to return to our trusty RV, it occurred to me that it might be wise to set up a ventilator in case Carolyn weakened during the night. This request of the nursing personnel was met with puzzled looks.

"But, Doctor Roode, didn't anybody tell you that our respirator is broken and hasn't been used for years?"

I now felt the sinking sensation that perhaps is analogous to the girl who has had unprotected sex with her new boyfriend only to hear him tell her that he was lying about his HIV status. Carolyn's GP was so damned anxious for a return to the "good old days" when they did everything locally, without interference from the hated specialists, that he had either consciously lied to me or exaggerated the capability of their hospital. Or maybe he didn't even know what equipment they had or how to use it. Now I was on the hook, holding a tiger by its tail. If anything were to go wrong with Carolyn's breathing, what would I do? The answer was that Carolyn would have to be loaded into an ambulance and transferred to larger better-equipped hospital.

Well, that wouldn't be so bad, I thought.

The other town I was covering was a mere eighteen miles away. They had a respirator, and I was on the staff there. If Carolyn went bad, they could send her over to me at the larger hospital.

"No," I was informed. Hospital policy was that patients must only be transferred to other Mercy-affiliated hospitals or to larger medical centers if it was beyond a local Mercy affiliate's capability. So if Carolyn needed better care than they could provide, she'd have to bypass the nearest hospital that could care for her in order to go to another hospital in the Mercy network. Corporate politics. Policies made without regard to the patient's welfare. We physicians have no say in these matters.

I am happy to report that Carolyn made an uneventful recovery, and I resolved to be a wee bit more suspicious in the future.

Encounter in a Chinese Restaurant

It was the dead of winter, and I was staying in a local motel. That meant restaurant food. As was the usual case in a small town, everybody knows everybody. That bearded white-haired fella sitting in the corner was a surgeon from Florida, filling in for Dr. S. He didn't much like the cold. He always ate with chopsticks, liked his food spicy hot, and frequently read a book while eating.

Last night, the book was *The Effendi*, a 1904 historical romance about the Battle of Omdourman in the Sudan in 1898.

High-school aged waitress, being sociable, "What are you reading?

I replied, "Oh, it's just a historical novel."

"I like history. What is it about?"

"The battle of Omdourman."

The waitress had a blank look.

I explained, "Well, it was over a hundred years ago in a country called the Sudan."

"Oh."

Trying to be helpful, I asked, "Did you ever hear of Winston Churchill?"

"Yes."

"Good. He was in a battle there."

She said brightly, "Oh."

Me, dubiously, "Do you know who Winston Churchill was?"

After a long pause, she said somewhat hopefully, "One of our presidents?"

"Um… Er… Well, not really."

"I'm going to be a teacher someday."

"Good for you."

Gertrude Anderson (A Tylenol Overdose)

Some things are just a crying shame, and that's about all you can say about them. The legislators, the politicians, the government regulators all fantasize that rules and regulations will prevent problems. And goodness knows, hundreds of such regulations are enacted every year. Lawyers love to initiate lawsuits, all in the name of justice or in the pursuit of compensation for injured victims. Punitive awards are demanded to "prevent recurrences of negligence" (not to mention the remunerative rewards for the lawyers themselves…).

How then does one comprehend the following mindless tragedy or devise a rule to prevent a similar incident in the future? Take an elderly lady, Gertrude Anderson—no doubt with a degree of failing intellect (early Alzheimer's?)—still living alone but in a controlled environment, in a supervised apartment for independent living. Now add in a painful medical condition. For Gertrude, it happened to be trigeminal neuralgia, but it could have easily been a fractured osteoporotic bone or even degenerative arthritis. Now add a concerned son who lives many miles away and who visits her as often as he can. Because of the pain and in order to avoid stronger medicine, such as a narcotic, he purchases a bottle of extra-strength Tylenol for her. He not only carefully explains to her how many she can take a day, but

266

he even writes it in large letters on a paper he tapes to the bottle. The stage is now set.

Snap ahead a mere two days. The son returned to visit his mother and found that she was stuporous, lying on the floor in a pool of diarrhea and blood. He also discovered, to his horror, that there were only twenty-eight extra-strength Tylenols left in the bottle! Could it be? Had she taken seventy-two tablets in a mere two days? Well, it seemed that she had. An ambulance was called. She was rushed to the hospital, where she was promptly admitted to the ICU for her massive liver failure. You see, Tylenol is toxic to the liver, and she had just about completely wiped out her liver.

I first learned of Gertrude when the ICU nurse called me because of her falling blood pressure. The internist wanted a surgical consult. I knew nothing of her Tylenol ingestion. The nurse told me about the falling blood pressure and then mentioned that the family wanted no surgery or other heroic measures.

"So why are they calling me?" I muttered to myself. To the nurse, however, all I said was "I'll be right in." If another physician wants me to see a patient, I can only respect his request…there must be a good reason for it.

After I spent a little time in the ICU, learned of the Tylenol poisoning, reviewed the chart, talked to the nurse, talked to the patient's son, and looked at the lab work. It was all too clear to me that she was bleeding because of the liver failure and not an ulcer. And so whether the family did or did not desire surgery was a moot point. Surgery would not help her.

This woman had committed suicide as surely as if she'd shot herself in the head with a gun, and ironically, she did it all unknowingly. She had pain. She took a pain pill. The pain continued. Because of her Alzheimer's, she forgot she'd taken a pill. She took another. And another. And another. Now put yourself into the mind of a bureaucratic regulator. How would you devise a law to prevent this sort of needless tragedy?

Was the son wrong to leave medicine with his mother? Is it wrong for a drug store to sell a medicine that could be harmful? Must you someday have a certificate of responsibility (or perhaps freedom from Alzheimer's) to purchase even aspirin or Tylenol? Should the supervised apartment complex snoop into every resident's room to prevent such accidents without violating any of a hundred other rules designed to preserve elderly people's privacy?

As for lawsuits to prevent this kind of tragedy, who could you sue? And who would be entitled to any monetary rewards? How would such a lawsuit prevent a future recurrence of this kind of tragedy?

What we have here is just a pointless, stupid tragedy. Things like this simply just happen and are perhaps best just simply forgotten...

I dunno.

Bad Day for the Burton Household

The beeper went off one evening. As usual, it was an inconvenient time: at 10:30 p.m. to be specific. It was the ER asking me (with a peculiar bit of urgency) to please come in without bothering to ask for any details.

In the ER, I was greeted with the case of Joseph Burton, sixty-five years old and recently retired from a lifetime of teaching government to every high school student in town. He had been home, minding his own business, sitting at the kitchen table, getting ready to retire, when suddenly and for no apparent reason, he experienced the sudden onset of severe abdominal pain. After a few minutes of confusion and anxiety, his wife decided to quickly drive him to the hospital rather than call 911. They clocked in at ten twenty.

The ER doctor did not like what he saw. He ordered lab tests, X-rays, and then asked them to call me in. I dressed hurriedly and was at the ER by ten forty. My suspicions were the same as his. The sudden onset of severe abdominal pain, accompanied by signs of shock and now a steadily increasing abdominal girth, all point to a ruptured abdominal aortic aneurysm. (Odd, I thought at the time, that he had no back pain.)

What to do next? If our suspicions were correct, it would be far more than we could handle here in this small rural Iowa hospital. Our only choice would be to transfer him to the nearest major medical center. Should we make the call, asking them to launch their expensive helicopter based only on our suspicion? Or should we call in the ultrasound technician to confirm our suspicion? But an ultrasound will only waste precious additional time. I suggested we go on our clinical hunch alone and call the nearest Mayo Clinic affiliate, asking them to launch their helicopter. And get blood available.

Perhaps the reason for my being asked to come in was to lend a bit of moral support to the ER physician in case the Mayo people were dubious. He could then say, "Well, my surgeon made the diagnosis and suggested the transfer."

Mayo did its usual bang-up job. After arrival, they were on the ground for only eleven minutes. (Helicopters elsewhere took much longer. Once, in another state, precisely the same kind of patient with the same diagnosis bled to death while the major medical center fiddled with the paperwork to be sure it was all in order.)

Later, I learned that the Mayo surgeons, agreeing with us, took him directly to the OR. They found the expected huge amount of blood filling the abdominal cavity. But his aorta was perfectly normal! Huh! What he had was a rare malignancy that had eaten a hole in another artery. He died on their OR table.

Like people of yesteryear, we are still helpless in the face of many illnesses. True, we understand things a whole lot better, but understanding is not curing. Now I know why he had no back pain. Duh! It wasn't an aneurysm. But while I have more understanding of what had happened, Mr. Burton, the high school teacher, still died. Similar scenarios have played themselves out in the past. Denied power to change things, we humans crave understanding and answers.

"Why did this happen?" the grieving widow asks the priest, medicine man, or shaman, who then tries to come up with an answer. While we smile at the answers, it's wise to remember that all of us, with all our scientific understanding, are often as helpless as they are.

24

Medical Potpourri

Benjamin Colby (Regional Helicopter Woes)

For the most part, the practice of medicine is quite uniform around the country. Occasionally, however, I'd notice, and often even be shocked, at how differently the same problem is approached in different communities. The problem at hand is the transfer of patients from one hospital to another. It wouldn't matter so much if we are shipping groceries to the supermarket. But when you have a critically ill or injured patient, you cannot afford the least amount of carelessness. This is a story of a man who may well have survived his illness had he merely chanced to live in a different part of the country.

Benjamin Colby presented at the ER with the sudden onset of tearing back pain. His blood pressure was low and his pulse high. His abdominal X-ray showed the telltale calcific shadow of an aortic aneurysm. So the diagnosis wasn't terribly difficult. His aorta, the main artery carrying blood from his heart to the lower half of his body, compromised by arteriosclerosis, had dangerously bloated into an aneurysm. Eventually, blood began to leak through the thin weakened walls of his aneurysm. The blood invaded the surrounding tissues, causing his excruciating back pain. As the leak worsened, he went into shock. The next stage would be the rupture of the aneurysm, leading to his immediate death.

The treatment for a leaking aneurysm is immediate emergency surgery, during which it is removed and replaced with a Dacron tube.

(Aside: That was the standard of care back in 1993 when this took place. Today, a replacement can sometimes be inserted endo-vascularly—that is, a tubular graft can be slid in through an artery. No abdominal incision is necessary.) Of course, the small hospital in which I was working did not have the capability of performing any kind of vascular surgery at all. So Benjamin's only chance was an emergency transfer to a larger hospital.

I'd like to report that things went well. When I have encountered medical or surgical emergencies in various geographic areas of this country, I cannot help but be impressed by regional differences. Some major medical centers, such as the Mayo Clinic or Meritcare in Fargo, North Dakota, are extremely efficient at rapid deployment of their medevac helicopters. Both will launch its helicopter on the request of virtually anybody at the local hospital. They realize that the attending medical personnel may have their hands full and don't always have the time to engage in a telephone interview in which the local physician seeks to justify his or her request. If the request has been made, then it must be a genuine emergency, and the best course of action is to get the transfer process underway as rapidly as possible.

It would be nice if this was the situation across the country. But in this southern area of the country, which shall remain unspecified, the procedure turned out to be vastly different. I had been called into the ER to see Ben. I had helped make the diagnosis. We then made contact with the nearest large medical center, one that holds itself forth as being able to perform emergency vascular surgery twenty-four hours a day. It happened to be only seventeen minutes by air from our small hospital. You would expect that Benjamin could be there well under an hour: two one-way trips and maybe ten or fifteen minutes on the ground at our end to get him into the helicopter.

What struck me in this case was that the medical center seemed to be more concerned about following the rules than expeditiously rescuing the patient in a desperate situation. Its helicopter would not be launched unless the local ER doctor himself broke away from the care he was providing and personally talked to the physician in the medical center, the one who would both accept the patient in transfer and agree to provide his care. Then the helicopter dispatcher must also personally speak to that accepting surgeon to verify that this was indeed the case. Tonight a phone call was dropped. Finally, we were able to talk to their surgeon, who agreed to accept Ben. Then the helicopter dispatcher could not immediately locate the surgeon who accepted Ben in transfer, to verify that he had indeed accepted the patient.

In all, nearly forty minutes elapsed between the time we tried to initiate a transfer and their helicopter even being launched. What a far cry from the standards set by Mayo Clinic or St. Luke's Hospital in Fargo, North Dakota!

Unfortunately, just as it was touching down at our hospital, Ben's weakened, leaking aneurysm burst. He went into deep shock and became unconscious. And so we had to take the time to intubate him.[1] He was barely alive when the helicopter landed at the medical center, and died as they were rushing him to the OR. In all, three hours had elapsed between the time of his pain onset and his arrival at the medical center. I'd like to think he would have survived had we been able to get him to the medical center more expeditiously. I'd also like to imagine that things have improved in this particular part of the country since I last worked there.

Eric Kelly

The evolution of all-terrain vehicles has gone from the original "three-wheelers" being replaced by the more stable "four-wheelers." But if you try hard enough, you can even crash the newer "four-wheelers," as Eric, a fifteen-year-old lad, did one day in rural Tennessee. He was brought to our ER with an obviously broken left arm and "stomach cramps." His arm was set, but his stomach cramps persisted. The ER doctor obtained a CT scan of the abdomen. It was negative. Nonetheless, because of his abdominal pain, the ER doctor called me at 11 p.m. We both felt that he needed admission for

---

[1]   We needed to insert a plastic tube into his trachea to enable us to breathe for him.

observation. Since the CT scan was normal and his vital signs were stable, the ER doctor considerately offered to write the admission orders so I wouldn't have to come in.

Barely an hour later, the floor nurse called to tell me that Eric had vomited 500 cc of undigested food, with blood in it. Well, considerate ER doctor or not, I felt I should see him. And so I heaved out of bed, dressed, and hustled right in. His exam was basically reassuring, with stable vital signs as well as a soft and only slightly tender abdomen. He had a few epigastric abrasions. I placed a nasogastric tube, and it irrigated clearly. A bloody nose could have easily accounted for the blood in his vomitus.

The next morning, he was still clinically stable, but now the right upper quadrant of his abdomen was painful. His lab tests remained normal all that day, but his abdomen remained tender. As I examined him repeatedly during the day, his abdomen gradually became firm. There were no bowel sounds audible in my stethoscope. He developed abdominal guarding.[2] By evening, his examination showed peritoneal signs,[3] and so despite his normal blood count and despite the normal CT scan, I recommended exploratory surgery.

In talking to his parents, I faced the usual parental anxiety.

"Who is this guy from Florida anyway? And where is our beloved Dr. C when we really need him?"

In the end, however, they accepted with my recommendation for surgery.

At surgery, I found a lot of free dark fluid that seemed to be originating from near his hepatic flexure.[4] The injury seemed to be in his retroperitoneum, and so I reflected the right colon to the left to visualize the entire duodenal sweep. There I found it: a 1 cm laceration on the back side of the duodenum behind the SMA[5] and right over his spine. Once located and exposed, repair was easy, but

---

[2]   The abdominal muscles either voluntarily or involuntarily would contract when I palpated his abdomen.

[3]   Signs of peritonitis.

[4]   In the right upper quadrant of the abdomen, where the colon lies near the liver.

[5]   Superior Mesenteric Artery.

I must say I'd never encountered this type of injury in this location. How it could have occurred in a vehicular accident without leaving traces of other intra-abdominal injuries or even any external signs of injury to his abdomen was a mystery to me.

He did well, and the parents were ever so grateful. They gave Betty and me a home-cured ham and, maybe best of all, gave me a "genuine" Davy Crockett-style coonskin hat that I proudly wore back in our hometown OR on my next assignment there. Perhaps most unusual (and gratifying!) of all was that they were extremely reluctant for me to relinquish his care to their beloved Dr. C, for upon his return, they went to the hospital administrator, asking him to have me stay on until their son was discharged.

Shirley Daly (Saved by an Ounce of Urine)

There is value in obtaining additional, supplementary data even after you have reached a tentative diagnosis. If the additional data is confirmatory you can proceed with confidence. On some occasions, however, an isolated lab test result or X-ray may be inconsistent with all the other assembled data, physical findings, and diagnostic impressions. Obviously at least some of your information is errone-ous, but which is it? The challenge, of course, is to sort through your data and decide which to keep and which to discard. The story of Shirley Daly illustrates this sometimes delicious complexity.

In a very small rural town in Virginia, late at night, I was called to the ER by no less than a full Professor of Surgery! He said he had a "hot appendix" for me. Now what in the world was a Northwestern University Professor of Surgery doing in this little (population four thousand) town? It seemed that a number of years ago, he'd resigned his professorship in Chicago to return to his native India to help found a medical college. However, his move to India proved to be financially unrewarding. And so he periodically returned to the USA to work in this Virginia ER. Like me, he was a *locum tenens* physician!

Midnight found me seeing an acutely ill, obese young woman in the ER.

Our patients do not come to us with their diagnosis written on their foreheads. The disease process resides deep within, hidden from our eyes and prying fingers. The lab helps but sometimes in unexpected ways. Reaching the correct medical diagnosis and determining the proper treatment is akin to puzzle solving. Selecting a diagnosis is not unlike choosing a road to travel upon. As we progress down our chosen road, we gather clues that tell us we are either on the correct path or hint to us that our initial choice may have been in error and that we ought to consider an alternative path. What is scary to me is how far down a road I sometimes travel before it dawns on me that I have selected the wrong one.

In this case, my initial thoughts were colored by the vaunted Professor of Surgery; surely he couldn't be wrong. And so I had gone into the examining room with appendicitis on my mind.

As I talked to and examined Shirley, I was reassured that she indeed was suffering from appendicitis. It had the typical onset—loss of appetite and vague epigastric pain that later localized to the right lower abdominal quadrant. The lab test results also fit well—a high white count at over 19,000. Her exam showed right-sided tenderness, perhaps a trifle high, but definitely on the right and below the umbilicus. There were even signs of early peritonitis.

I remember thinking, *I'd better do this one tonight. I would rather wait until morning so as not to have to call in the crew. But with the rebound tenderness and the high white count, I'd better not delay.*

Only, unbeknownst to me, her appendix was perfectly normal. The Great Surgeon in the Sky was probably having a good belly laugh at my expense. I still shudder to think how close I came to taking a toxic young woman to the operating room, making the wrong incision, and fishing out a normal appendix. What would I have then done? I wouldn't have had a clue as to what was going on. Can you imagine a more inauspicious start for a bearded stranger, a vagabond Floridian surgeon, in a small town in rural Virginia?

What saved me was a fluke. All the test results pointed to or were consistent with acute appendicitis. All told, as I later counted, the detailed components of her tests came to forty-three pieces of information available for my review. Only one, a minor component of the urinalysis, was a little out of line. There was evidence of bile in her urine. How tempting it was to discard that information as erroneous. There were forty-two other items that were matter-of-factly saying "appendicitis."

I had gone back to the ER desk and was about to call the evening supervisor to schedule the emergency appendectomy when I saw that isolated minor urine anomaly.

"What does this mean?" I found myself asking the lab tech who was sitting there in the ER, sipping coffee before going home. She wanted to be sure I wouldn't want any other tests before heading to the OR. I nudged the lab test sheet over to her.

"We find that once in a while in normal patients" was her reply. "We think it might be a colorimetric error in our laboratory test equipment."

"Do me a favor," I replied. "Humor me and run a bilirubin."

She did, and it was 3.4.

Hmm... That's odd. It doesn't fit with appendicitis. What's really going on? Maybe I should re-examine the patient.

I did. Was I imagining it, or was her pain a little higher in her abdomen? Thus, plans for surgery were scrapped. I simply admitted the patient, started IV antibiotics, and scheduled an ultrasound for the morning.

The ultrasound showed gallstones. Later that day, I did take my sick patient to the OR, but instead of making an embarrassing incision in her lower right abdomen to remove her appendix, I removed an acutely inflamed gallbladder.

So what to make of this little tale? Recovery from acute illness is routinely expected these days. But the public (not to mention their elected representatives) want it done ever more cheaply, hence the popularity of HMOs (Health Maintenance Organizations). To keep health costs down, HMOs devote considerable time and effort to the elimination of "unnecessary" tests. On many of my assignments, I would be given a list of tests that could not be obtained without a specific clinical suspicion that must be justified by a specific symptom.

There is a value, however, in the screening test. Who, for example, knows her mammogram will be abnormal? The patient has no symptoms of breast cancer. That is why we have invented these tests.

It could not be suspected that a routine appendicitis patient would have bile in her urine. The only reason that the bile test even exists as a component of the routine urinalysis is that it comes as part of the kit. If it could be separated out and if the kit could thereby be made cheaper, then that's the one that HMOs would mandate. Shirley was saved from the wrong operation by an "unnecessary" test, one with a result that happened to be totally out of line from what would be expected.

Locomotive Lore

Dan, an executive of the DM&E (Dakotas, Minnesota, and Eastern) railroad, came to the clinic in South Dakota because a growth on his face had recently enlarged. He showed it to his family physician, who advised its removal. It was done in the office, a minor procedure done under local anesthesia, and all went well. And no, it wasn't cancerous.

What I am recording here is only peripherally related to the practice of medicine. It is nothing more than an example of the conversations that transpire between a physician and his patient even during an outpatient procedure.

There were a number of questions regarding railroads that I've wondered about over the years. For example, have you ever sat at a railroad crossing, watching a slow freight train pass by, and wondered how far the locomotive could go on a tank of fuel?

After expressing my delight that he could do something for me while I was simultaneously doing something for him, I asked him, "Say, how big are the fuel tanks on a locomotive?" And it turned out that when the engineer pulls into a fuel stop and says "Fill 'er up!" he can expect to get up to two thousand gallons. And as an interesting bit of trivia, that turns out to be about how much blood the average heart pumps in an average day! Think about it the next time you see a locomotive go by with that huge black fuel tank slung under it, right over the rails.

"How far can a locomotive drive on a tank of fuel?"

Dan hedged on that one, because it depends on how big a train is being pulled. For example, idling, a typical locomotive burns only 6 gallons/hour. A quick calculation shows that a locomotive could therefore idle its engine for about two weeks. But at maximum power output starting up on an upgrade, the diesel engines gulp fuel at a whopping 168 gallons/hour. If it were to continue at this rate, a locomotive would run through the entire 2,000 gallons in something like 12 hours. A typical locomotive pulling a typical train travels somewhat less than 1,000 miles on a tank of fuel. That figures out to about half a mile per gallon until you realize that there are often two or three locomotives per train, and so a better measure is gallons per mile. They burn 6 to 8 gallons per mile. And to improve economy, believe it or not, yes, they do a lot of coasting when going downhill!

I know it is hard to believe, but things became even more interesting. For example, it turned out that they refueled all locomotives automatically, once a day, no matter what. That way, they would never run out of fuel. Well, almost never. You see, they don't have fuel gauges in these things! Now that startled me. Locomotives must cost half a million bucks, and they don't put in fuel gauges?

I asked an open-ended question, "Say, have you ever had a locomotive run out of gas?"

He replied, "Well, er...not often. Maybe once a year."

And in sharp contrast to the aviation industry, running out of gas is not looked upon with horror. It's one of those things that happens from time to time. Annoying to be sure, but all they have to do is send out a fuel truck. No reports are required to any federal agencies.

"Do they still have those so-called 'deadman' switches on locomotives?" (You know, the switch the engineer had to hold shut all day long so that if he fell over dead, the switch would open and the train would come to a screeching halt.)

Answer: "No, they aren't required. We don't have them, but they do out east." And then he volunteered (helpfully) that locomotives are equipped these days with a black box, like airliners, so that accidents can be reconstructed.

And now to the grand finale. Why does the front of a locomotive look vaguely like a car or a truck? It has a crew cab, complete with windshield and wipers. Then there is that box-like thing sticking out front. It looks for all the world like a small engine compartment. But we all know that the huge engines are behind the engineers.

"What's up in front of the engineer, the thing he looks over when he's driving?" I asked Dan.

You would *never* guess the answer.

It's the bathroom! Yup, there is a commode up front in the nose of every locomotive! Heretofore, there has been a degree of elegance in the classic railroad crossing accident. I now realized that, in reality, it involves the ignominy of a collision with a high-speed commode! Sigh...

25
CHAPTER

On Being a Nice Bastard

Five weeks were spent in a small hospital in Virginia where I covered for the lone surgeon who was away. Our trusty fifth-wheel RV was parked right on the hospital grounds at the outskirts of town. It was an idyllic setting, surrounded by open fields nestled up against low rolling hills.

Paul Pierson

One day in early June, I stopped by medical records to see if, perchance, I might have received a letter from Betty. No such luck, but there was an official-looking hospital envelope in my slot—a carefully sealed envelope. Odd. Most hospital paperwork was slipped into the slot wide open. The letter was from the Hospital Risk Manager. It seemed that a complaint had been lodged against me by a Mr. Pierson. He had called in to Administration and angrily complained that I'd been "rude" to him in the ER, that I had called him a drug addict, and that I had said he wasn't getting any "dope" from me. He'd even made veiled threats to contact his attorney. The Risk Manager invited my response to these allegations.

I remembered Paul well. On Saturday of the Memorial Day weekend, having nothing better to do, I'd gone over to the ER and was making small talk with the physician covering the ER. He was a young gastroenterologist just starting up a practice in Washington, DC. Due to an abundance of physicians in the nation's capital, it was slow going. He had kids to feed and apartment rent to pay. And so he supplemented his meager income by working weekends in this remote Virginia ER. As we chatted, he mentioned his current problem. The ER agency that hired him was unable to provide his shift relief. He was being asked to work and additional five hours until a different relief ER physician could arrive. That meant he'd miss his flight back to Washington. He asked me if I'd be willing to cover the ER for him for five hours. I agreed, with the proviso that he must find a secondary backup for the ER, in the unlikely event I had to go to the OR. He did, and the deal was set.

And so Sunday afternoon found me manning the ER. In the course of five hours, I saw fifteen patients, one of whom was Paul. The shift nurse, a grizzled old veteran, warned me that he was one of their "regular" customers and was widely regarded as seeking drugs. Thus, it was that I entered the exam room with a jaundiced view. I asked him what I could do for him, and he replied that he needed something for pain.

"What hurts?" I asked.

"This," he said, holding up what appeared to me to be a perfectly normal right hand. "I was recently diagnosed as having a carpal tunnel, Doc," he continued, "and the pain is killing me."

What Paul apparently didn't know was that the carpal tunnel syndrome, caused by a pinched median nerve in the wrist, more often manifests itself as numbness and tingling in the hand and fingers rather than sharp pain shooting clear up to his elbow. I knew I had to proceed cautiously.

I started off carefully. "You are already using the maximum safe dose of pain killers that your carpal tunnel doctor prescribed. The only thing stronger that I can give you is a narcotic. Is that what you want?"

Now maybe that last question was provocative, and maybe I shouldn't have asked it. But I had a reason. Most people are inwardly leery of narcotics. In fact, such is the fear of addiction that I often have to convince patients with legitimate pain that it is safe to take a narcotic.

No such reticence on Paul's part. He grinned and said, "Sure, Doc. Whatever it takes!"

Suspicions confirmed.

We are all the products of our past. One of my best friends, a family physician in Iowa, ran afoul the law a number of years ago. His office secretary asked him for a prescription for her husband. It was for a controlled medication (narcotics? sleeping pill?). Being the "nice guy," he obliged her. A couple of weeks later, she was back for more. He scribbled out another prescription. He finally realized what was going on and confronted her. Her response was to inform him that he'd broken the law by writing several prescriptions for a person he'd never seen, and if he didn't refill the script, she would turn him in. He refilled it and agonized over how he'd gotten himself into such a pretty pickle. The upshot of the whole affair was that somewhere he found the courage to refuse his secretary. She carried through with her threat. He was arrested, tried, convicted, and spent time in a federal penitentiary. He told me that the judge apologized to him before handing down the sentence, explaining to my friend that mandatory federal guidelines allowed him no discretion in sentencing. He will carry that criminal record with him for the rest of his life and all for being a "nice guy."

"Nice guys," as Leo Durocher once said, "often finish last."

And the office secretary? She got off with a plea bargain.

Snap back to the present, to Paul sitting there, grinning idiotically in front of me...

"Well, I have a problem with that" was my response. "I'm reluctant to give you a narcotic when your regular doctor has chosen not to. As a matter of fact, I can't do it."

He got up abruptly and walked out of the ER. He called the hospital two days later to complain about my "rudeness." I wrote a letter to the Risk Manager, giving my version of the incident, all of which would be forwarded to the insurance company against the day a lawyer might call. In this case, however, I knew that there would be no lawyer, no lawsuit. Why? Well, it seemed that, a week later, Paul was arrested in West Virginia and charged with altering a doctor's prescription for a narcotic. Aha! It wasn't the narcotics he was after but a signed prescription!

Laundromat (Small Towns Are All the Same)

Saturday morning, I'd been in town for ten days now. It was time to do the laundry. And so I rose early; gathered my laundry, detergent, and quarters; and drove to the town's only Laundromat, hoping to beat the crowd. Gradually, other customers drifted in, all bent on similar missions. More and more of the machines were put into use. The Laundromat was populated by a cross section of the town's poor folk. As I was folding my clothing, an elderly man shuffled up, dragging his left leg awkwardly behind. The relic of a stroke or perhaps a long-ago accident? We had never met.

"Say!" he blurted out. "Jes what kinda doc are you anyhow?"

I was not surprised by the question from a perfect stranger. It had happened to me so many times before. I looked up, bemused. Everybody in the Laundromat was staring at me—an obese housewife who obviously needed a bath as much as her clothing, a coal miner in the corner, an elderly woman. I had said nothing at all to anybody. I was dressed in sweatpants and a T-shirt. I drove a dirty one-ton Ford "dually" that I bought used from a cement contractor in Iowa. But in a small town, there are no secrets. Everybody watches everybody else, from the town cop on down to the street dweller. They not only knew who I was, but also where I lived and what I did for a living. I had gone to the grocery store last evening, and they undoubtedly knew about it. They probably even knew what I purchased. This has happened to me countless times in countless small towns.

"A travelin' doc," I replied with a grin. "I drift around the country. They call me Old Drifter."

My interrogator seemed to be satisfied, and he shuffled off. The other patrons returned to the TV, tattered magazines, or their laundry. Such is life in a small town.

Kristi Hurd (Small Hospital Challenges)

Saturday evening. Nothing to do. Once again, I wandered over to the ER and engaged in idle chatter with the ER doctor. As I was planning to leave, the radio scanner came alive. There had been a motor vehicle accident with personal injuries. The ER doctor looked at me with a silent plea in her eyes. She was great with the little ones, but trauma was not her forte.

"I'll stay," I assured her.

The scanner continued. There were three victims trapped in the vehicle. They would need to use the "Jaws of Life" to extract them. Later, I was to learn that the three young girls had been out driving at a high rate of speed on a lonely country gravel road. No, they weren't drinking, but they might as well have been. You see, the driver (Kristi) had only gotten her license a mere two weeks before.

"What parents in their right mind will let a newly licensed sixteen-year-old drive late at night?" I wondered.

It was not till twenty minutes after midnight that the first ambulance backed in. A sixteen-year-old girl was unloaded, with a bloody towel across her face.

"No cervical collar,"[1] I noted.

"Two more on the way, Doc," one attendant told me as they moved their patient into the ER. Once inside, I removed the bloody towel and saw a five- to six-inch laceration across her forehead. Portions of her eyelids were missing. She had pain in the eyes themselves. The remaining portion of her forehead was pockmarked in the fashion that only a shattering windshield could make. Evidently, she was not wearing her seat belt. I quickly checked her for life-threatening conditions. Heart. Lungs. Abdomen. No signs of serious internal hemorrhaging. Her right leg was broken, so she'd need that tended to.

"This one needs to go to a plastic surgeon," I told the ER doctor. "And perhaps an ophthalmologist as well."

We had neither of these specialists available locally, and the forehead of a pretty girl, her eyelids, and her eyes were a responsibility that one ought not to assume casually.

"Oh, I can sew that up," responded the ER doctor brightly.

I was somewhat startled. She was a family physician, but who was I to protest? She knew her capabilities, and if she could handle a severe laceration that other family doctors would send to a specialist, who was I to disagree? She is on the staff here, while I was merely a "hired hand."

She happily set about sewing the large laceration, as well as those on her eyelids. This occupied her for the next two hours—two hours in which she was *not* available to help with the other more seriously injured victims of this accident. How clever of her! I wound up being all alone with the other two victims. And as it later turned out, the family wanted that first victim, the one with the facial laceration and the broken leg, to be transferred to a larger hospital. The ER doctor arranged for this transfer after she had finished her attempted repair

---

[1] Anytime a person's head hits something with enough force to lacerate the forehead and cause unconsciousness, a protective collar ought to have been placed by the ambulance crew. The neck could have been fractured. The slightest subsequent movement could have resulted in permanent paralysis. Evidently the local ambulance crew lagged behind their brethren elsewhere in the country.

of the patient's facial laceration. And there, in that larger hospital, the orthopedic surgeon took one look at the patient's face and reached the same conclusion I did. He consulted a plastic surgeon, who had to take the patient to the OR, remove all the ER doctor's sutures, and replace them properly.

Soon, the second ambulance backed in with the second victim, Kristi. I didn't know it at the time, but I would be awake for most of the next forty-eight hours with her. When I first saw her, however, she was conscious, stable, and had a reassuring abdominal and chest exam. Her right femur was broken, and her right ankle was twisted inwardly in a grotesque fashion. A fracture dislocation it is called, and if left as it was for more than a few moments, it could sometimes cause loss of the foot. I pulled it straight, the broken bones grating together under my gloved hands. Kristi screamed, then was quiet again as I applied a plaster splint that would hold her ankle stable until an orthopedic surgeon could see her. While this was going on, the third ambulance had delivered its charge. At that time it looked like Kristi's main injuries were going to be orthopedic.

I was interrupted by a nurse who told me that the third victim, Allison, looked "real bad." Once again, her nursing instinct was correct.

"Akoury!"[2] I yelled across the trauma bay. "I've got to run into three! We have one deteriorating. Please take care of this one!"

As soon as I examined the third victim, it was clear to me that she was the worst of the lot. Her abdomen was rigid and silent.

No doubt there's blood in there, I thought. *I'll have to tap her, and then we are probably off to the OR.*

"Get the OR crew in here!"

"What do I tell 'em we're doing?" asked the ward clerk.

"G——dammit. Just get them in here! I'll tell 'em what we're gonna do when I figger it out."

---

[2] Name of the ER doctor.

In preparation, I have them insert a Foley catheter.[3] *Hello!* Pure blood. Allison has therefore at least two intra-abdominal injuries. And worse, there was no urologist available in this town. This one needed to go to a larger hospital. But did we have the time? Would it be safe? Transfers of bleeding patients are always a huge gamble, especially when you don't know how fast they are bleeding. In this case, Allison was stable, and I decided to take a chance on transferring her to a hospital better equipped to care for her.

"Do not leave here!" I told the ambulance crew as I set about attending the details of the transfer.

After various phone calls were made, a larger hospital with a urologist on staff twenty miles to the east accepted her in transfer. And now we ran into one of those maddening paperwork delays, one directly attributable to governmental meddling into medicine.

A number of years ago, it was the practice of disreputable, for-profit hospitals to "dump" undesirable[4] patients onto public or university hospitals. Indeed, in the most outrageous examples, women in labor were placed in ambulances and sometimes even gave birth while en route to a hospital hundreds of miles away. There was no way you could justify this type of behavior, but the government solution was, perhaps, worse. A draconian law was passed.

Why did senators and congressmen think that enactment of a detailed, complex law, full of heavy penalties, would solve any given problem? Now there are several phone calls and innumerable forms to fill out before a patient can be transferred. Everything ground to a halt while the paperwork was neatly finished up. All the while, Allison quietly continued to bleed, and I continued to hover over her in case my decision that she was stable enough to withstand the transfer turned out to be wrong. If that was the case, then I'd be forced to take her to the OR here in this small hospital. There was simply nothing I could do to speed things up.

---

[3] Rubber drainage tube inserted into the bladder to decompress the bladder and make my next planned test, the DPL, safe.

[4] Read: those without insurance.

"They have accepted her in transfer. Can't we send her now and *fax* the paper to the hospital?" They looked to me with horror. "We can't take that responsibility." So there you have it. Paper is more important than people.

How did Allison do? It turned out that the hospital to the east did a CT scan and was alarmed by the findings. They, in turn, had her flown to Charleston, WV, where she underwent surgery for a fractured pancreas and liver.

How easy it would have been for me to have decided to take her to our little OR here. And if I had, there would have been absolutely nothing that I could have done. What saved me from this nightmare? The bloody urine.

After I finally succeeded in getting Allison safely transferred, I returned to the trauma bay to see how Kristi was doing. I found to my surprise that Kristi's physical exam had changed. She now had a tender, silent[5] abdomen. Clearly, she had more than mere orthopedic injuries. All this while, our ER doctor was *(plod, plod, plod)* sewing on the face of the first victim, stitches that would all have to be removed and replaced at the medical center to which she was sent by the orthopedic surgeon. I had relied on her to at least get some lab values. Evidently it was simply business as usual—first come, first served...no sense of urgency...no sense of prioritization to see the most severely injured first. Dang! How I longed to be back in Fargo! Why was I running their ER?

In a larger hospital, the next step would be a CT scan (in the case of a stable patient) or perhaps a DPL[6] (in the case of an unstable patient that might need more urgent surgery). Kristi looked stable to me, and so I (foolishly as it turned out) opted for the CT scan. I forgot. They were not used to doing CT scans in the middle of the

---

[5]   One of the responses of an abdomen to injury, internal bleeding, etc., is to cease normal peristalsis. We can detect that with the lowly stethoscope. Of course, we still need the fancy X-ray tests to show precisely what is going on in our patients.

[6]   Diagnostic Peritoneal Lavage. In this test, a small plastic catheter is inserted with local anesthesia into the patient's abdomen. We can then run IV fluid in, withdraw it, and sample it for blood or other substances.

night. They had no radiologist here to read them. The tech came over to be sure that I was actually requesting an unheard-of, after-hours CT scan. She informed me that she'd turn the machine on, but it would have to warm up for fifteen minutes. Later, she came back to inquire about contrast.[7]

"Yes, by all means," I replied. "Use it!"

She thought it over. Time crawled by. The patient still hadn't been given the contrast. The tech returned to say that she had further checked the policy manual and she couldn't give contrast to a patient that might be going to the OR. Huh! The author of that policy manual was copying advice pertaining to routine surgery when we like our patients to have empty stomachs. In trauma situations, we operate all the time on patients with fluid[8] in their stomachs. But I kept forgetting… This was rural, small-time western Virginia.

Another half an hour drifted by, and still there were no movements toward X-ray for the CT scan! I was walking down the hall to the X-ray department to see what the delay could possibly be when it suddenly dawned on me that I was heading for trouble. Ordinarily, a CT scan should take only fifteen minutes or so, time that was easily affordable in getting a patient to the OR. This one looked like it could easily take much more than an hour. They were clearly not used to doing urgent CT scans in the middle of the night on trauma patients. How sure was I that my patient would remain stable throughout that time?

At this point, I gave serious thought to sending Kristi to that larger hospital to the east. But the rapidity with which she had deteriorated gave me pause to worry that she could deteriorate during the transfer. And so I hurried back to the ER. "We're gonna do a DPL," I announce to the ER nurse.

DPLs are less accurate than a CT scan. You only get a yes or no answer. Either there is or there is not blood present in the abdo-

---

[7]   A mixture of barium that the patient swallows. It shows up on the X-ray as a bright white substance outlining the shape of various organs, such as stomach, intestines, etc. And best of all, if one is ruptured, the contrast will leak out, and the problem will be evident to all concerned.

[8]   Read: BEER.

men. You can't tell where it is coming from. The elegance of the CT scan is that you can see exactly which organs are injured and how badly. That is why they are so popular all around the country. Here, I smelled only trouble if I persisted with the elegant test. Best to fall back into the 1970s and do the quick and dirty DPL. At least, if it was negative, then I'd know that it would be safe to let the X-ray department screw around for an hour or two. If it was positive, then it was an immediate trip to the OR without all the fancy diagnostic information.

Well, the tap turned out to be positive. Had I persisted with the CT scan, we could have easily have had a patient in shock in the X-ray department. Already her blood pressure was beginning to fall.

"We need to go to the OR," I announced. "What do we have for labs?"

To my horror, while I had been taking care of Allison, the worthless ER doctor who I had asked to see Kristi had done nothing at all. Kristi had been lying in the ER with not a single lab test having been done! There wasn't even any blood available to give her a transfusion! But I could not be angry. It was my own damn fault. I'd forgotten that I was in a backward, rural part of western Virginia. Elsewhere, trauma patients automatically had labs drawn. Here, they did absolutely nothing unless specifically told what to do. Hastily I set about rectifying my egregious omission. Meanwhile, the worthless ER doctor was still sitting there *(plod, plod, plod)*, sewing on the girl's face, which manifestly needed to be seen by a plastic surgeon.

The OR crew, which had been called in earlier, was notified, and off we went to surgery. On the way out the door, a supervisor ventured to inform me that we didn't have permission to go to surgery! This girl's mother and guardian happened to be visiting relatives in Vermont and couldn't be reached by phone. "What should we do? I asked her. "Sit around and watch Kristi bleed to death? Do we treat paperwork or people?"

It was now well past three in the morning. At last, all had been assembled in the OR. Kristi was asleep. Her blood pressure was low but was holding steady. So far, I had the feeling of extreme luckiness this evening. I had trod through the minefield (so far) without managing to blow my foot off. I opened Kristi's abdomen and found the expected blood. The damage was to her liver, high up, under her ribcage, right where the steering wheel caught her. Once again, the lack of a seat belt bit the patient. But the laceration was smallish, maybe only two or three inches long. It had bled merrily for an hour or so but now had ceased to bleed. There was nothing for me to do but carefully inspect all other organs, wash out the blood, and send Kristi to the ICU.

Her main problem was going to be, I suspected, pulmonary. The steering wheel had no doubt also bruised her lungs, and her long bone fractures were likely to ooze fatty marrow into her bloodstream. It would be filtered out in her lungs and would further compromise their function. Events over the next thirty-six hours would not only confirm my pulmonary fears but would take an unexpected turn.

By now, it is 5 a.m. on Sunday morning. I caught two quick hours of sleep, and then was back in the ICU. There was the matter of her broken bones to be tended to. I filled out a consult to the local orthopedic surgeon on call. Kristi had received two units of blood, and her vital signs were stable. At 1 p.m., Kristi, the orthopedic surgeon, and myself were back in the OR, where we inserted a metal rod down the length of the femur to stabilize it. A plate and screws were also placed into her ankle. All went well, and I permitted myself to breathe easy.

On Sunday afternoon, I was back in ICU to check on Kristi before going back to my trusty RV to cook supper. Kristi's temperature was 103°. Peculiar. *Now what?* I wondered. It was much too early for infection. Could it be her lungs? What to do? I mulled it over and, despite the lack of a clear diagnosis, decided to start her on an antibiotic. I then headed home to supper, hoping that this would be the end of Kristi's adventures. Maybe she wouldn't even make it into my memorable patients file. I hoped. Later than night, I heard a rub[9] in her chest. I repeated the X-ray. No change. Maybe I worry too much. On the domestic front, Kristi's mother had arrived from

---

[9]   This is a grating-like sound made by a bruised lung as it rubs against the inside of a patient's chest.

New England and was simultaneously grateful for her daughter's care and worried that everything must turn out well. We talked about transferring her to a larger hospital, but we opted to continue her care here for now. If Kristi deteriorated, I'd be the first to know, and I'd keep the mom informed.

On Monday morning, thirty hours into this tale, Kristi's lungs were only so-so. She needed the oxygen we had been giving her. This morning, at least her rub was gone. The X-ray showed the contusions were stable, but still serious. Her abdominal exam was reassuring, and I took the NGT[10] out. We got her out of bed into a chair so as to help prevent the formation of blood clots in her legs. She also had compression stockings on, but I had held off the low-dose blood thinners for fear of abdominal bleeding. Blood clots tend to form in traumatized patients, and if they break loose, they can migrate to the lungs and really cause problems. I went off to the office, hoping that we would have clear sailing the rest of her stay. But I was uneasy… There was her pulse for one thing. Why had it remained 130 to 140 ever since surgery? There was no evidence that she was bleeding. The lab tests were normal. Her heart shouldn't be racing so. I hoped it would soon settle down.

All day Monday, Kristi's blood count had been slowly dropping. I received a phone report at noon. After office hours, I checked her. Her heart was still racing. I was still worried but couldn't put my fingers on what was going wrong. By 8 p.m., the blood count had fallen further—ten grams of hemoglobin this morning, nine grams at noon, now under eight grams. She was losing blood somewhere for sure. The big question was where. Could it be back in the abdomen? Could I have missed an injury? Had her liver started to bleed again? Could it be in her leg, around the fracture sites?

It was an off-hand remark from the lab tech that jolted me into action. "Doc, her platelets look awfully low on the CBC machine."

We hadn't done a whole lot of lab tests, only those that were necessary to monitor her progress. Thank God for alert, helpful lab techs! I quickly ordered a slew of tests, and the results served to

---

[10] Nasogastric tube.

quantify my unease. Kristi platelets had fallen from 269,000 to a mere 87,000. Ordinarily, they should rise in the early post-op period. Something was consuming them. And her P-time was prolonged.[11]

What could explain these laboratory abnormalities? One that immediately occurred to me was DIC.[12] This was a dread complication of major trauma, liver injury, shock, pancreatitis, transfusion reactions, and even cancer. A number of research studies reported a mortality of 80 percent. We needed one more test to confirm that diagnosis—a D Dimer test.

"We don't do that here," the lab tech informed me. "We do get fibrin split products, but they have to be sent out. You wouldn't get the result for two days at least."

"I need it a lot sooner than that" was my reply.

And as for the fibrin split products, that one is falsely elevated if there are fat globules in the lung. No, what I needed was D Dimer itself. And so we drew the sample and had the hospital rent a taxicab to run the specimen twenty-seven miles east on to the nearest place that could run that test. In the meantime, I arranged for a second X-ray tech to come in and fire up the CT scanner. The very worst thing a surgeon could do was blame a falling hemoglobin on a coagulation abnormality when the true problem was simply a blood vessel bleeding somewhere in the chest or belly. If Kristi were hemorrhaging again, I meant to find out properly this time. She wasn't in shock this time. We had the time to safely do the CT scan event in this hospital. I also began a third unit of blood and two of fresh frozen plasma. We weren't going to let Kristi slip into shock again.

---

[11] A measure of the "thinness" of her blood. Patients who take "blood thinners" for medical reasons have this test done routinely to be sure their blood is of the right "thinness." This test showed that even without medication Kristi had managed to become anti-coagulated. She was bleeding and, worse, she could no longer make clots to stop the bleeding.

[12] Disseminated Intravascular Coagulation. In this disease the body gets "carried away" and makes clots way too enthusiastically. They form in all sorts of places. If they form in the brain, you can have a stroke. After that process has been going on sufficiently long, the clot forming mechanism becomes exhausted and the patient then begins to bleed uncontrollably.

At 10:30 p.m., I now had all the results back. For starters, the D Dimer was positive, meaning we did have a DIC situation, hopefully a mild case. The CT scan showed fluid around surprisingly good-looking lungs and that a smallish amount of a blood/serum mixture had collected in the pelvis. No massive, hidden intra-abdominal hemorrhage. No need to operate. Yet. If the DIC was severe, it could cause the liver to start rebleeding.

"Lookee here, Doc," Donna the ICU nurse called out to me.

Kristi's leg surgery incision had quietly begun to bleed. That settled it for me. We were dealing with DIC for sure. It was time to send her to a genuine trauma center. Not that they could do anything for it that we couldn't.[13] But still in all, parents feel better if their children die in a major trauma center, comforted that indeed all that could have been done was done.

It was simple now that I had reached a diagnosis, but incredibly, my evening was far from over. I laid out the various possibilities to the mom, and to nobody's surprise, she asked me to transfer her daughter. So once again we had to deal with the governmental transfer forms, but the nearest medical center was unable to accept her. Perhaps they had no free beds? I had to look elsewhere—Roanoke, Virginia, or Bristol, Tennessee. The mother's choice was Roanoke. I called Dr. G, the trauma surgeon on call there, and described the case to her. She readily accepted Kristi in transfer but then told me that they couldn't send the helicopter right then. Roanoke, it seemed, was getting blasted with a thunderstorm at the moment.

"Fine" was my response. "She isn't in shock. We'll arrange ground transportation."

I then asked the nurse to get an ambulance here. Incredible as it might seem, we contacted three ambulance services, and all three turned us down.

---

[13] The condition is essentially untreatable, though some hardy souls have tried to give a blood thinner to a bleeding patient on the theory that the initial problem is too many clots and if you can prevent any more of them from happening, then you might (hopefully) stop the bleeding. That is sort of like pouring gasoline on a fire in the hope that if you do it fast enough you can somehow drown the fire by robbing it of oxygen.

"We have a run in the morning. If our crew takes your patient to Roanoke, they'll be tired tomorrow," whined the first one.

"We have only one ambulance on call and have to save it for emergencies." I guessed Kristi was not considered to be a true emergency?

"We're not available this evening."

This was getting frustrating. I next called Bristol, Tennessee, and spoke to their trauma surgeon. He, too, readily accepted Kristi in transfer, and since the thunderstorms had passed through Bristol a number of hours earlier, there was no problem with them sending my friend the helicopter. It took two hours to arrange a transfer!

It was precisely thirty-eight minutes past midnight that the state police helicopter touched down. No, they didn't have a medevac helicopter in this part of the country, so they used the state police helicopter. A hugely obese paramedic, followed by a most diminutive nurse, clambered out of the helicopter and sauntered into the hospital. They took over forty minutes getting Kristi back into the helicopter.

"Lucky she isn't in shock," I muttered under my breath.

But the crowning touch of the entire evening was when the obese paramedic demanded to see the X-rays. He proceeded to riffle through the CT scans.

"Good God!" I muttered under my breath. "His boss has already accepted Kristi in transfer. He has to transport her. What is this bozo looking at the CT scans for?"

He finally found what he was looking for—a chest X-ray.

Aha! I thought. *I was wrong. I am actually in the presence of a genius. This guy must be really good. I bet he is making sure that Kristi doesn't have an occult pneumothorax that will worsen at altitude.*

And so I said to him, most politely, "We did a CT scan, and there is no pneumothorax."

He looked up at me blankly and went back to the chest X-ray. He held it to the ceiling light. He peered at all corners. He rotated it forty-five degrees. He counted the ribs. I really didn't know what he was doing (except wasting time. Maybe he gets paid by the hour?)

But it's a good show, I thought. He had mostly everybody impressed—everybody but me. You see, I was intimately familiar with every one of Kristi X-rays. I'd studied them over and over again. Our noble paramedic was looking at a chest X-ray that was nearly forty-eight hours old, the very first one that was taken when she got to the ER! God knows what he expected to find, but whatever it was, the old X-ray no longer applied to the situation at hand!

Finally, they left. Kristi made a safe arrival in Bristol where she continued to hold her own in their ICU. Over the next several days she slowly improved, in their ICU. In retrospect, she would have improved here had we chosen not to transfer her. Her family is happy. Did she have DIC? Probably only a mild case, if at all. What caused it? Well, in retrospect, when we gave her the third unit of blood in the ICU that evening, her temperature shot up again. I looked at the list of causes of DIC. "Transfusion reaction" jumped out of the page at me! Of course. How simple the explanation after the fact. As usual. The blood wasn't perfectly matched for her. There are hundreds of antibodies out there, and the standard type and cross match detects only the most common. Of course, I could never prove that was the cause, but it sat easiest on my mind. And Bristol assured the mother that we did a pretty good job up here in the backwoods of Virginia.

Funny though. After all the excitement had died down, and I sat down to record these events and emotions, there was one picture that danced in my mind. It was the obese paramedic peering at an obsolete X-ray late at night in our ICU. Sometimes that image faded and was replaced by one of a chimpanzee in a zoo somewhere, peering intently at a physics textbook, holding it upside down.

Steve Fox (The Necessity of Being a *Nice* Bastard)

Steve, disabled from an old mine accident, was out in the woods one fine Saturday morning cutting firewood. As he explained to me, he didn't have "nuttin' else to do." The dead tree he was cutting chanced to fall onto and become entangled with an adjacent tree, and somehow in his efforts to free it, it fell, striking him on his right shoulder and back, doubling him over and then flipping him down into a small ravine. He got up, dusted himself off, had a smoke, and decided to call it a day in the woods.

Several hours later, when the pain in his chest and back refused to let up and when he began to notice his increasing shortness of breath, he went into the ER, where X-rays revealed that the tree had fractured his ninth rib on the right. Worse than that, the jagged end had then punctured his lung, partially collapsing it. And to top things off, when the tree had forcibly doubled him over, it broke his back. Not a complete break, just the compression fracture of one lumbar vertebra. There was no injury to his spinal cord, which was why he was able to get up, dust himself off, and return home.

Called to the ER, I found him to be in pain but not much respiratory distress. What distressed him most was his desire for a "smoke."

"Ya can't do that with oxygen running, Steve," I replied.

His vital signs were stable, but the lab results showed blood in the urine. Not a lot. It was a warning signal that ought to be further investigated. The spinal fracture was at the level of L1, meaning right at the level of the kidneys. Anytime something strikes the human body with enough force to fracture a bone, you have to wonder about the adjacent soft tissues. A CT scan was in order, to be sure that the lumbar vertebra fracture did not have fragments about to compress his precious spinal cord and also to rule out any associated intra-abdominal injuries. So the appropriate requests were made, and by and by, Steve was transported to the X-ray department.

Later, as I sat reviewing the films with the radiologist, he told me that he saw no evidence of any bleeding or other significant injuries to Steve's internal organs.

"How about the kidneys?" I asked.

"Oh, they look fine."

"Yeah, but are they functioning?"

"Well, I hadn't planned on giving any contrast."[14]

"Oh, why not?"

"Well, it's awfully expensive."

"Yeah, but how do I know the kidneys are working?"

"Well, they look okay."

"He has blood in his urine."

"Do you really want me to give contrast?"

"Yes, I do."

And so he did, and yes, the kidneys were fine. While those films were being developed, the radiologist proceeded to tell me that it would cost the hospital nearly $300 for the contrast material. And since Steve was on Social Security Disability, they wouldn't get fully reimbursed for the contrast material.

"I have to watch my budget and justify each expenditure, you know" was how he explained his reluctance to use the contrast material.

"You know what?" I responded. "I couldn't care less how much it costs you or your hospital or your HMO. If I miss a kidney injury, the resulting lawsuit will cost me and my insurance company hundreds of thousands of dollars. There is no percentage at all for me to save costs since it merely increases my risk."

And so now I had a reputation around the hospital of being an unreasonable and somewhat obnoxious bastard. It was Carl Konvolinka, the surgeon I most admired in my surgical training too many years ago at Geisinger Medical Center, who had an aphorism based on that well-worn Leo Durocher quote: "Nice guys finish last, and the patients of nice physicians do likewise."

The next day, one of the local internists, a hospital employee, took me aside and mentioned that word was getting around that I had the impression that I thought that their hospital somehow didn't measure up. (Well, duh! Can you even imagine?) There were hurt

---

[14]   Contrast is a radio-opaque dye given before X-rays are done to reveal if the kidneys are functioning properly. I once diagnosed an unsuspected major kidney injury by using this test in an airplane accident victim in Alaska, who had precisely the same type of back injury that Steve had—a compression fracture of L1.

feelings, she told me. I apologized and said I'd try not to convey that impression. After all, if a complaint against me was sent to the *locum* agency that hired me, they, being in a poor position to evaluate such a complaint, might assume that I truly was a bastard. They can't afford to lose one of their customers. In the *locum* business, it seems, one has to develop the knack of being a nice bastard.

Ah, well. Next time you are in a clinic or hospital or, God forbid, a car accident, you might want to ensure that you get an bastard for a surgeon. Otherwise, an administrative type is going to try to cut corners. We take a dim view of cost-cutting measures when it comes to running an airline. We should take an equally dim view of cost-cutting measures in running a hospital.

CHAPTER 26

Taking Chances

A two-week assignment at a small hospital in Iowa illustrates another challenge a *locum* surgeon can face. There are times when we take personal chances for our patients.

The lone, foreign-born surgeon who worked in this town was not board certified. Like others I had met over the years, he was insecure. He had spent his entire career in the United States at this one location, coming here upon the retirement of the town's beloved icon. He was grudgingly respected but not loved by the medical staff. And so it was not surprising that he opposed the administration's plan to hire me for a two-week period when he was going to be out of town.

"We no need temporary surgeon" was his comment.

Was he worried I'd make him look bad? Or perhaps he feared that I was hunting around for a place to settle down. If so, he'd have competition. The administration felt that hiring me made economic sense, and so it was done.

Prior to my arrival, I had no clue as to this political climate. It was my practice to arrive in town before the staff surgeon departs so that he could go over his patients with me and tell me of any problems. I could also get a sense on how he liked things done so that I could fit in with the least amount of disruption. My first clue on local politics was when the local surgeon flatly refused to even see me.

Helen Winfield

A variety of different operations can often be done for any one condition. Alas, we do not live in a simplistic world in which each disease has one widely accepted, effective treatment. A surgeon must weigh the pros and cons of various options. Many factors enter into the decision-making process—the age and physical condition of the patient, the extent of the disease, the likelihood of complications, etc. For *locum* surgeons, this has to also include the (often unknown) strengths and weaknesses of the particular hospital they find themselves in, especially if it is a small country hospital. And strange as it may seem, on rare occasions, some of the available choices can even represent a danger to the surgeon.

The case of Helen illustrates the complex nature of the decision process. A choice is made. A particular operation is recommended. If things turn out well, the patient may never appreciate that the surgeon took a personal chance.

Helen was a tough eighty-five-year-old lady who was admitted to the hospital by her family physician. Abdominal pain was the problem. She lived alone, and her family had begun to worry about her.

"She seems to be slipping, Doc," her son said to me.

Early Alzheimer's? As for the pain, well, it started the night before and had progressed to waves of pain, accompanied by nausea and vomiting. The initial X-rays were interpreted by the radiologist as an "ileus" (paralysis of the bowels), and so that was the admitting diagnosis. The family physician requested a surgical consult.

I examined Mrs. Winfield and talked to her son. To me, it seemed more like a bowel obstruction than an ileus. But there it was, on the chart. The typed radiology report clearly said, "Ileus."

"I'm going to go look at her X-rays myself," I announced to the family if for no other reason than to give myself time to consider various possibilities. In the X-ray department, I had a look at the films, which had a pattern of much dilated bowel, both large and small.

"Can you be sure this isn't a sigmoid volvulus?"[1] I asked the radiologist.

"Yes. Ummm... Well, ah... Pretty sure..."

"Why don't you give her some barium just to humor me?" was my reply.

And he agreed.

Well, guess what. It was neither an ileus nor a volvulus but a bowel obstruction caused by an obstructing colon cancer. Okay. The diagnosis was now clear. What should be done about it? There was more than one possible operation, each with advantages and disadvantages.

A bit of review for the uninitiated seems to be in order. If the flow of waste material in the colon is obstructed, well, it doesn't idly sit there. The body tries to eliminate the waste by turning it into diarrhea to force it through the narrowed area. The strong contractions of the obstructed bowel are what cause the pain the patient experiences. If the diarrhea "trick" doesn't work, then things back clear up to the stomach, and the patient will vomit. One way or another, the body will eliminate its wastes.

Surgeons are naturally concerned with cleanliness and prevention of infection. One of the steps taken prior to colon surgery is to "clean out" the waste material. Enemas, laxatives, and antibiotics are used to this end. In this way, chances of contamination during surgery are reduced. However, this is not possible in patients with a bowel obstruction. Enemas and laxatives cannot remove the waste material above the obstruction. And so, at surgery, the surgeon will then face a swollen, tense bowel chock full of poisonous diarrhea! If he were to accidentally spill it during surgery, the patient would surely get a horrid peritonitis. What to do?

One option is to divert the obstructed feces, the diarrhea, so that it would drain outside the body. In other words, the patient would receive the dread colostomy. This would guarantee that the patient must have a second operation at a later date to close the colostomy.

---

[1] The sigmoid colon manages to flop itself around, twisting into an obstructing loop.

There is, however, another way. One can, in selected patients, seal both ends of the dilated, obstructed, diarrhea-filled colon with stapling instruments and then remove the whole of it in its entirety. This is a much bigger operation. Much normal colon is, perforce, removed along with the cancerous segment. But if things go well, it is then safe to immediately rejoin the small intestine back to the remaining colon and presto, you are done. No colostomy. No need for a second operation. Despite the fact that this is a much bigger operation than the removal of the cancer and colostomy, many surgeons consider this to be the "operation of choice" for obstructing left-sided colon cancers.

But there is a downside. About 5 percent of such patients will be troubled by diarrhea for the rest of their lives. I had done this operation nine times in the previous twenty years, and so far, had nine delighted patients. Could Helen be number ten?

Here is what ran through my mind as I walked back to her room from the X-ray department:

1. Avoiding a colostomy in a patient that may be developing Alzheimer's disease is no small consideration. A colostomy in such a patient might be all it takes to push her into a nursing home.

2. She is eighty-five, and a subtotal colectomy is a big operation. Can she stand it?

3. The safest thing is to do the colostomy. You can't go wrong by choosing the safest thing. Nobody can criticize you for doing the standard, tried-and-true operation. Sure there will be two operations, but those are the breaks of the game for the patient. Tough for her.

4. *Subtotal colectomy... Hmm...* I wonder if they have ever done such an operation in this small hospital. Certainly, they don't have the equipment I'll need. They'll have to send out to get me the staplers that I'd need to safely do this operation in the shortest possible time, with minimal risk of spillage.

5. What if I do the operation, and there is a complication? I won't be here to take care of it. She'll be under the care of the "regular" surgeon, who likely has never done this operation. Worse, I know that he actively opposed hiring me for *locum tenens* coverage: "We no need temporary surgeon. We do fine like in past." All it would take would be a stray, off-hand remark to the effect that he doesn't do this kind of "dangerous" operation. He does the "safe" operation. If he had been here, none of this would have happened.

6. Why take a chance on somebody I hardly know? Do the safe thing. If this lady has to live with a colostomy, well, that's their problem. Why should I, a temporary, itinerant surgeon who they'll never see again, stick my neck out and take a chance for the patient? If things go wrong, the family will turn on me in a flash, and I'll get sued. I'll make an ideal candidate for their ire at mother's illness and complication. They may not ever sue a beloved local doctor, but who cares about a transient from out of town?

7. If it were my mother, I'd do the subtotal. I *know* I can do it safely, and the chances of a leak in my hands are less than 5 percent. I *know* this because I keep track of my statistics.

8. Nobody here knows about my statistics. For them, it will be a strange big operation.

What to do? What to do? What is in it for me to take on a *personal* risk on behalf of my patient? Nothing really, except that she is, after all, another human being and I want to do what is best for her, regardless of my own personal risk. Wonder if the accursed lawyers even *faintly* understand this?

And so what did I do? Well, I did the subtotal colectomy because that was what I'd want for my mother. And I left town two days later after the town's regular surgeon had returned. And I wondered and wondered during my next *locum* assignment, *How is she doing now?* One thing I was quite certain of was that she and her family would never appreciate that I took a risk for her. They simply assumed that there was but one operation per disease and that the surgeon did it, and the patient got better.

Much later, I learned via a circuitous route that not only did the patient do well but was also grateful.

An Infant with a Hernia

My second example of risk-taking on the part of the surgeon involved a case when I was still in training many years ago at Geisinger Medical Center in Central Pennsylvania. In this case, my personal risk was much greater. I could well have been arrested for assault and battery, perhaps even losing my medical license. However, the problem with surgery is that often a decision *must* be made, no matter how difficult. Sitting on your hands is not an option if it results in harm or death to another human being. Many years ago, I made just such a difficult decision, and happily everything turned out well. Here is this curious story.

One night when I was on surgery call, I was called to the ER to see a baby with its intestines lying out on the abdominal wall.

Huh?

Yep. It seemed that this child had been born to a local Amish family. The infant had a large hernia, one that involved his umbilicus. A few days later, the father, out in the barn tending to his animals, happened to notice that when a sheep delivered, the new lamb was enclosed in a membrane (the amniotic membrane). He cut it away to let the new lamb breathe. As he stood there in the barn, he had this *vision*: Such he was to do to his son. He went to the house, and in front of his horrified wife, took out a razor and proceeded to slash the infant's umbilical hernia open. Naturally, the kid screamed, blood ran all over the place, and his son's intestines spilled out— all over his abdomen and bed. There must have been a great fuss. Much against the father's wishes, the infant was transported to the Emergency Room, and I was called in.

By this stage in my training, I was the Chief Surgical Resident and could operate independently. Oh, that heady glory! It looked like a simple problem to me—merely take the infant to the OR, wash and reinsert the intestines, and repair the hernia. And so it was proposed to the parents.

"No."

"What?"

"God doesn't want you to do this to my son" was the father's calm reply.

The mother was anxiously wringing her hands, but she had no say in this particular Amish family. Now here was something that I hadn't been taught. What to do? Hiding my confusion, I retired to the nursing station and asked the grizzled old ER nurse, Flossie, what I should do.

"Oh, you should call the county mental health workers," she quickly replied. "They can get a court order, and then you are off the hook."

And so it was done. And you know what? The judge said he'd hold a hearing on the matter *in the morning*!

In the rashness of my youth, I exclaimed, "Well, piss on the judge! And the father too! I'm going to surgery!"

Somebody warned me, "Doctor, you can't do that without parental permission!"

"The hell I can't! That baby is going to get peritonitis and *die* if I don't operate! Who is going to stop me?"

Silence. I glared at everybody. Nobody even looked back at me.

I took that little tyke to surgery and fixed his hernia without his parents' permission, indeed with the father's express forbiddance. The kid did fine and went home. And I never heard "boo" from the family, the courts, the judge, the staff surgeons, nor the administration.

CHAPTER 27

Conclusion

I hope that my stories have been informative and enlightening to many and at least entertaining to all. It is my hope that the public will see that the practice of surgery does not always automate well. Sometimes diagnoses remain obscure. Sometimes they must be arrived at in the face of conflicting evidence. Lab tests or X-rays can be falsely normal or abnormal. "What to leave in, what to leave out" in the words of the popular song "Against the Wind."

Another factor, perhaps even worse, is that frequently one's decisions must be made quickly in the face of a deteriorating situation. At such times, you simply don't have the time to gather more data to guide your decision. You face the twin dangers of failing to recommend surgery if it is needed, as opposed to rushing to surgery when it is not needed. You dare not be wrong in either situation. A patient can be harmed by your failure to operate if it is needed, as opposed to being harmed by an operation that is not needed. It is in these situations that you must rely upon your past experience and your gut instinct.

Another aspect of surgery that might not be apparent to the general public is that even after a diagnosis has been decided upon, one particular operation is not automatically in order. There are often several different possible operations for any given condition, each with advantages and disadvantages that have to be carefully weighed for each particular patient, considering his or her age and ancillary medical conditions. I hope that my stories have illustrated both the difficulty in arriving at a diagnosis and then choosing the most appropriate surgical operation.

And always, after the fact, the situation is perfectly crystal clear. Your successes and failures lie out in the open for all to see. It is then obvious exactly what you should or should not have done.

There is yet another aspect of surgery that is not well appreciated by the general public. A few decisions represent a degree of risk to the surgeon! If you make a choice that does not work out well, you could be blamed. I chose two such stories for Chapter 26; in one of them, I agonized which operation to perform. In my second story, I did what I thought to be ethically moral but could have easily been arrested for assault and battery.

Lastly, in this book, I have also tried to give examples of how bureaucracy often has a negative impact on the practice of medicine. The ever-present threat of lawsuits results in unnecessary tests. Balanced against this are instances in which desirable tests are prohibited in a regulatory attempt to keep costs down. All this exacts a toll upon the public whether we realize it or not. It is for the politicians and ultimately the public to guide the adoption of governmental regulations that ensure quality results without having adverse consequences.

I thoroughly enjoyed the seventeen years of traveling and doing surgery in small rural hospitals, helping patients who otherwise would have had to travel to larger cities. I also take a certain measure of pride in the fact that many severely injured patients simply would not have survived had I not been where I was, when I was.

There is merit in retiring when your health is still good. You can expect time to enjoy retirement with your beloved. I have known far too many colleagues who held on, held on, perhaps afraid to retire. When I was a first-year surgical resident in training, one of the patients I helped care for was a family physician from a nearby town. His diagnosis was stage IV colon cancer. One day, when I saw him on rounds, he fixed me with a stare and solemnly pointed a finger at me. "Young man, if there is something you wish to do, don't put it off until it is too late!" He had always longed to visit China, and he kept putting it off because of all the sick people he felt he had to tend to. Now his cancer was denying him his lifelong dream. And the beloved Milt Barrent, who once was my senior surgical partner in Iowa, was diagnosed with inoperable pancreatic cancer only three months into his retirement.

And so it was that in the summer of 2007, age sixty-seven, we made the decision that it was time for me to retire. Fortunately, our health was still fine. Betty and I have heartily enjoyed our retirement, finding time to travel, visit friends and relatives, and participate in nine overseas charity medical trips. Retirement also afforded me the time to volunteer for Angel Flights, a nonprofit organization that provides free air transportation to major medical centers for patients with severe illness.

Glossary

abscess. The collection of a pool of pus from an infection. Abscesses must be drained in order for them to heal.

acetabulum. That cuplike socket in your pelvis, which accepts the ball at the top of your femur (thigh bone).

ACLS (advanced cardiac life support). An intensive course on the initial care and stabilization of heart-attack victims.

acute abdomen. Any serious medical or surgical condition causing abdominal pain. This is often (but not always!) a surgical emergency. The diagnostic dilemma is to sort out and exclude medical conditions that present this way and do not require surgery.

adhesion. Scar tissue developing after surgery, causing loops of small bowel to adhere to each other or to the abdominal wall. Adhesions can pinch off bowel continuity, causing a bowel obstruction. And of course, they make any surgery much more difficult.

afebrile. Literally "not having a fever"—that is, having a normal body temperature.

AIDS (acquired immunodeficiency syndrome). It's a disease caused by HIV (human immunodeficiency virus).

anastomosis. The surgical joining of two tubular structures (most commonly either blood vessels or the bowel). It's necessary after a diseased segment has been removed. The sutures have to be meticulously placed so that the joint is leak-tight. A dread complication of this operation is an anastamotic leak, in which some of the contents leak through the suture line, causing blood loss or an infection.

anemia. Low red blood cell count. It can be caused by nutritional problems, bone marrow disease, or a chronic, slow blood loss—say, from a tumor in the colon.

aneurysm. This is the ballooning in the diameter of an artery, usually the aorta, due to either a birth defect or weakness caused by arteriosclerosis. If an aortic aneurysm ruptures, you can rapidly bleed to death.

angiocath. A needle covered by a plastic sheath. After insertion into a vein, the needle is removed, leaving the plastic sheath behind. Then IV fluids can be run through the plastic sheath.

aorta. The large blood vessel through which the heart pumps blood to the body.

aphasia. The inability to speak, most commonly caused by a stroke.

appendix. A small tubular organ attached to the cecum at the very beginning of the colon in the right lower quadrant of the abdomen. When infected, it will swell and can burst.

arteriogram. A special X-ray taken after a radio-opaque dye is injected into the arteries to show their outline, patency, continuity, etc.

arteriosclerosis. The so-called "hardening" of the arteries. Calcium and cholesterol are deposited in the artery walls. The artery can thus narrow, interfering with blood flow.

ascending colon. The large bowel on the right side of the abdomen that joins to the transverse colon.

asystole. The condition in which a heart has stopped beating.

ataxia. The loss of normal balance leading to a staggering gait.

ATLS (advanced trauma life support). An intensive course on the initial care and support of injured patients.

avulse. To rip away. To tear from its foundation.

barium enema. Barium, a non-soluble radio-opaque substance, is injected into a patient's rectum for the purpose of outlining the shape of the colon during the subsequent X-rays. See *gastrografin enema* below.

bile. The discharge from the liver containing waste products that the liver has filtered from the blood.

bilirubin. One of the waste products excreted by the liver. If the common bile duct is obstructed, it will back up into the bloodstream, where it can be detected by a suitable blood test. Since it is colored orange, it also shows in the "whites" of a patient's eyes, which become "jaundiced."

blood count. A microscopic report on the numbers and concentration of the various cells (white cells, red cells) that make up the composition of our blood. An elevated white count is indicative of an infection; a low red count is diagnostic of anemia.

bollard. A short but thick bulbous metal post mounted on a dock to which a ship's mooring ropes can be secured.

bradycardia. Slow heartbeat.

breech. A situation where an infant lies in the uterus in a head-up position. Delivery is still possible but much more difficult as the largest part of the fetus (its head) delivers last and may become stuck half-in and half-out of the uterus.

bronchoscope. A flexible fiber-optic examination tube that is inserted into a patient's trachea, then down to the bronchi. Biopsies can be obtained through it, and obstructions are sucked out.

cachectic. An emaciated condition either because of starvation or severe disease.

CBC (complete blood cell count). This will detect the presence of many diseases.

CBD (common bile duct). The sole drainage path through which the liver discharges the waste products it has filtered from the blood into the bowel so that they can be eliminated.

CCU (coronary care unit).

cecum. The beginning of the large bowel. It is located in the right lower quadrant of the abdomen. The appendix is attached to it.

cellulitis. An inflammation or infection of the soft tissues of the body, most often due to bacterial infection.

central line. An intravenous line inserted through one of the large vessels in the neck or under the collar bone. The tip of this line lies in the superior vena cava, a large vein right outside the heart. This line can be used to infuse concentrated nutrients for those patients who cannot tolerate oral feeding. It is also used in severe trauma to measure the blood pressure at the entrance to the heart.

central venous pressure (CVP). The blood pressure at the entrance to the heart. It is used to monitor and adjust the treatment of severely injured patients.

cervical spine. Your neck bones.

chest tube. A simple plastic tube ranging in size from a quarter inch to half an inch in diameter. It is surgically inserted between two ribs into the space between the lung and chest wall. The lungs are not directly attached to the chest wall; instead, they are held there by a slight vacuum. Anything that destroys that vacuum will result in the lung collapsing and becoming nonfunctional. The chest tube can re-establish this slight vacuum, as well as remove any abnormal fluid that might be surrounding the lung.

chole. Medical slang for cholecystectomy; the operation to remove a diseased gallbladder.

cholecystectomy. Surgical removal of the gallbladder.

cholecystitis. Inflammation or infection of the gallbladder.

cholelithiasis. The condition of having gallstones in one's gallbladder; indicative of chronic disease.

chromic. A type of suture made of "catgut," which, by the way, does not come from cats.

circulating nurse. The person who is able to move about the operating room and is the one who would handle non-sterile supplies as needed during surgery.

cirrhosis. Scar tissue that builds up in the liver, usually as the result of alcohol abuse; also can form after a long-term infection with a virus.

clavicle. The collarbone.

code. A medical emergency declaration, often over a hospital's loudspeakers, to the effect that there is a cardiac emergency (CPR) in process. There are definite protocols on who responds and what is done during a code.

colectomy. Surgical removal of the colon, the large intestine. A colectomy can be either partial or total.

colon. The large intestine, which takes the liquid discharge from the small intestine and concentrates it by removing excess water. It originates at the right lower quadrant of a person's abdomen, rises upward toward the liver, where it is known as the hepatic flexure. It then goes to the left, across the upper abdomen (splenic flexure), before turning down, eventually ending in the rectum and anus. That portion immediately above the rectum is known as the sigmoid colon.

colonoscope. A flexible fiber-optic tube that can be inserted through a patient's rectum (under suitable sedation!) and guided through the entire length of the colon, allowing both examination and biopsies to make a diagnosis.

colostomy. If the colon is divided to remove a diseased portion, the surgeon then faces the decision on the next step. In many cases, it is safe to rejoin the severed ends. In other cases (severe infection), it is safer to bring the ends out to the abdominal surface through smaller incisions. There it is sutured in place. A suitable plastic bag can be glued to the skin, and all fecal material will empty into the bag. The distal end is also sutured in place but carries no contents. It termed a mucous fistula. Once sufficient healing has occurred, it may be possible (during a second operation) to rejoin the two ends of the colon (re-establish intestinal continuity).

common bile duct. The one and only channel for the liver to discharge its toxic waste products into the bowel, where they are ultimately eliminated.

COPD (chronic obstructive pulmonary disease). Most commonly brought on by smoking.

CPR (cardio-pulmonary resuscitation). This may involve compressions to the patient's chest or an application of an electrical shock to the heart.

CRNA (certified registered nurse anesthetist). A registered nurse who has received additional training so that he or she is able to administer general anesthesia.

C-section. The surgical delivery of an infant through an incision through the abdominal wall. This is done when normal vaginal delivery is not possible. Speed is often a necessity, especially if this is done because of fetal distress.

CSF (cerebral-spinal fluid). The brain "floats" in CSF within the skull.

C-spine (cervical spine). The bones in your neck.

CT (computed tomography). Computer-guided X-rays that give exquisite detail of the body. These X-ray "slices" can then be mentally reconstructed to yield a three-dimensional picture of the disease processes at hand.

CVP (central venous pressure). That venous blood pressure measured through a central line or subclavian line.

cystic duct. The small duct connecting the gallbladder to the side of the common bile duct. The gallbladder is essentially a storage vessel off to the side of the common bile duct. The cystic duct is necessarily divided upon removal of the gallbladder. During this process, extreme care is taken to avoid injury to the vital common bile duct, which is the only route for the liver to discharge toxic waste products into the intestines for ultimate elimination.

DCIS (ductal carcinoma in situ). A precancerous breast disease.

debride. The surgical process of trimming obviously dead tissue out of a ragged, dirty wound prior to its repair.

descending colon. The large bowel on the left side of the abdomen that joins to the sigmoid colon.

DIC (disseminated intravascular coagulation). A serious hematological complication in which clots form far and wide within a patient's vascular system.

diverticula. Little outpouchings on the surface of the colon. They can appear anywhere, but most are on the left. There is an increasing frequency with age. If infected, they can lead to the condition of diverticulitis, which can then progress to peritonitis.

diverticulitis. Inflammation of little outpouchings (diverticuli) on the colon; it's more common on the left compared to the right.

DOA (dead on arrival). A term used to describe a patient who has died prior to arrival at the emergency room.

DPL (diagnostic peritoneal lavage). A small plastic tube is inserted into the abdomen of a trauma victim. Clear saline solution is run in and then aspirated back to see if there is blood lying anywhere within the abdominal cavity. This has the advantage of being quick but lacks the more complete information one obtains from a CT scan of the abdomen. I used it chiefly in small hospitals, especially those with inadequate CT equipment, in order to assure myself that transfer of a seriously injured patient to a larger hospital was safe.

ectopic pregnancy. Normally, when a woman ovulates, the ovum (egg) enters the fallopian tube leading to the uterus. Fertilization, if it is going to take place, happens within the fallopian tube. The now-fertilized ovum must then continue its journey to the uterus, where it implants and grows into a fetus. Sometimes, however, the progress of that fertilized ovum is interrupted. It halts and then begins to grow within the fallopian tube. If this happens, the fallopian tube will eventually rupture and the patient will begin to hemorrhage. Urgent surgery is then necessary to prevent the woman from bleeding to death.

EGD (esophagogastroduodenoscopy). Use of a flexible fiber-optic endoscope to examine the esophagus, stomach, and upper part of the duodenum.

EKG (electrocardiogram). Used to assess cardiac health or disease of the heart.

emphysema. A chronic lung disease often caused by smoking. Air gets trapped in the lungs because of the loss of normal tissue that supports and keeps the small air passages open during exhalation. Patients have difficulty breathing because their lungs are constantly over filled.

empyema. A severe infection of the gallbladder in which it literally fills with pus.

EMT (emergency medical technician).

endoscope. A flexible fiber-optic tube that can be used to examine either the upper or lower digestive system.

endotracheal tube. A plastic tube inserted into a patient's trachea. This is then connected to a mechanical ventilator so that it can breathe for him or her.

epigastric. Pertaining to the upper part of the abdomen.

ER (emergency room).

ERCP (endoscopic retrograde cholangio-pancreatogram). This procedure is performed by a gastroenterologist using an endoscope to inject dye into the lower end of the common bile duct. X-rays can then reveal the anatomy and any diseases in the ducts and liver.

esophagitis. Inflammation of the esophagus. It can be due to a failure of the valve at its lower end, allowing acidic gastric contents to reflux up into its delicate and unprotected lining.

fecal diversion. Known as either a colostomy or ileostomy, this is an operation designed to interrupt the flow of feces through the colon. It is done when a diseased portion of the colon has been removed and the surgeon judges that it is not safe to rejoin (anastomose) the ends of divided intestine.

femur. Thigh bone.

fetal distress. A condition that can develop during childbirth, usually when the fetus is deprived of sufficient oxygen. When this situation develops, an immediate delivery, usually by C-section, is in order.

flail chest. A severe injury to the chest in which ribs are broken in two places. The segment of the chest wall between those two fracture sites cannot move with the rest of the chest. As the chest expands, the flail segment remains immobile or even moves in the opposite direction. Usually, the underlying lung is also severely bruised.

Foley catheter. A soft rubber tube with an inflatable balloon at the tip. It is inserted into the bladder so that urine can be collected in badly injured or very sick patients.

gallbladder. A small hollow organ that serves to store bile, the waste product of the liver. It drains via the cystic duct into the common bile duct and thence into the intestines, where eventually it is eliminated from the body.

gastrectomy. Surgical removal of the stomach. It can be partial or total.

gastritis. Inflammation of the lining of the stomach.

gastroenterologist. A medical doctor specializing in diseases of the liver, stomach, and intestines. This is not a surgeon.

gastrografin enema. In principle, it's the same as a barium enema, only a different contrast material is used. Gastrografin is water soluble and is safe to use if one suspects that a perforation of the colon has occurred.

gastroscope. A flexible fiber-optic tube that can be inserted through a patient's esophagus and into the stomach. The esophagus, stomach, and upper part of the duodenum can be examined, and biopsies can be obtained to make a diagnosis.

GI bleed. Bleeding from anywhere in a patient's gastrointestinal tract, esophagus, stomach, the small or large intestines.

GI. Refers to the gastrointestinal tract from the mouth to the anus.

GP (general practitioner). Also known as a family practitioner.

H+P. A history and physical exam report. It's part of a patient's chart in which the admitting physician records the results of his interview with the patient, as well as the physical findings on examination.

hemopneumothorax. It's similar to the simple pneumothorax, only now there is blood freely filling the pleural space.

hemostat. It's a surgical instrument that looks like a pair of scissors, but instead of blades, it has jaws somewhat like those in a pair of pliers. It is normally used to clamp bleeding blood vessels during surgery, but a hemostat can also be used to grasp any number of things. Fishermen are especially fond of using a hemostat to remove hooks from fish.

hepatic flexure. That portion of your colon that lies in the right upper quadrant immediately beneath your liver.

hernia. Any abnormal opening in the abdominal wall that leads to a cavity (sac) outside the abdominal wall but still under the skin. Hernias occur in the inguinal (groin) region (especially in males), in the umbilicus, or anywhere in the abdominal wall, where there is a defect resulting from prior surgery or injury. They are dangerous when the opening into this cavity is narrow, for then any bowel that protrudes into the sac can become trapped there. If the trapped bowel swells, it can have its blood supply cut off, and gangrene will then set in.

HIDA scan. A test used to evaluate the function of your liver. It tracks the flow of bile from the liver down into the intestine. It also shows whether the gallbladder is functioning properly.

HIV (human immunodeficiency virus). The cause of AIDS.

HMO (health maintenance organization).

hyperalimentation. Concentrated nutrients are infused into a patient who is unable to eat. These IV solutions are so concentrated that they can only be given via a central line, which is an IV that has been inserted peripherally and then guided into the great vessels leading to the heart.

hypertension. High blood pressure.

hypotension. Low blood pressure.

hypovolemia. A condition in which the intravascular blood volume is low. It can be caused by hemorrhage or even simple dehydration. Hypovolemia often results in shock or low blood pressure.

hysterectomy. Surgical removal of the uterus.

I+D (incision and drainage). An operation done to drain pus from an infected site. Treatment for an abscess.

IBW (ideal body weight).

ICU (intensive care unit).

ileostomy. The bringing of a divided end of the small bowel to the surface of the abdomen to divert its contents away from diseased bowel lower in the GI tract.

ileus. Paralysis of the bowels that accompanies many serious illnesses. Surgery for this condition is usually not warranted. On the other hand, if the patient is actually suffering from a bowel obstruction, then surgery indeed is necessary. Distinguishing between these two can be tricky.

incarcerated. When referring to a hernia, it means that the bowel has filled the hernia sac and become trapped there. If the neck of the hernia is small and if the bowel swells, then its circulation can be cut off, leading to gangrene. The only safe hernias are those that have a sufficiently large neck that any bowel in them can be easily squished back into the abdominal cavity.

intercostal space. The space between the ribs.

intubation. The insertion of a plastic tube is inserted into a patient's trachea and connected to a mechanical ventilator, which will breathe for him or her.

IV (intravenous). Usually, it refers to a solution that can be run through a plastic tube into a patient's veins to correct dehydration, restore blood pressure, or deliver drugs.

IVC (inferior vena cava). A large vein within the abdomen and lower chest that drains blood coming from the lower body. It empties into the heart.

IVP (intravenous pyelogram). A contrast-enhanced X-ray of the kidneys to determine if they are functioning properly.

jaundice. The yellow discoloration in a person's skin or eye whites. It is due to a high level of the toxic waste product that the liver produces (bilirubin). If the common bile duct that drains the liver becomes obstructed—say, by a stone or a tumor—then bilirubin backs up into the bloodstream, and the patient is said to be jaundiced.

lap chole. Removal of the gallbladder (cholecystectomy) using minimally invasive (laparoscopic) instruments. These slender instruments can be inserted through mere half-inch incisions, and the operation is done using a video camera, thin graspers, cautery, scissors, clip appliers, etc.

laparoscope. A long, thin instrument with a solid-state camera at the tip. It can be inserted through a quarter-inch puncture of the abdomen and used to inspect the abdominal contents or guide the performance of many different types of minimally invasive surgery.

laparotomy. Exploratory abdominal surgery.

large intestine. See *colon*.

left hemicolectomy. Surgical removal of the left side of the colon.

liver. The largest solid organ in the body. It lies in the right upper quadrant of the abdomen. Immediately beneath it lies the gallbladder, a temporary storage area for bile.

LLQ (left lower quadrant). Part of the abdomen. Under this area is the sigmoid colon.

locum tenens. A Latin expression best translated as "taking the place of…" In medicine, it refers to a doctor temporarily filling in for another who is away from his or her practice.

lumbar spine. The lower backbone.

LUQ (left upper quadrant). Part of the abdomen. Here lies the easily damaged spleen and a portion of the left colon.

mesentery. The blood vessels that nourish the small bowel travel from the great blood vessels that lie behind the abdominal contents out to the bowels, encased in a wide ribbon of peritoneum and fat.

mucosa. The soft cellular lining of a hollow organ, such as the colon or bladder.

mucous fistula. When a segment of the colon must be removed and when it is deemed unsafe to rejoin the ends, then both ends are brought out onto the abdominal wall through suitably placed small incisions. The proximal (upper) end will discharge waste material into a plastic bag glued to the abdomen (the dread colostomy). The distal end carries no content. It is termed a mucous fistula.

MVA (motor vehicle accident).

necrotic. Gangrenous; dead.

NGT (nasogastric tube). This tube is made of plastic and used to empty a patient's stomach. It is commonly inserted through a patient's nose and goes down the esophagus to the stomach.

NPO. (Latin: *non per os*). In English, it means "nothing by mouth." It's a term designating those patients who, because of their condition, are dangerous to feed.

omentum. An apron of fat that drapes down from the transverse colon, covering abdominal contents. It frequently is referred to as the "policeman of the abdomen" because it can seal perforations and wall off abscesses so they don't spread throughout the abdomen.

OR (operating room).

OR crew. A team of professionals. Titles of team members and their duties may be unfamiliar to the layperson. There are four, sometimes five, categories of healthcare givers present and working together during any operation.

- Scrub Nurse. The person who wears a cap, mask, sterile gloves. and sterile outer gown. He or she must remain within the sterile environment that surrounds the operating table. This team member arranges the sterile surgical instruments on a "back table" as well as on a nearby small portable stand and hands them to the surgeon to use.
- Circulating Nurse. The person who is able to move about the operating room and is the one who would handle non-sterile supplies as needed during surgery.
- Anesthesia is administered by either another physician or a specially trained nurse (CRNA). The vital signs of the patient are continuously monitored. He or she is always in close communication with the surgeon.
- The surgeon is in charge of the operation. He or she may be performing the actual operation or supervising another.
- The assistant(s): one or more people who provide the extra hands often needed for the operation. May be other physicians or specially trained OR technicians.

osteoporosis. The thinning and weakening of bones as we age. This is especially severe in elderly women.

pancreatitis. Inflammation of the pancreas gland. This can range from mild to so severe that a patient's life is in danger. The pancreas gland makes the enzyme that enables your digestive juices to dissolve protein. If it leaks out of the inflamed gland, you commence to digest your own insides.

peptic ulcer disease. The common ulcers we read and talk about. Once thought to be caused by stress, we now know they are caused by a bacterium (H. Pylori). And so the treatment is now antibiotics and antacids, not surgery, unless an emergency condition arises.

peritoneum. The membrane that lines the abdominal cavity, which is therefore also known as the peritoneal cavity.

peritonitis. Inflammation of the abdominal cavity.

pleural space. The lungs are not actually attached to the inner chest wall. Instead, they are held there by a slight vacuum. Normally, this is only a potential space. However, if the vacuum is destroyed, the lung collapses, and this potential space is now be filled with either air or fluid.

pleurodesis. A surgical procedure in which dense adhesions are created between the lung and the inner chest wall. This prevents the lungs from collapsing if the slight vacuum that ordinarily holds the lungs inflated is destroyed. Pleurodesis is performed for patients who have had repeated episodes of collapsed lungs (pneumothoraces) in order to prevent future occurrences.

pneumothorax. A condition in which the slight vacuum within the pleural space (the space between the lung and inner chest wall) has been destroyed, either by disease or an injury to the lung. When this happens, the lung collapses. The treatment is to insert a chest tube to re-expand the lung. Pneumothoraces come in three varieties: "simple" as described above, "tension pneumothoraxes," and "hemopneumothoraxes," in which blood is also freely present in the pleural space.

psoas. Vertical muscles that parallel the spinal column on the inside of the abdomen.

PUD (peptic ulcer disease).

radio-opaque. A substance that X-rays cannot penetrate. It is infused into hollow organs, such as the stomach or colon, so that the outline of these normally invisible organs can be seen.

RBC (red blood cell) count. The number of red blood cells per millionth of a liter of blood. The red blood cells carry oxygen from our lungs to our tissues. A low RBC count is called anemia.

rectus abdominis muscle. A pair of muscles running vertically on the anterior wall of the abdomen.

renal dialysis. A treatment for patients with kidney failure. Their blood is temporarily routed through an artificial kidney to remove toxic substances.

retractor. A surgical instrument looking roughly like a small garden hoe. With it, the incision can be held open by an assistant so that the surgeon can perform the operation. Retractors come in a variety of sizes and configurations. Some are merely handheld, while others can be attached to a framework clamped to the edge of the OR table to free up OR personnel to better participate in the operation at hand.

retroperitoneum. The abdominal space behind all the organs. The kidneys, great blood vessels (aorta and vena cava), as well as various muscles live there.

right hemicolectomy. Surgical removal of the right colon.

RLQ (right lower quadrant). Part of the abdomen, the "home" of the appendix.

road rash. Irregular and often dirt-filled deep abrasions and/or lacerations that a person receives when hitting the earth or pavement at high speed. The dirt and foreign material in road rash often is usually ground into the wound.

RUQ (right upper quadrant). Part of the abdomen. Under this region lies the liver, gallbladder, and a portion of the right colon.

sacrum. The lower end of the spinal column. It is part of the pelvis.

scrub nurse. The person who wears a cap, mask, sterile gloves. and sterile outer gown. He or she must remain within the sterile environment that surrounds the operating table. This team member arranges the sterile surgical instruments on a "back table" as well as on a nearby small portable stand and hands them to the surgeon to use.

sebaceous cyst. A round cystic structure filled with a cheesy, foul-smelling substance that forms when the pore of a sebaceous gland becomes obstructed. The easiest treatment is excision of the cyst under local anesthesia.

seborrheic keratosis. A common, noncancerous skin growth.

septic. A potentially life-threatening condition caused by the body's response to an infection.

serum electrolytes. A measurement of various ions in the blood: sodium, chlorides, potassium, etc.

sigmoid colon. The lower part of the left colon. The upper part is joined to the descending colon, while the lower end joins to the rectum. The site of most instances of diverticulitis.

SMA (superior mesenteric artery). It provides blood to the intestines.

spleen. A fragile blood-filled organ with many immunological functions to protect against infection. It is located in the left upper quadrant of the abdominal cavity. Surgical teaching was once that any injury at all to this organ mandated its removal to prevent hemorrhage. We have now learned how to preserve it in many instances.

splenic flexure. That portion of your colon lying in the left upper quadrant of your abdomen, adjacent to the spleen.

subclavian line. An intravenous line inserted into the large vein that lies beneath the clavicle (collarbone). It can be used to infuse concentrated nutrients in patients who cannot tolerate oral feeding. Also frequently used in critically ill patients to measure the pressure in the superior vena cava at the entrance to the heart. Also known as a central line.

superior vena cava. The large vein located within the chest that carries blood draining from the head and arms into the heart.

sutures. The thread used in sutures is made of a variety of materials.

tension pneumothorax. It's similar to a simple pneumothorax, only now pressure builds up in the pleural space and forces the chest contents to the opposite side, compressing and interfering with their function.

tertiary health-care center. A center capable of offering the full spectrum of health care specialties to handle complex cases. These centers rarely need to transfer a patient to another care center.

thoracotomy. A thoracic operation in which the chest is opened to perform surgery either upon the lungs or heart.

TPN (total peripheral nutrition). See *hyperalimentation.*

transverse colon. That part of the large intestine that stretches across the upper abdomen from right to left.

transverse lie. A situation that can develop during childbirth. Usually, the fetus is either head up or head down (vertex or breech). In both of these situations, the infant can be delivered. A third possibility is when the fetus is oriented crosswise in the uterus. When stuck in that position, delivery cannot take place.

The infant must either be rotated to vertex or breech position or be delivered by C-section.

trauma center levels. Level I trauma centers have on staff all the medical and surgical specialties needed to completely care for severely injured patients. These specialists are on duty 24/7 and are actually within the hospital at all times. Level II trauma centers also have on staff medical and surgical specialists to completely care for severely injured patients, though a few of the specialists may not be physically present in the hospital around the clock. Level III centers lack some specialists and often must transfer seriously injured patients to larger centers.

trigeminal neuralgia. A chronic disorder of the trigeminal nerve in your face. It causes what has been described as the most excruciating pain known to humanity.

trocar. A sharp metal rod inside a plastic tube to facilitate insertion of the plastic tube into a patient. The sharp trocar penetrates the abdominal or chest wall and then is removed, leaving the plastic tube in place. Trocars are also used to create the passageways into the abdomen for introducing laparoscopic instruments. There is an accompanying danger that the trocar can injure an organ in the process.

UGI. A series of X-rays of the upper gastrointestinal system. The patient swallows a radio-opaque contrast material that outlines the shape of the stomach and duodenum on the X-rays.

ultrasound. A diagnostic machine that beams ultrasonic sound waves into the body and records the echoes they produce. Like an X-ray, it gives information on disease processes within the body. The machine is portable and can be employed anywhere in the hospital.

umbilical hernia. A hernia, usually of congenital origin, in which there is an abdominal defect under the umbilicus that allows intestines to protrude out and come to rest beneath the skin.

ureter. The tube that conveys urine from the kidneys to the bladder, where it is stored until voided.

VA (Veterans Affairs). It operates a countrywide network of hospitals and clinics to care for our military veterans.

VBAC (vaginal birth after a C-section). The fear in the 1990s was that, for a woman who has had a prior C-section, the uterine scar, which is potentially a weak point, could rupture during labor, creating a life-threatening emergency. So for a long time, the mandate was "once a C-section, always a C-section." Those that tried a VBAC had to ensure there was surgical backup immediately available in case the uterus did indeed rupture. Because of the development of a low transverse uterine incision, nowadays, VBACs rarely result in rupture.

vena cava. The large vein that drains blood into the heart. The superior vena cava drains the upper body and lies within the chest. The inferior vena cava drains the lower body and lies within the abdominal cavity and the chest.

vertex. An infant lies in the uterus in a head down position. This is the most common position and vaginal birth can proceed, unless there is a size disparity between the mother's pelvis and the fetal head.

WBC (white blood cell) count. The number of infection-fighting white blood cells per one millionth of a liter of blood. If this value is elevated, it is a sign of infection. Normally, the value is below 10,000.

Xylocaine. A local anesthetic that is an injectable drug used for minor procedures. Your dentist uses it before drilling and filling your teeth. For reasons that I don't understand, it is often called Novocain, the name of a now-obsolete precursor to this drug.

YO. A common medical abbreviation meaning "year old."

About the Author

I spent most of my childhood in Africa, where my father worked as a physician in the South Sudan. Obviously, that is not a lucrative field, and so, while attending a boarding high school on Long Island, I found myself entirely "on my own" with regard to obtaining a college education. I was lucky enough to receive a full scholarship courtesy of the Navy and chose to attend Rensselaer Polytechnic Institute, where I majored in physics, graduating in 1962. The scholarship then had to be repaid by my serving four years' active duty. Because of my college major, I applied for the Navy's Nuclear Power Program. This necessitated an interview with the renowned Admiral Rickover, founder of the Nuclear Navy. The preliminary interviews did not seem to go well for me at all. I kept being sent for additional interviews. Surely, I thought, I was not going to be accepted. To my surprise, at the end of the day, I was offered an assignment in Washington, DC, at the Naval Reactors Branch of the Atomic Energy Commission. I snapped up that opportunity despite the fact that it would require an additional year of service.

And so, for five years, I worked in the "N" building at Main Navy, right across the hall from Admiral Rickover himself. I was responsible for radiation testing of nuclear fuel materials as well as design of the 120-ton lead-shielded casks we used to transport highly radioactive spent fuel from submarines to a storage facility in Idaho. In medicine, we deal with microcuries of radioactive substances; in each of these spent fuel shipping containers, we had 50 million curies! To this day, nobody knows how to process or dispose of that spent fuel. It will have to be stored for the next 1,000 years.

During my time with the Naval Reactors Program, I pondered how I really wanted to spend the rest of my life. How much more rewarding would it be to devote myself to directly helping people rather than being part of a military organization. Alas, I had no pre-med courses to my credit. So I enrolled in evening classes at George Washington University. My other preparation was to read every single article in the previous fifteen years of *Scientific American* that dealt with medicine or biology. Thus, I achieved a fairly good score on the MCAT (Medical College Admission Test).

Then came the time to apply to medical schools. What would I do for a recommendation to medical schools? Well, I went to the Navy infirmary and asked to see the physician on duty. I told him I needed a recommendation to get into medical school. Intrigued, we had a nice long visit, after which he gladly fabricated a glowing letter for me! I duly made application to Johns Hopkins, Case Western, Albany Medical Center, and… What was this? A new medical school, Penn State University, College of Medicine, was being founded in Hershey, Pennsylvania. I was both attracted to it and more than a little suspicious—attracted because of its rural location.

At that time, I had two small children and didn't want to raise them in a major city. However, I also knew that new enterprises often are often beset with huge problems. In any case, the fall of 1966 found me being interviewed in one of Milton Hershey's orphanage buildings next to a cornfield in Hershey. Wonder of wonders, I was accepted into the Pioneer Class. Only 40 of about 1,600 applicants were accepted that year. Now for the difficult part, should I accept the invitation? I thought long and hard before agreeing. And to my surprise, the start-up problems were minimal, thanks in no small part to nearby Harrisburg and Polyclinic Hospitals.

When Admiral Rickover heard of my intention to quit working for him, he was furious and summoned me into his office. After I told him I was leaving to attend medical school, his only comment was "Very good." (Aside: Medicine was one of the few professions Rickover respected because there was never any doubt as to who the responsible party was. He would challenge people to determine who was to blame for the engineering error that caused the wings to come off those first Lockheed Electra airliners. He often told congressmen that if anything ever went wrong with a nuclear submarine reactor, he was the responsible person.)